P. M. ABBEY
G. M. MACDONALD

'O' LEVEL COOKERY

Methuen Educational

First published in 1963
by Methuen and Co Ltd
Reprinted three times
Second edition 1965
Reprinted in 1965
Third (colour) edition 1968
Reprinted nine times
Fourth (metric) edition 1976
Reprinted seven times
Reprinted with revisions 1984
by Methuen Educational Ltd
11 New Fetter Lane, London, EC4P 4EE
© 1963, 1965, 1968 and 1976 P. M. Abbey and G. M. Macdonald
Printed in Great Britain
by Butler & Tanner Ltd
Frome and London
ISBN 0 423 88620 7

Miss Abbey was formerly principal lecturer
at the F. L. Calder College of Education.
Miss Macdonald was formerly Adviser in
Domestic Science to the London boroughs of
Redbridge, Barking and Havering.

Illustrations by Christopher Neal

CONTENTS

INTRODUCTION

This course in domestic cookery is for students who are studying the subject to GCE 'O' level and equivalent examinations. The text is as concise as possible so that the essential facts can be absorbed readily either in class or by private study. This should leave more time for practical cookery and experimental work, for wider reading and for discussion about various issues.

The authors and publisher would like to thank Mr. D. H. Fry for checking the food science, Miss Anne Dare for supplying the chapter on Home Freezing, and for information on Meat Cookery, and Miss Elizabeth Gilbert for the information on convenience and alternative foods.

They gratefully acknowledge too the generous help with checking and updating the text given by: The Milk Marketing Board, The Electrical Association for Women, British Gas Corporation, the Prestige Group Consumer Advisory Service, the New Zealand Lamb Information Bureau and ROSPA Safety Education Division.

Grateful acknowledgment for permission to reproduce diagrams or information goes to: The British Standards Institution for the diagrams and information on the Kitemark and Safety Mark; British Electrotechnical Approvals Board for the BEAB mark; British Gas Corporation for their Seal of Service; British Sugar Bureau for the information on sugar; Mothercare for a photograph of a cooker guard and Fishing News for information and a photograph of coley, from which drawings were made; J. M. Dent and Sons Ltd. for the diagrams on steaming from the book *Look and Cook* by lecturers from the Gloucestershire Training College of Domestic Science; Waitrose for information on cuts of meat; Porosan (D.I.Y) Ltd. for information on Porosan caps; Meat Promotion Executive for the diagrams of beef, lamb and pork in chapter 3.

INTRODUCTION TO THE FOURTH EDITION

This edition of 'O' Level Cookery uses metric units throughout. There is no direct conversion of ounces to grams in recipes. All proportions have been worked out using a 25 gram base unit which appears to be the accepted unit by most authorities. Recipes have been tested and the teaspoon used is the standard 5 millilitre spoon. Temperatures are given in degrees Celsius (Centigrade) but a diagram of a thermometer showing both Celsius and Fahrenheit scales appears below. The term kilocalorie has been used because the joule (SI unit) is not yet in common use.

Metric Units

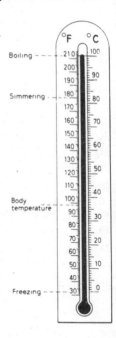

SI Units: SI units are the International System of Units which are standardised for international use.
Temperature: °C = degree Celsius.

Quantity of heat and energy: the joule is the SI unit for heat and energy – J is the symbol. The Calorie or kilorie are metric units but not SI units.
1 kilocalorie = 4.186 kilojoules.

Capacity	*Length*
ml = millilitre	mm = millimetre
dl = decilitre	cm = centimetre
l = litre	m = metre

Weight	*Area*
mg = milligram	cm^2 = square centimetre
g = gram	m^2 = square metre
kg= kilogram	
μg = microgram	*Volume*
	dm^3 = cubic decimetre
	cm^3 = cubic centimetre

1. PRINCIPLES OF NUTRITION

A widespread interest in nutrition is essential for a nation's health and well-being. This knowledge is the basis for meal planning.

DEFINITION OF TERMS USED IN NUTRITION

1. *Nutrition*. Study of all the processes of growth, maintenance and repair of living bodies which depend on the intake of food.

2. *Dietetics*. Study of nutrition in relation to the human body both in health and disease.

3. *Malnutrition*. Results when the body receives the wrong amount or proportion of nutrients.

4. *Under-nutrition*. Results if the body receives an insufficient total amount of nutrients.

5. *Food*. Any solid or liquid which, when swallowed, provides the body with material enabling it to carry out one or more of the following functions:

a) Growth and repair.

b) Energy production (including the liberation of heat).

c) Regulation of body processes involved in a) and b).

6. *Metabolism*. The name for all the chemical changes that occur in living cells and tissues resulting in:

a) Their growth and repair.

b) The release of energy and its use by the cells to promote all their activities, using the chemical substances (nutrients) obtained from digested foods together with oxygen taken in by the lungs.

SOURCES OF FOOD

Plants take in carbon dioxide from air through their leaves and absorb water, with dissolved mineral elements from the soil, through the roots.

The green colouring matter in leaves, called chlorophyll, enables them to absorb energy from the sun. This energy is used to convert carbon dioxide and water into carbohydrates. From these and mineral elements, all other substances in the plant are formed.

Animals either feed on green plants, i.e. are herbivorous, or prey on other animals, i.e. are carnivorous (but these are also dependent in the first instance on plants for their food).

Man is both herbivorous and carnivorous, i.e. *omnivorous*.
Note: A mixed diet is best for most people.

NUTRIENTS

All food is made up of chemical substances called nutrients.
Nutrients are:

1. *Proteins*. Provide material for body growth and repair, and are also used as a source of energy.

2. *Carbohydrates*. Provide energy which is needed for all bodily activities. Some energy is liberated as heat.

3. *Fats*. As above. They also act as insulators when stored in fatty tissues.

4. *Minerals*. Provide material for growth and repair and regulation of body processes.

5. *Vitamins*. Assist resistance to disease and regulation of body processes.

6. *Water*. Forms a large proportion of all body materials – needed for various secretions in the body, so may be classed as a regulator. Transports materials within the body.

Note: *Fibre*. Not digested, so not a nutrient, but needed to help digestive action.

Standard measurements

To calculate the amounts of different nutrients it is necessary to use standard units.

Gram (g) is used for measuring protein, fat and carbohydrate. 28.35 grams = 1 ounce.

Milligram (mg) is used for measuring minerals and vitamins. 1,000 mg = 1 g.

Microgram (μg) is used for measuring vitamins A and D. 1,000 μg = 1 mg.

Balanced diet. The table on page 3 shows that while foods contain various nutrients, no one food contains sufficient of all nutrients for perfect health, so variety is essential for perfect nutrition, i.e. a balanced diet. The various nutrients must be studied to know their value to the body, sources, recommended daily intakes, etc.

PROTEIN

The word protein is from the Greek meaning 'I am first'.

Proteins are essential to life as all living cells are built up of protoplasm which consists of protein, among other substances.

Proteins are made up of the elements carbon, hydrogen, oxygen, nitrogen and usually sulphur. In addition other elements may be present in, or associated with, some proteins.

The nutritive value supplied by 100 g of some foods

		Milk	Butter	Cod (steamed)	Sugar	Cabbage (cooked)	Chicken (roast)	Wholemeal bread
protein	g	3.3	0.5	18.0	0	0.8	29.6	8.8
fat	g	3.8	82.5	0.9	0	0	7.3	2.7
carbohydrate	g	4.8	trace	0	100	1.3	0	41.8
kcal		65	745	69	394	8	184	216
kJ		272	3122	289	1651	34	771	918
calcium	mg	120	15	14.6	0	58	15	23
iron	mg	trace	trace	trace	0	0.5	2.6	2.5
vitamin A	μg	44	995	0	0	50	trace	0
vitamin B thiamin	mg	.04	0 ·	.09	0	.03	.08	0.26
riboflavin	mg	.19	0	.09	0	.03	.19	.06
nicotinic acid	mg	.08	0	5.6	0	.5	12.8	5.6
vitamin C	mg	trace	0	0	0	20	0	0
vitamin D	μg	0.05	1.25	0	0	0	trace	0

Amino-acids

These are the simpler substances which make up protein. There are 22 amino-acids and different proteins contain different numbers and combinations.

There are 8 essential amino-acids which the adult body needs for growth and repair, and 9 needed by the growing child.

High biological value proteins. These contain all the essential amino-acids in good supply.

Low biological value proteins. One or more of the essential amino-acids is in a limited supply.

Note: Proteins can compensate for each other's deficiencies if taken together, e.g. cheese and bread – the protein in cheese is deficient in different amino-acids than bread so they complement each other. Another combination is rice and lentils.

Sources of protein

High biological value protein is found mainly in animal foods:

```
Meat:    myosin, collagen
Fish:    myosin
Eggs:    white – albumen, yolk – vitellin, globulin
Milk:    caseinogen, globulin
Cheese:  caseinogen
```

Low biological value protein is found mainly in vegetable foods:

```
Cereals: wheat – glutenin and gliadin
         barley – hordin
Pulses:  (peas, beans, lentils) legumin
```

Digestion of proteins. See notes on digestion.

Functions of protein

1. For growth and tissue repair especially for children, expectant and nursing mothers, and invalids.

2. Secondary source of energy.

Note the danger in slimming diets of cutting down too much on fats and carbohydrates, and not providing sufficient protein for growth and repair and energy.

Recommended daily protein amounts for average adult in normal health

```
Average      55–85 g per day
Sedentary    65  ..  ..  ..
Moderately
  active     75  ..  ..  ..
```

Active   83 .. .. ..
Very active   90 .. .. ..

These recommendations assume that the proteins are a mixture of high and low biological value.

Proportion of high and low biological value protein needed

A third to a half of daily protein intake should be of animal origin (i.e. of high biological value). Animal foods are fairly expensive so a mixture of animal and vegetable foods supplying protein should be taken.

Cheaper cuts of meat and fish are as nutritious as expensive cuts if correctly cooked and if there is not too much waste.

Alternative protein foods

Protein in alternative forms derived from soya, wheat and other vegetable sources is being produced. (See page 209.)

FAT

Fats are composed of carbon, hydrogen and oxygen, the same elements as in carbohydrates, but in a different proportion. They are the most concentrated energy food.

Plants store fats in the form of oil droplets or as solid fat.

Animals and humans store fat which may be derived from fatty foods or from excess carbohydrates.

Simple chemistry of fat

Fats and oils are made up of two groups of simpler substances.

a) *Glycerol or glycerine*. A sweet sticky liquid.

b) *Fatty acids*. There is a large variety, about 25 kinds distributed among both animal and vegetable fats.

1 molecule of fat = 1 unit glycerol + 3 units fatty acids.

The fatty acids present determine the consistency of the fat or oil.

Fats are solid at room temperature.

Oils are liquid at room temperature.

Rancid fats

a) *Hydrolytic* – caused by the glycerol splitting from the fatty acids. The smell of rancid fat depends on the fatty acid present. It is especially noticeable in rancid butter.

b) *Oxidative* –the breakdown of particular fatty acids in reaction with oxygen with the release of substances that have an unpleasant taste and smell.

Sources of fat

Animal.

> Milk fat – cream, cheese, butter.
> Meat fat – lard, dripping, suet.
> Egg yolk
> Oily fish.

Note: Margarine may be a mixture of animal fat and vegetable fats and oils.

Vegetable

> Nut and seed oils.
> Margarine (for vegetarians) – rape, nut, cottonseed and sunflower oils.
> Olive oil.

Note: Milk and egg fat are in the form of a fine emulsion and so are easily digested. (See later notes on milk and eggs.)

Chemical changes on heating. If heated over 190°C most fat begins to decompose into fatty acids and glycerol, gives off smoke, burns and discolours. The substances produced irritate the stomach so burnt fat should not be used.

Frying fat and oil have been treated in such a way that they will heat up to approximately 220°C before burning. (See chapter 12 'Fats and Oils' on page 102.)

Functions of fat

Fat is the body's most concentrated source of fuel and energy, but it may not be the best source as a large amount cannot be tolerated especially with poor digestion. Climate affects intake.

Fat forms a fuel reserve. It is stored in small amounts in almost every part of the body but the main storage, accounting for the bulk of body fat, is in the subcutaneous layer of fatty (adipose) tissue. Animal fats convey the fat-soluble vitamins A, D, E, K. Fish liver oils used as medicinal supplements provide vitamins A and D. Fat acts as an insulator round the body and prevents loss of heat. Cooking in fat increases the energy value of food. This is inadvisable where there is a tendency to obesity.

Intake of fat in the diet

The fat intake of most people in Britain supplies over 40% of their energy. This is now considered to be too high. Fat intake should be restricted so that less than 30% of the energy comes from fat. A reduction in fat intake could be made by a change in eating habits – boiled or baked potatoes instead of fried or roasted; less butter or margarine; grilled food instead of fried, etc.

Sources of fat in the diet (visible and invisible)

Fat content of protein rich foods – milk, cheese, eggs, meat, fish (oily).

Fat content of made-up dishes – cakes and puddings.
Fat used for cooking.
Fat served with carbohydrate foods, e.g. butter with bread.
To help digestion. Fat foods should always be eaten with carbohydrate foods, e.g. bread and cheese, chipped potatoes.

CARBOHYDRATES

Carbohydrates are composed of the same elements as fats – carbon, hydrogen and oxygen. ('Hydrate' because the same proportion of H and O as water – H_2O.)

They are usually plant products, and contain stored energy which the plant has obtained from the sunlight with the help of chlorophyll.

Carbon dioxide + water + energy = carbohydrates + oxygen.

Monosaccharides

1. *Glucose or Dextrose*. Found naturally in ripe fruits and in some vegetables, and honey. Glucose is manufactured commercially from starch for sweets, etc. All carbohydrate foods digested in the body are converted to simple sugar which can circulate in blood – blood sugar (the commonest of these is glucose). The amount of glucose in the blood is controlled by insulin from the pancreas. If there is insufficient insulin to control the level of sugar, diabetes results.

Since glucose manufactured from starch is not as sweet as cane sugar, it may be added to foods or drinks to increase their energy content without making them over sweet, and may be used in an invalid diet. (See page 34.)

(See later notes on digestion of carbohydrates page 20.)

2. *Fructose*. Similar to glucose. Found in fruits (fruit sugar) honey, plant juices.

3. *Galactose*. Formed during the digestion of lactose (milk sugar).

Disaccharides

1. *Sucrose*. Formed from 1 molecule of glucose and 1 molecule of fructose. It is obtained from sugar-cane and beet, and is also present in fruits and certain vegetables.

2. *Lactose*. Milk sugar. It is not so sweet as sucrose. It is formed from 1 molecule of glucose and 1 molecule of galactose.

3. *Maltose*. Malt sugar – formed from starch in the germination of the barley grain.

Polysaccharides (Complex carbohydrates)

1. *Starch*. Many plants store starch as their principal food reserve, e.g. in the stem of the sago palm, in cassava root (tapioca), in the potato tuber and in seeds such as cereals and pulses.

2. *Dextrin*. Formed from starch which has been changed by cooking, e.g. toast, breakfast cereals, crust of loaves. It is more soluble than starch.

3. *Glycogen*. This is an animal carbohydrate. Glucose is converted into glycogen for temporary storage in small amounts in the liver and muscle tissues of animals and humans. It can be converted to glucose again for use by the body.

4. *Cellulose* forms the structural framework of plants. Humans are unable to digest cellulose. It can be digested by herbivorous animals. It is found in the skins and framework of fruits and vegetables, and skins of cereals.

5. *Hemicellulose* is found in fruits and vegetables.

6. *Pectin* (see pages 168–171).

Dietary fibre consists of cellulose, hemicellulose and pectin.

Sources of carbohydrate in the diet

1. *Starch*. The principal carbohydrate eaten. It is obtained chiefly from cereals; wheat in the form of bread in this country, rice in the Far East. Potatoes are also a good source, and cakes, biscuits, puddings, breakfast cereals, etc. (See cereal notes for more detail.)

2. *Sugar*. Eaten in the form of cane or beet sugar, and as a sweetening in drinks or in cooked food. Also present in fruit, vegetables, honey, jam, syrup, and in processed foods, e.g. tinned and packet soups, tinned vegetables.

Average intake.

At least 70% of total kilocalories should come from carbohydrates – most of which should be complex carbohydrates. Sugar intake in Britain needs to be reduced.

Functions of carbohydrates in the body

1. For the production of energy used for all bodily activities. Energy can be measured in kilocalories.

2. Fibre which stimulates the digestive tract.

Storage in the body.

A small supply is stored in the liver and muscles in the form of glycogen if not utilised by the body. Excess is converted into fat on the body.

Digestion of carbohydrates.

(See later notes page 20.)

Effect on cooking.

(See note on the effect of heat on nutrients page 108.)

VITAMINS

Discovery

Vitamins have been identified during this century. Before this it was believed that a diet of protein, carbohydrate, fat, minerals and water was all that was needed to maintain health and activity. This was tested by experiments. Animals were fed on pure materials prepared in the laboratory providing the above nutrients. All attempts to keep the rats alive on diets of pure materials failed. So what was missing was vital to life and health, although only in minute quantities. These unknown substances were called accessory food factors.

Until about 1910 it was believed that many illnesses were caused by microbes, and foods were cooked for a long time to kill any bacteria present. This long cooking would, of course, destroy much of the vitamin content of certain foods, especially vitamin C.

Early records of the curative effects of certain foods are available, e.g. fruit juice – lime and lemons, etc. for scurvy (vitamin C supplied); fish, meat, for beriberi (vitamin B group supplied); fat for rickets (vitamin D supplied).

In 1912 Dr. Funk coined the name Vitamine (vital amine) for a factor curing beriberi. Further research has shown that this term is incorrect, but the word vitamin is used. At first it was thought that there was only one missing factor, but in 1915 two further factors were discovered and named fat-soluble A, and water-soluble B. More new vitamins were isolated, and were named alphabetically as they still are, although they are now distinguished by chemical names. Vitamins cannot usually be manufactured by the body.

Severe deficiency diseases are practically unknown in this country, but prolonged lack of any vitamin will cause death.

Individual vitamin needs vary considerably. Not all of the intake may be utilised by the body, and there is a health danger in taking supplements of some vitamins. A sound mixed diet should provide all the necessary vitamins unless there is a medical reason for a supplement.

Types of vitamin

Fat soluble. Vitamins A, D, E, K.
Water soluble. Vitamins B group, C.

Vitamin A

Retinol. Fat soluble.

Functions in the body

1. Necessary for health of mucous membranes in linings of the throat, digestive and excretory tracts, etc. and of skin, thus helping resistance to infection.
2. Necessary for growth in children especially their bones and teeth.
3. It helps vision, especially in dim light.

Effects of a deficiency of vitamin A

Vitamin A is essential for the manufacture of the pigment 'visual purple' needed to see in dim light. A prolonged deficiency could result in blindness caused by ulcerated cornea (xerophthalmia).

Note: There could be a health risk in taking too much vitamin A as a supplement.

Main sources in the diet
May be supplied as retinol or as carotene, part of which is converted by the body to vitamin A. Retinol is supplied by animal foods. Carotene is supplied by vegetables. The body can store vitamin A in the liver.

Animal sources (Retinol)	*Vegetable sources (Carotene)*
Fish-liver oils (cod-liver, etc.)	Carrots
Butter	Green vegetables
Cheese	Spinach, watercress,
Eggs	cabbage, green peas,
Liver and kidney	parsley, kale.
Herrings	Apricots, prunes
Fresh and powdered milk	Tomatoes
Vitaminised margarine	

Vitamin A in dairy foods is formed by cows from carotene in the green grass eaten, so there is more in summer milk and butter.

The amount of carotene present depends on the amount of sunshine received by the fruit or vegetable. Outer leaves of cabbage are a good source of carotene but the inner heart may contain none.

Vitamin A is not naturally present in vegetable fats.

Effect of cooking
Retinol and carotene are insoluble in water so are not leached out by the moist methods of cooking – boiling or steaming, or by soaking. So boiled vegetables contain just as much carotene as raw vegetables.

Dehydrated foods are often cited as particularly good sources of nutrients but this is only an apparent comparative richness due to the concentration effects of water removal. Reconstitution restores the water, dilutes the solid matter and thus returns the food to virtually its original composition.

Vitamin D

Cholecalciferol. Ergocalciferol (sunshine vitamin). Anti-rachitic. Fat soluble.

Functions in the body
Vitamin D, in conjunction with calcium and phosphorous, is necessary for the formation of sound bones and teeth. It helps in the laying down of calcium

phosphate in the cartilage of babies and young children during the process of bone formation.

It is called the calcifying vitamin.

Formation of sound bones and teeth depends on sufficient calcium, phosphorus and vitamin D in the diet.

Effects of a deficiency of vitamin D

Deficiency of vitamin D or of calcium and phosphorus could cause the deficiency disease rickets to occur. Rickets is characterised by the softening of the bones due to the inadequate deposition of calcium, causing malformation of the bones. Symptoms are bow legs, knock knees, etc. Rickets can develop in a baby's body before birth if the mother's diet is deficient in vitamin D. Rickets is uncommon in tropical countries, except where purdah operates, but was very prevalent in overcrowded industrial cities in Britain before the cause was known and the cure discovered. There is some evidence of rickets in Asian familes in Britain. Vitamin D helps to prevent dental decay. Lack of vitamin D may cause senile oseoporosis.

Main sources

Is obtained from two main sources: food, and the action of sunlight on dehydrocholesterol under the skin.

Food. Animal fats – fish-liver oils, especially tunny fish oils, halibut and cod.

Oily fish – herrings, mackerel, sardines, salmon.

Dairy fats (small supply, more in summer because of effect of sunlight on cows).

Vitaminised margarine (vitamin D added).

Sunlight. Beneath the skin is a layer of fat containing dehydrocholesterol. When the body is exposed to sunlight, dehydrocholesterol is converted to vitamin D – cholecalciferol – which is stored and utilised by the body. Ultra-violet rays cause this change.

Effect of cooking. Vitamin D is not destroyed by heat or lost by solubility.

Vitamin E (Tocopherol)

Fat soluble. It aids the healthy functioning of muscles, blood and skin, and has been used to treat women who have had a series of miscarriages. The chief sources are wheatgerm oil, green vegetables and whole grain cereals, but a balanced diet provides a good supply.

Vitamin K

Fat soluble. Vitamin K is the anti-haemorrhagic or coagulation vitamin and it enables blood to clot, but it is not the only blood coagulating factor in the body.

There is no standard recommended intake level. If vitamins A and C are present in sufficient quantities there will be enough vitamin K because it is usually found in association with them.

Vitamin B Group

Water soluble. Cannot be stored in the body. There are a number of vitamins in the B group but only the most important will be considered. All are soluble in water and are usually found together in the same type of foods, but not always. The body is not able to store these vitamins because of their solubility in water, so a daily supply is recommended.

Thiamin (B₁)

Functions in the body
1 It is connected with the liberation of energy from glucose.
2. Necessary for growth and general good health.

Effects of a deficiency of thiamin
1. Very slight deficiency leads to arrested growth in children. At all ages it can lead to loss of appetite, fatigue, nausea, indigestion, general fatigue, constipation, nervous irritability and a type of neuritis (inflammation of the nerves).
2. Prolonged deficiency may result in the disease beriberi, which attacks the nervous system and causes a type of paralysis.

Sources in the diet
Widely distributed in foods but usually in small amounts.
Food made from fortified or wholemeal flour.
Wheatgerm.
Yeast and yeast extracts, e.g. Marmite.
Oatmeal. Nuts.
Lean meat. Pork and bacon. Liver, heart and kidney.
Fish and roes. Eggs.
Peas, beans and lentils.

Most 'natural' foods give a supply of thiamin, but foods which have been over-refined are usually deficient, e.g. white bread, sugar, honey, glucose, polished rice (skins removed).

Effect of cooking. The vitamin is soluble in water and about half will dissolve in the cooking liquid. Alkalis in baking powder, etc. will cause some destruction. Destroyed by high temperatures, e.g. pressure cooking, and canning. Despite cooking losses a reasonable amount of this vitamin is usually retained in the food.

Diet requirements. People on heavy work needing a good supply of carbohydrate food will need more thiamin. More of the vitamin is needed by growing children and expectant and nursing mothers. If a mixed diet is eaten with plenty of natural foodstuffs, the daily requirement should be met easily.

Riboflavin (B₂)

Functions in the body
It is concerned with the release of energy from foods by oxidation and with the utilisation of food fats and amino-acids.

Effects of a deficiency of riboflavin
1. A check in growth of children.
2. Inflammation of the mouth and tongue.
3. Nervous depression, unhealthy skin and digestive disturbances.
4. Cornea may become misted and vision impaired.

Sources in the diet
The vitamin is found in a great number of foods and is usually present with thiamin.
  Important sources are:
  Yeast and yeast products, e.g. Marmite, beer.
  Liver, heart, kidney, lean meat, fish.
  Wheatgerm.
  Cheese, milk and milk products, eggs.
  Pulses, nuts. Rice meal. Oat meal.
  Potato, spinach. A supply in other vegetables.
  The vitamin is present in such a variety of foods that there is little likelihood of a shortage if a mixed diet is taken.

Effect of cooking. Riboflavin is soluble so it will dissolve out in the cooking water. Some is lost during normal cooking, but more losses occur when high temperature cooking takes place, e.g. canning, pressure cooking, etc. Some is lost when milk is exposed to strong sunlight.

Nicotinic acid

Niacin. Anti-pellagra vitamin.
  Note: The body is capable of converting one of the amino-acids (constituents of protein) to nicotinic acid. Thus, supplies of the preformed vitamin in a food are likely to be enhanced by any protein present. Therefore, sources are both richer and of greater variety than those listed for just the performed vitamin. (Nicotine in tobacco is a poison and cannot be converted to the vitamin, but nicotinic acid is chemically related, hence the name.)

Function in the body. As in the case of the other B group of vitamins, nicotinic acid helps in the release of energy from carbohydrate foods.

Deficiency of the vitamin leads to:
1. Arrested growth in children.
2. Diarrhoea and digestive troubles.
3. Rough, raw, red sore skin.
4. In extreme cases mental disorders and pellagra.
   (Disease of the 3 D's – dementia, dermatitis, diarrhoea.)

Sources in the diet
Similar to other B group, especially riboflavin, but milk products do not give a good supply.

Effect of cooking. Nicotinic acid is soluble so it dissolves to some extent in cooking liquid. It is stable in the presence of heat but is easily oxidised.

Other B group vitamins
B_5 (calcium pantothenate)

Aids wound healing and helps fight infection. Reduces fatigue.
Sources – meat, whole grain, kidney, liver, heart, green vegetables, yeast.

B_6 (Pyridoxine)

Aids the assimilation of protein and fat, and helps in some nervous and skin disorders.
Sources – yeast, wheat grain, bran, liver, kidney, heart, cabbage.

B_{12} (Cobalamin)

Helps to maintain the health of the nervous system.
Sources – liver, beef, eggs, milk, cheese.

Folic acid

Necessary for the formation of red blood cells and to prevent anaemia. Aids in lactation. Acts as an analgesic for pain.
Sources – green vegetables, carrots, liver, egg yolk, whole wheat.

Vitamin C

Ascorbic acid. Anti-scorbutic (against scurvy) vitamin. Water soluble.
This is an important vitamin which is essential in the diet and is easily destroyed.

Functions in the body
1. For healthy body tissues.
2. To help heal wounds.
3. Healthy teeth and gums (with calcium, phosphorus, vitamins A and D).
4. To prevent scurvy.

A deficiency of vitamin C leads to:
1. Bad skin.
2. Easily infected gums and teeth.
3. Slow healing of wounds and fractures.
4. A check in growth of children.
5. Laziness, gloom and irritability.
6. In severe cases, scurvy.

Scurvy is a very serious and sometimes fatal disease affecting the whole system, particularly blood vessels, bones, teeth and gums. It is not common now, but was on early sailing ships and expeditions, where it was not possible to obtain fresh fruit and vegetables.

Sources in the diet
Fruit and vegetables, *but* amounts vary considerably.
Fruit. Good sources: rose hips, blackcurrants. (Ribena.)
   Fairly good: citrus fruits, strawberries, gooseberries, redcurrants, tomatoes, raspberries.
Other fresh fruit supplies some vitamin C. Dried fruit does not.
Vegetables. Rich supply: brussels sprouts, kale.
   Very good: cabbage, spinach, cauliflower, watercress, broccoli, new potatoes.
   Some in other fresh vegetables. None in dried vegetables.
Fresh milk contains a little vitamin C but it is lost before it reaches the consumer.

Effect of cooking on vitamin C. Because of the ease with which the vitamin is destroyed or lost, great care must be taken to preserve it as much as possible.
   1. Vitamin C is very soluble and so is easily dissolved in cleaning or cooking (avoid soaking). Therefore use the cooking liquid for sauces, etc. Cook in a little water as quickly as possible.
   2. The vitamin is destroyed by heat, so cook quickly.
   3. As it oxidises to form a substance which is useless to the body, food containing it should be stored for as short a time as possible. Use the food fresh – straight from the garden is best. Cook with the lid on to minimise oxidation. Dish up quickly.
   4. There is an enzyme present with vitamin C in foods which, once the cells of the plant are damaged by bruising, cutting, or cooking, begins to destroy vitamin C by oxidising it. Most destruction takes place between 65°C and 85°C; so, if the

vegetable is put into boiling water this activity will not occur and the enzyme will be quickly destroyed. Use unbruised vegetables and do not cut up too finely *except* to ensure quick cooking.

Raw fruit and vegetables contain most vitamin C but some must be cooked to be digested more easily.

Dried peas and beans, etc. do not contain any vitamin C, but dehydrated vegetables processed by modern methods may give a normal supply.

Modern methods of canning do not cause much destruction of vitamin C – about as much as household boiling. The canning liquid should be used.

Modern quick freezing methods conserve vitamin C.

Fruit and vegetables must be included in the diet and care must be taken in cooking to ensure the best conservation of this vitamin which is most likely to be deficient in the diet in this country.

The vitamin cannot be stored in the body, so a daily supply is recommended.

MINERAL ELEMENTS

These are the elements other than carbon, hydrogen, oxygen and nitrogen that are found in the body. There are 19 remaining when the body is reduced to ash. Minerals are the components of the substances forming many parts of the body, e.g. calcium and phosphorus are present in teeth, bone and blood. They also form an important part of many secretions, e.g. iodine is present in thyroid secretion and sodium and chlorine are present in certain digestive juices. The principal mineral elements are:– calcium, phosphorus, potassium, sulphur, chlorine, sodium, magnesium, iron, manganese, iodine, cobalt, copper, fluorine, nickel, zinc, selenium, chromium, molybdenum.

Function of mineral elements

1. They are essential for the proper functions of many parts of the body.

2. They enter into the structural framework of the body, e.g. calcium and phosphorus are present in bones.

3. They form constituents of body cells such as muscle fibres, nerve cells, blood corpuscles, liver cells, etc.

4. As soluble salts in body fluids they contribute to the composition and stability of the fluids, e.g. sodium helps to maintain the water balance in blood.

Supply of elements. Many foods contain inorganic elements and it is not likely that a deficiency would occur in normal diets, as most elements are needed in such small amounts. Care must be taken, however, to ensure that calcium and iron are in adequate supply.

Calcium

Main funtions are carried in conjunction with phosphorus.

Functions in the body

1. It plays a part in the proper development and growth of bones and teeth. It is needed in conjunction with phosphorus and vitamin D and vitamin C.
2. To help in the clotting of blood.
3. To help in the functioning of muscles.

A deficiency of calcium leads to:

1. Rickets and badly formed teeth in children.
2. In old age, calcium may be withdrawn from the bones to meet other bodily requirements. The bones become very brittle and break easily.

Sources of calcium

Milk; cheese; fish eaten with bones, e.g. sardines, salmon; bread fortified by calcium carbonate; hard water, green vegetables.

Phosphorus

Functions in the body

1. It plays an essential part in energy production.
2. In conjunction with calcium it helps the development of bones and teeth.
3. It helps to regulate the acid balance in the body.

Sources. In a normal diet the supply will be adequate. Phosphorus is present in most proteins.

Iron

Functions in the body

Iron is needed for the formation of haemoglobin which gives blood its red colour, and is essential for transporting oxygen in the blood.

A deficiency of iron leads to: poor health and anaemia.

Iron is lost from the body by general body wear and tear; in excretion; in bleeding.

Sources in the diet

Liver; kidney; egg yolk; meat, especially corned beef; wholemeal and white bread; dried fruit; beans; green vegetables.

Intake. Everybody needs a basic supply of iron, but in some circumstances extra is needed, e.g. in pregnancy and lactation. Adolescent girls with heavy periods may need more. Babies are born with a supply of iron to last 6 months. After this time they need iron, which may be supplied by finely minced liver, egg yolk or sieved green vegetables.

Iodine

Functions in the body
It is part of the hormone thyroxin produced by the thyroid gland which is situated in the neck. Thyroxin controls the metabolic rate. In adults deficiency leads to the gland increasing in size in an effort to produce more thyroxin. This condition is known as a goitre. Babies born to women suffering from a serious deficiency may be cretins.

Sources. Fish (sea); foods grown near the sea; water.

Sodium and chlorine (from common salt)

Sodium. Required for the correct composition of the body fluids.

Chlorine. Helps to form the hydrochloric acid secreted by the stomach. Necessary for the correct composition of the body fluids.

Medical authorities now recommend a low salt intake because there is evidence of a relationship between sodium and high blood pressure. Heavy workers need more salt to make up the loss by perspiration. Some, e.g. steel workers or people in the tropics, take salt tablets.

Fluorine

Functions in the body
1. Needed for the healthy formation of bones and teeth.
2. Helps to decrease dental decay.
Needed in very small amounts.

Sources
Found in drinking water in varying amounts; and in fish.
Excessive amounts cause mottling on teeth.

WATER

Functions in the body
Water is vital to life. The body needs water second only to air. Two-thirds of the body's weight is water, and it forms a part of protoplasm.

Water is needed by the body
1. For blood and for all body secretions and digestive juices.
2. To assist digestion, absorption and assimilation of food.
3. To assist in the excretion of waste and elimination from the kidneys.
4. To help to regulate body temperature.
5. To act as a lubricant in joints and membranes.

Approximate loss of water from the body every day:

By perspiration to regulate body temperature		500 ml
By expiration from the lungs (breathing out)		350 ml
In the urine		1.25 l
From the bowels		100 ml
	Total loss	2.2 l

Approximate daily sources of water:

Water content of drinks	1.2 l
Foods with high liquid content, e.g. fruit	750 ml
Oxidation of foods	350 ml

DIETARY FIBRE

This is unavailable carbohydrate, i.e. the cellulose content of plants. It is too complex to be digested by humans, but is of some value to animals and insects.

Fibre increases the bulk of food and stimulates the movements of some of the digestive organs. It encourages peristalsis, which is movement of the digestive tract, and helps in elimination.

Found in cell walls of fruit, vegetables, skins, pith of fruit and vegetables, and cereals.

DIGESTION AND ABSORPTION

The nutrients in food which are required by the body for purposes of growth, repair, to give energy and warmth and resistance to illness have been discussed already.

Definition of food

Food is any substance which when swallowed provides the body with material which enables it to function. Food does not become part of the body and cannot fulfil any of its functions until it has entered the bloodstream through the walls of the digestive tract. Before this absorption into the bloodstream can take place the foods must be converted into simple soluble substances.

Digestion is the process of breakdown of foods into simple substances which will dissolve in water.

Absorption is the process of the passage of the products of digestion through the walls of the digestive tract.

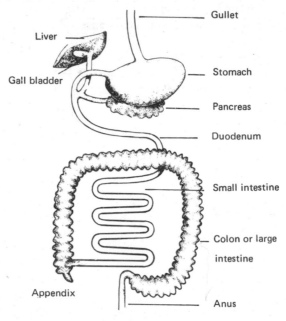

The Alimentary canal

The digestive tract

The alimentary canal or digestive tract is a long tube open at both ends – the mouth and the anus.

It consists of: mouth, gullet (oesophagus), stomach, small intestine, large intestine, rectum. The liver, pancreas and gall bladder are accessory digestive organs.

The small intestine in an adult is over 6 metres long. The large intestine in an adult is over 1.75 metres.

Digestive juices

Digestive juices are secreted by various glands in parts of the digestive system. These juices contain enzymes which break down the food by chemical action. Different enzymes act upon different food substances.

In the mouth. Salivary glands secrete saliva. This contains the enzyme *salivary amylase* which breaks down some cooked starch into maltose and dextrin (first stage in the breakdown of carbohydrates to glucose).

In the stomach. Between 2 and 3 litres of gastric juices are produced each day by the gastric glands. The juice contains 0.2–0.4% of hydrochloric acid. Gastric juice contains the enzyme *pepsin*. Pepsin in the presence of hydrochloric acid converts protein into peptones. The enzyme *rennin* is also present in the juice in babies and young children. This curdles milk and keeps it longer in the stomach.

In the small intestine. Food comes in contact with:

1) Pancreatic juice from the pancreas.

2) Bile from the liver.

3) Intestinal juice from the small intestine.

Pancreatic juice contains:

a) *Trypsinogen.* This is converted by enterokinase in the intestinal juice into trypsin which is responsible for the breakdown of proteins and peptones into amino-acids.

b) The enzyme *pancreatic amylase*. This breaks down starch into maltose.

c) The enzyme *lipase*. This breaks fat into fatty acids and glycerol.

Bile contains alkaline bile salts which emulsify fats, i.e. break fats up into minute globules.

Intestinal juices complete the following tasks:

a) Conversion of starch and sugar into glucose.

b) Conversion of proteins and peptones into constituent amino-acids.

Absorption is almost entirely carried out in the small intestine. Only relatively small quantities of material are absorbed through the walls of the stomach. Absorption in the mouth is negligible. Small quantities of sugar, soluble mineral elements, soluble vitamins B and C and water may be absorbed through the walls of the stomach. Proteins, carbohydrates, fats, minerals, vitamins and water are almost completely absorbed in the small intestine.

Large intestine. Its main function is the absorption of water from the indigestible residue of foodstuffs and digestive juices. These then form the faeces which are passed out of the body.

Digestion (in more detail)

1. **Digestion in the mouth.** First stage of digestion takes place – food enters the digestive tract and is exposed to the action of digestive juices.

The process of mastication helps reduce food to a small size – teeth cut and grind the food, and the tongue and mouth muscles move to mix up the food with saliva from the salivary glands. The flow of saliva is stimulated by the smell and sight of appetising food (mouth-watering). Emotions of fear, worry, etc. may stop secretion of saliva (mouth dries up). Saliva acts as a moistener and lubricator so as to allow the soft bolus of food to pass easily down the gullet or oesophagus.

The enzyme *salivary amylase* begins the breakdown of cooked starch into sugar by converting the cooked starch into dextrin and maltose. *Not* uncooked starch. Saliva is alkaline and the action of salivary amylase continues in the stomach until the alkaline saliva taken down with the bolus of food is neutralised by hydrochloric acid in the stomach juices. If the food is swallowed hastily without chewing, salivary amylase does not have time to do its job and indigestion may result.

2. **Digestion in the stomach.** The stomach has various functions, but it is not primarily an organ in which a great deal of digestion takes place. It is a receptacle which receives food via the mouth, brings its contents into a form acceptable to the next organ in the digestive system, and then passes the products on for further digestion in appropriate quantities.

Foods of different temperatures are all brought to the temperature of the body, 37°C, and fats are melted. Hydrochloric acid act as a powerful antiseptic. Salivary amylase continues the work begun in the mouth until neutralised by the acid. Enzyme *pepsin* in association with hydrochloric acid starts the conversion of proteins into peptones. In the stomachs of babies and small children rennin curdles milk in readiness for the next process of digestion.

The action of the stomach muscles together with the gastric juices helps to reduce the food to a soft consistency and it is then known as 'chyme'. Different food stays in the stomach for different times (2–4 hours), then the ring of muscle at the lower end of the stomach opens and allows small amounts of the semi-liquid food to pass into the small intestine.

3. **Digestion in the small intestine.** Chyme, containing gastric juice which is acid, passes to the first part of the small intestine – the duodenum. The reaction is alkaline in the small intestine. The result of the admission of acid is the stimulation of the flow of pancreatic juice and bile.

Pancreatic juice is the most powerful of the digestive juices. It contains 3 enzymes which do the following work:

a) *Trypsin* – originally secreted as trypsinogen – continues the work of pepsin and converts proteins into peptones and finally into their constituent amino-acids.

b) *Pancreatic amylase* continues the work of salivary amylase on starch, breaking it down into maltose.

c) *Lipase* acts on fats and, after they have been emulsified by the alkaline action of the bile, splits them up into fatty acids and glycerol.

Intestinal juices contain the enzymes:

Erepsin which converts peptones into amino-acids.

Maltase which converts maltose into glucose.

Lactase which converts lactose to glucose.

Invertase which converts cane sugar to glucose and fructose.

Enterokinase which converts trypsinogen into trypsin.

The food, now called 'chyle', is moved along the length of the small intestine by the peristaltic action of the muscles, ready for absorption through the walls.

4. **Digestion in the large intestine.** The large intestine contains no digestive juices, but is rich in bacteria. All digestible food has been absorbed by the time the mass of residue reaches it. A large proportion of this residue is fibre together with the remains of digestive juices and bacteria. Water is absorbed from this mass as it passes along the large intestine and when it reaches the rectum it is in a more or less solid form, ready to be expelled from the body. Bacteria in the large intestine produce certain B vitamins, so supplementing the body's supply.

Absorption (in more detail)

Absorption is the term applied to the passage of the products of digestion through the walls of the digestive tract.

Absorption takes place mainly in the small intestine. The broken down products of food are absorbed through its wall into the bloodstream. The lining of the small intestine consists of tiny projections called *villi*. Each *villus* contains a small lymph-vessel called a lacteal and a network of capillaries (capillary blood vessels).

The *villi* are surrounded by chyle containing the final products of digestion – amino-acids, glucose, fatty acids and glycerol. These are absorbed into the lacteals and capillaries.

a) Glucose and amino-acids pass via the capillaries and portal vein into the liver and thence if required into the general blood circulation.

b) Fatty acids and glycerol pass into the lacteals of the *villi* where they are at once reconstituted as fats. They join the lymphatic system which opens into the thoracic duct. From this the milky emulsion of fats enters the bloodstream without first passing through the liver.

c) Mineral elements are absorbed into the capillaries.

d) Fat-soluble vitamins A and D are absorbed by the small intestine. Excess of body's requirements are stored in the liver.

Water-soluble vitamins are absorbed by the stomach and the small intestine. Any excess passes out of the body via the kidneys after absorption.

Summary of passage of nutrients in the body

(See previous notes for details.)

Proteins. Pass through the mouth chemically unchanged.

Partly broken up in the stomach.

Process of change to amino-acids completed in the small intestine.

Absorbed in the small intestine, pass through the walls into the blood and carried to the liver. The liver removes any excess.

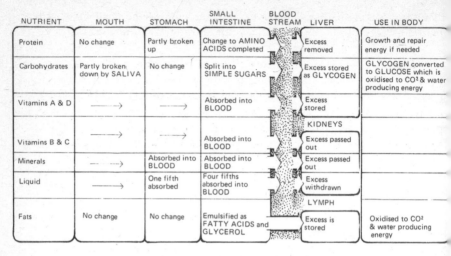

NUTRIENT	MOUTH	STOMACH	SMALL INTESTINE	BLOOD STREAM	LIVER	USE IN BODY
Protein	No change	Partly broken up	Change to AMINO ACIDS completed		Excess removed	Growth and repair energy if needed
Carbohydrates	Partly broken down by SALIVA	No change	Split into SIMPLE SUGARS		Excess stored as GLYCOGEN	GLYCOGEN converted to GLUCOSE which is oxidised to CO_2 & water producing energy
Vitamins A & D	⟶	⟶	Absorbed into BLOOD		Excess stored	
					KIDNEYS	
Vitamins B & C	⟶	⟶	Absorbed into BLOOD		Excess passed out	
Minerals	⟶	Absorbed into BLOOD	Absorbed into BLOOD		Excess passed out	
Liquid	⟶	One fifth absorbed	Four fifths absorbed into BLOOD		Excess withdrawn	
					LYMPH	
Fats	No change	No change	Emulsified as FATTY ACIDS and GLYCEROL		Excess is stored	Oxidised to CO_2 & water producing energy

Chart showing the passage of nutrients in the body

The remainder is used by tissues for growth and repair. May be oxidised for production of energy, if needed.

Carbohydrates. Partly broken down by saliva in the mouth.

No change by stomach juices.

Split into simple sugars in the small intestine.

Absorbed through the walls of the small intestine into the blood.

Carried to the liver where excess is stored as glycogen. When the body needs energy, the glycogen is converted back to glucose, for use by the body cells and tissues. With the production of energy of various types, glucose is oxidised to carbon dioxide and water.

Fats. Pass unchanged chemically through the mouth and stomach.

In the small intestine, fat is finely divided, until completely emulsified, broken into fatty acids and glycerol, and absorbed through the walls of the small intestine into the lymph. Excess is stored.

The remainder is taken to the cells to be oxidised to carbon dioxide and water with the production of energy.

Minerals. Soluble salts are absorbed by the stomach or the small intestine, into the blood. Excess passes out via the kidneys.

Vitamins. Water-soluble B and C absorbed in the stomach and the small intestine into the blood. Little is stored and excess passes out through kidneys. Fat-soluble A and D absorbed in the small intestine into the blood. Excess stored in the liver.

Liquids. (Water) About one-fifth of the total absorbed by the stomach and four-fifths through small intestine into blood. Excess is withdrawn by the kidneys automatically to maintain proper composition of blood.

ENERGY VALUE OF FOODS

Energy provided by food is required by the body for many purposes:
1. To maintain normal temperature 37°C.
2. For all physical activity.
3. To maintain the action of the heart, the circulation of the blood, respiration, and other movements of internal organs.
4. To maintain chemical processes within the body cells, e.g. secretion.

Each of the three nutrients (carbohydrate, fat and protein) can provide this energy. Many foods contain a mixture of these three nutrients so the energy supplied by each of these nutrients added together is the total in the particular food.

To measure the energy in food
The energy value of food is measured in terms of heat units called kilocalories (kcal). A kilocalorie is the amount of heat required to raise 1 kilogram of water through 1°C. The term Calorie is still sometimes used in nutrition instead of kilocalorie.

Energy value of nutrients

Carbohydrates	1 gram yields 4 kcal – 25 grams yield 100 kcal
Fats	1 gram yields 9 kcal – 25 grams yield 225 kcal
Proteins	1 gram yields 4 kcal – 25 grams yield 100 kcal

The joule (J) is the SI unit for heat and energy.
  4.186 kilojoules = 1 kilocalorie
  4.186 megajoules = 1,000 kilocalories
Nutrition tables usually give measurements in kilocalories and kilojoules or megajoules.

Daily energy recommendations

The amount of energy used by different people depends on the amount of their living tissue, i.e. surface area of individual bodies; also on the amount of physical activity, age and sex.

Note: Children are small but may be very active and so need many kilocalories in proportion to their size.

Man	2,100 – 3,600 kcal
Woman	1,900 – 2,700 kcal
Child	1,200 – 3,000 kcal

Calculating energy value of different foods

Egg (average 57 g)
Nutrients in weight per 100 grams:

Nutrient	Quantity in g	Energy value per g	Kcal	Total kcal per 100 g	Energy value 57 g egg
Carbohydrate	1.0	4	4.0		
Fat	12.3	9	110.7		
Protein	11.9	4	47.6		
				162.3	$\frac{57}{100} \times 162.3 = 93$ kcal

Energy from fat = 68%

Cabbage (75 g portion)
Nutrients in weight per 100 grams:

Nutrient	Quantity in g	Energy value per g	Kcal	Total kcal per 100 g	Energy value 75 g cabbage
Carbohydrate	1.3	4	5.2		
Fat	0	9	0		
Protein	0.8	4	3.2		
				8.4	$\frac{75}{100} \times 8.4 = 6$ kcal

Energy from fat = 0%

Cheese (75 g portion Cheshire cheese)
Nutrients in weight per 100 grams:

Nutrient	Quantity in g	Energy value per g	Kcal	Total kcal per 100 g	Energy value 75 g cheese
Carbohydrate	0	4	0		
Fat	34.5	9	310.5		
Protein	25.4	4	101.6		
				412.1	$\frac{75}{100} \times 412.1 = 309$ kcal

Energy from fat = 75%

Basal metabolism and energy requirements. The rate at which the essential involuntary body processes proceed varies with the individual but will be approximately 70 kcal per hour for an average man and 60 kcal per hour for an average woman during sleep.

Additional energy needed for everyday activities in kilocalories per hour

Sitting	15	Writing	20
Standing	20	Typing	30
Walking slowly	115	Cycling	125
Walking downstairs	290	Carpentry	140
Walking upstairs	1,000	Mining	350

It will be seen that the energy requirements are sharply increased as the work involves more muscular activity – e.g. writing, 20 kilocalories; mining, 350 kilocalories.

Energy value of a diet

If diet contains 400 g carbohydrate
100 g fat
100 g protein
the energy value is:

Carbohydrate	4 × 400 =	1,600
Fat	9 × 100 =	900
Protein	4 × 100 =	400
		2,900 kcal per day

Nutrients supplying kilocalories

Carbohydrates. Sugars, starches.
Must be converted to monosaccharides to be absorbed.
May be stored in the body as fat.

Fats. May be animal or vegetable. MINERAL oils which are chemically quite different from edible fats and oils are not usually suitable for human consumption. Fats are absorbed as fatty acids and glycerol through the small intestine into the lymphatic system and then into the bloodstream.
Plants and all animals can form their fat from carbohydrates.
Fats are stored in the body as fat.

Proteins. They are essential constituents of plant and animal cells needed for growth and repair. Animals cannot form their own amino-acids from which protein is formed, and so this must be obtained in the first instance from plants or other animals,

Animal protein is usually of high biological value as it contains the essential amino-acids. Vegetable protein may not be of such high biological value so more bulk has to be eaten to supply all the essential amino-acids. A mixture of both is advisable. Supplying energy is only a secondary function of protein.

Kilocalories and fatness

Excess carbohydrate and fat are stored in the body as fat. Excess protein is broken down. The nitrogen is removed and excreted as urea: the remainder is used as a source of energy.

The most fattening foods are those containing the most kilocalories.

2. MEAL PLANNING

A day's meals may vary considerably according to the circumstances of the family, the working hours of the family, the area lived in, etc. but generally speaking there is one main meal, either at midday or in the evening, and two other lighter meals, one being breakfast.

People plan meals to their own particular meal pattern. It is not enough to produce a few perfect dishes – it is a combination of dishes to produce suitable meals for particular occasions which is important.

The word 'menu' is French, and the translation is literally 'small or minute detail'. The English equivalent is 'bill of fare'. The making of menus is a great art, requiring correct technical knowledge and good judgement. Skill is needed to provide a meal which will combine a well-balanced diet with a pleasing colour scheme, which can be cooked adequately and served in the time allotted with the equipment available.

The meal chosen and the number of courses, etc. will depend on whether it is for an elaborate social occasion, a family meal or a simple type of entertaining. An appreciation of good food, well cooked and presented, is an important factor in social relationships. Meal-times should be enjoyable occasions for all concerned, including the cook. Experience will help in planning meals wisely in certain respects, but the following points must be considered:

1. The needs of individual members of the family – age, sex, work, health.

2. The nutritional aspect: some food from each of the three food groups (i.e. food for growth and repair, for energy and for regulation of body processes) should be served, with special attention to mineral elements, vitamins, water and fibre, with reference to point 1.

3. The occasion for which the meal is required, e.g. special occasion or family meal, and the number of people eating.

4. The money available for catering.

5. Time available for preparation and cooking. Someone who is out at work all day will need dishes which may be prepared the night before or in the morning, and may need to utilise convenience foods – canned, frozen or dehydrated.

6. Cooking facilities available, fuel economy, type of cooker, use of automatic oven-timing.

7. Season of the year, using foods which are cheapest and best. Use of home-grown produce. Food available in store.

8. Provide foods suitable for the time of year.

9. Shopping facilities – when food is fresh in local shops. If a refrigerator is available to store perishable food. Amount of storage space available for dry foods. Is a home freezer available?

10. Capabilities of the cook.

11. Give variety in meals. Consider flavour (do not repeat the same flavour, e.g. not pea soup and peas for vegetables) and colour. Texture should vary between soft and crisp foods for mastication. Variety of appearance, e.g. not shepherd's pie followed by apple crumble. Variety in cooking methods, e.g. not meat pie and fruit pie. Variety in garnishing to look colourful.

12. Make meals look and taste as attractive as possible.

Planning a menu for a day

A sensible guideline would be:

Protein – at least two servings of animal protein. (See vegetarian cookery pages 36–37.)

Liver, kidney or heart once a week if possible.

Milk – At least 500 ml per day for adults.

At least 750 ml for children.

Milk products may be used to replace part of the milk.

Butter cannot replace milk.

Fruit and Vegetables – four servings per day.

At least one serving of citrus fruit or a vegetable to supply vitamin C.

Dark green or deep yellow vegetable at least once a day for vitamins A and C.

Cereals – Bread, cake and cereals as appetite demands. Usually about 4 servings.

Fibre – encourages peristalsis (movement of the digestive tract) and aids elimination.

Water – 1.25 litres of water per day in all liquids taken.

Note: Care should be taken to supply an adequate breakfast as a start to the day, especially for young people and manual workers.

Average portions

The portion served depends upon the needs of the person eating the meal, the type of meal being served, and the cost. Weight given indicates the raw weight of commodities per person.

Soup	150–200 ml
Fruit juice	100 ml
Hors d'oeuvres	100 g
Fish (off the bone)	100 g
(on the bone)	150 g

Meat (off the bone)	100 g
(on the bone)	150 g
Cheese	50 g
Eggs (2 eggs)	100 g
Vegetables (more if a lot of wastage in preparation)	100 g
Potatoes (depending on appetite and nutritional needs)	200 g
Gravy	25 ml
Milk puddings	125 ml milk
Cold sweets	100 g
Fruit	100 g
Pastry flans, steamed and baked puddings using flour	25–40 g flour
Sweet sauces	50 g
Drinks	175 ml

NEEDS OF INDIVIDUALS IN A FAMILY

Needs may vary considerably:
  Father – may be manual worker or sedentary worker.
  Mother – may be at home or working, may be expectant or nursing.
  Small baby.
  Toddler.
  Boys and girls up to 13.
  Adolescents.
  Elderly people.
  Invalids and convalescents.
  Vegetarians.
  The aim in feeding is to provide each member of a family with all the nutrients required by his or her particular body in the correct proportion. These may vary considerably but the cook should be able to plan meals which can be adapted to suit the needs of all the members of the household.

Feeding the expectant mother

The diet must provide for the health of the mother and development of the infant and for the storage of some nutrients, e.g. iron to last until the child is weaned. A mixed diet is required with extra supplies of animal (high biological value) protein – milk, eggs, cheese, meat, fish. A good supply of vitamins – vitamin C (fresh fruit and vegetables and orange juice). Vitamin B group (supplied in most natural foods). Vitamins A and D for bone and teeth development (dairy foods and in tablets and drops supplied by clinics). A good supply of mineral elements, especially calcium for bone and teeth formation and iron for development of red blood cells and for storage in the infant's liver until weaned. (Calcium and iron are also present in the tablets supplied by the clinic.) Avoid strong tea, alcohol, highly seasoned foods and too much fried food.

Nursing mother

Diet is as for the expectant mother, but with a greater supply of protein, vitamins, calcium and iron.

Feeding the toddler

This is a period of rapid growth, but the appetite is often small; so avoid bulky foods and those of little nutritive value. Supply plenty of good-quality protein for body growth.

Milk, eggs, cheese, meat, fish.

Fresh fruit and vegetables for vitamins C and A and iron.

Dairy produce for vitamins A and D and calcium.

Food to give 'bite' – rusks, crusts, carrots, apples.

Fill up with carbohydrate foods. Meal-times should be a pleasure to toddlers. There should never be a feeling of tension. Children must not be over-tired when they sit down to a meal. Portions should be small and attractive – a second helping can always be given. Plenty of time should be allowed for meals. Introduce new foods and flavours carefully. Avoid highly spiced foods. Gay tableware, colourful cloths, attractively presented food will make meal-times more interesting. Training should be given to develop acceptable eating habits and recognised social behaviour.

Toddler's diet for one day

Breakfast. Porridge or cereal + sugar + milk
  Scrambled egg
  Crisp toast
  Butter or margarine
  Jam or honey
  Milk
Mid-morning. Fruit drink or milk drink.
Lunch. Fillets of fish baked in milk
  Creamed potatoes
  Spring cabbage

Fruit fool
Milk
Tea. Cheese sandwiches
Fruit and milk jelly
Biscuit or sponge cake
Milk or fruit juice
6 p.m. Drink of milk or fruit drink.

Feeding children aged 6–12 years

During this stage boys and girls are growing rapidly and are very active. Considerations for diet are the same as for toddlers but with increasingly large helpings. A much greater supply of kilocalories is needed especially at the end of the period, but care must be taken to avoid supplying carbohydrate instead of protein. New foods and flavourings should be introduced during this period. They should be served at the beginning of the meal when the child is hungry. 30% of the kilocalorie requirement should be supplied by fat to avoid too bulky a diet. School meals and milk at school could assist in providing a satisfactory diet.

Feeding the adolescent

The nutritional requirements of adolescents are higher in many cases than those of any other group. This is a period of rapid growth and development and great activity. Appetites are large. A good supply of animal protein must be provided. Milk is a valuable food for this group – supplying protein and calcium. Raw fruit and fresh vegetables must be supplied daily. 30% of the total kilocalories each day should be supplied as fat, or the diet will be too bulky. School meals and canteen meals could help to provide a balanced diet. In the lower income group there might be a tendency to provide too much carbohydrate instead of protein. Care must be taken with packed meals to ensure that there is not a deficiency of protein, calcium and vitamin C. Adolescent girls require a good supply of iron or they may suffer from anaemia if their periods are heavy.

Feeding the manual worker

An increased supply of kilocalories must be provided. At least 30% of the kilocalories should be supplied by fat, or the diet will be too bulky. Extra thiamin will be required to assist in the digestion and assimilation of carbohydrates. There should be some increase in the protein intake. Extra salt, water and vitamin C will be needed if the work is done in a humid atmosphere. 3 full meals a day and some snacks must be provided. Fried food, pulse foods and suet puddings, and all carbohydrate foods, are valuable in this diet, but not to the exclusion of protein.

Feeding elderly people

A supply of animal protein for body repair. Calcium and vitamin D to ensure healthy bones and avoid decalcification. Vitamins C and A to combat infection. Vitamin B group to assist the nerves. Iron must be supplied as there might be a tendency to anaemia.

Food must be easy to digest. Several small meals are better than one large one. Foods should be easy to eat as eyesight might be poor and dentures inadequate – avoid fish with bones, nuts, figs, etc. Milk should play an important part in this diet.

Malnutrition in the old is often caused by shopping difficulties in bad weather; making do with a cup of tea and a biscuit instead of a meal due to lack of interest and capability, and money; poor cooking and storage facilities. Some local authorities supply midday meals for elderly people in their homes, or will arrange to cook or shop for them.

INVALID COOKERY

Providing diets for special diseases needs training in dietetics, but it is necessary to know how to feed invalids not on special diets, or who are convalescent, in order to speed their recovery.

The main aim is to build up wasted tissues and to give a good supply of vitamins and minerals – vitamins C and A and B group, iron and calcium are especially valuable. Stress should be put upon protein food for body repair. Warmth and energy foods, e.g. the carbohydrates, are needed in much smaller supply, and so are the fats – greasy foods are generally avoided.

So it is necessary to know the food nutrients and their function in order to supply balanced meals suitable for the type of illness being treated. *But* doctors' orders must be obeyed.

There are usually three stages in an illness:

Early stage

Temperature is usually above normal and there is little appetite. A liquid diet is usually all that is needed until temperature drops.

Fruit juices, e.g. orange or lemon, blackcurrant juice.

Sweeten with glucose which can be absorbed directly into the bloodstream without much digestion. In the case of stomach disorders, strain the juice to avoid pulp which would irritate the stomach lining. Honey is also easily digested and can be used for sweetening.

Milk and milk drinks unless forbidden by the doctor, but these are not really thirst-quenching.

Barley water.

At least 2.5 litres of liquid per day are usually required at this stage. A supply of cold drink should be left at hand unless the patient is too ill.

Second stage

When temperature has dropped, a little solid food can normally be introduced, but this must be very light and easily digested.

Foods giving a supply of necessary mineral elements and vitamins, especially calcium and vitamin C, should be offered.

Egg dishes which are lightly cooked, e.g. scrambled egg.

Minced meat, chicken or white fish (not fried).

Milk and milk dishes.

Fruit and vegetables to give a good supply of vitamin C.

A good supply of liquid should still be given unless forbidden in the diet.

Third stage (convalescent stage)

A varied diet is now needed to build up the patient. Within reason he should eat what he wants, but the following are suggested.

White fish

Poultry

Dairy foods

Meat (pork may be indigestible)

Fruit

Vegetables

Potato or rice

Carbohydrate food as desired.

General rules

1. Doctor's instructions about diet must be obeyed.
2. Scrupulous cleanliness during preparation, cooking and serving.
3. Food must be fresh and of the best quality possible.
4. Punctual and regular meal-times.
5. All cooking should be done out of sight and smell of the sick-room, and should be a pleasant surprise to the patient.
6. Choose appetising easily digested foods. Give variety in kind, colour, flavour, as far as possible, and in methods of cooking and serving. Do not serve highly flavoured meals.
7. Avoid bulky foods, e.g. too much carbohydrate. Avoid fried or greasy foods as these are difficult to digest.
8. Serve small dainty portions – a little often rather than fewer, larger meals. Meals are a break in a long day for an invalid.

9. Make the food as attractive as possible to tempt the appetite. Never serve food left over from previous meal.

Foods which might be unsuitable.
   All fried food and greasy food.
   Rich pastry and fresh new bread.
   Pork and fat meat. Sausages.
   Highly seasoned foods, sauces and pickles.

Serving the meals. Everything must look as attractive as possible to tempt the appetite. Spotless tray, cloth, crockery, cutlery and napkin. Everything convenient for use and some colour introduced, e.g. with flowers, garnishes.
   Serve small portions in attractive individual dishes.
   Remove tray and all traces of food when meal is over. But always leave a drink within reach, covered.

Convalescent diet for one day

Breakfast   Fruit juice
          Scrambled egg
          Toast
          Marmalade
          Coffee or tea

Midday   Braised liver
          Carrots
          Creamed potatoes
          Fruit salad and cream
          Coffee or tea

Evening   Chicken casserole
          Mixed vegetables
          Rice
          Caramel custard
          Coffee or tea

VEGETARIAN COOKERY

Vegetarians are those who have conscientious, religious or aesthetic objections to using animal flesh as food. There are two main types of vegetarian.
   1. *Strict vegetarian*. This type will not eat animal products of any kind.
   2. *Lacto-vegetarian*. This type will not eat flesh, e.g. meat, fish or poultry, but will eat eggs, milk and cheese.

Strict vegetarian (vegan)

Such a diet is very limited in choice and could be monotonous, bulky and uninteresting. It could be difficult to adapt to such a diet and there are problems in supplying some nutrients.

The chief difficulty is to provide an adequate supply of the essential amino-acids without adding too much bulk, the fat-soluble vitamins A and D and the minerals calcium, phosphorus and iron.

Most difficult is the supply of protein. The best sources are the pulses, peas, beans, lentils, soya and nuts, but the protein is of low biological value, so more must be eaten. This will give a large bulk in the diet and digestion may be difficult because of the skins and the cellulose, and sometimes the sulphur present. Cereals also provide a small supply. Cellulose will offer decided resistance to the action of the digestive juices and cannot be digested. Some vegetables also absorb water and become more bulky when cooked. Because of the bulk which has to be eaten, the stomach is very full after each meal. This may lead to enlargements without increase in the activity of the enzymes. So there is extra work for the muscles of the alimentary canal, and other body parts may be deprived of their full share of energy.

Vitamin A is obtained in the form of carotene from vegetables, but more bulk is needed to give adequate supply. There is no vitamin A in vegetable fat.

Vitamin D is more difficult. Vitaminised margarine may be used or vitamin tablets, but if the added vitamins come from animal sources, a true vegetarian would not take this, so most vitamin D would have to be obtained from sunshine.

The important mineral elements calcium, iron and phosphorus will have to be supplied by green vegetables, e.g. watercress, kale, cabbage, and by nuts.

Vegetable oils, fats and certain margarines replace animal fats in the diet. Nuts contain a large percentage of oil.

Vegetable extracts, e.g. Marmite, replace meat extracts.

Agar-agar for gelatine replacement (from seaweed).

There should be no shortage of carbohydrates (may be too much) or of vitamins of the B group (except possibly vitamin B_{12}) and vitamin C.

But: Lack of variety – in kind and flavour. Lack of savour. Diet may be monotonous. Make it colourful and flavour it well with herbs and spices, celery, onions, curry powder, tomatoes, mushrooms.

Diet may be expensive. Medical advice should be sought before undertaking such a change in diet.

Lacto-vegetarian

It is much easier to achieve a balanced diet – animal protein will be supplied by cheese, milk and eggs, and all the vegetable protein foods mentioned above may be eaten, so that it is easier to supply all the essential amino-acids. Vitamins A and D and calcium will be provided by dairy foods. The diet can be more colourful and have more flavour, and is not so bulky.

SHOPPING

1. Think out meals or at least chief items for as far ahead as possible. This could economise in time and money, and ensure variety and balance.

2. Make sure of money available for housekeeping and what the money is to cover.

3. Buy the best quality which can be afforded for money available.

4. Buy at shops where turnover is quick and goods fresh.

5. Patronise clean shops (see food hygiene notes page 190).

6. Inspect larder before shopping to use up surplus food.

7. Buy and choose personally, if possible. If goods are delivered check with invoice.

8. Keep receipted accounts. Keep account book to see where money is being spent. Do not run up an account but pay cash if convenient.

9. Be methodical in shopping – use a list and plan a route.

10. Know appearance of various foods when fresh and at their best to obtain the best nutritive and economic value. Consider 'sell by' or 'best by' dates.

11. Study shop windows for any economies that can be made which are good value e.g. 'loss leaders'. May be economical sometimes to buy dry or canned goods in bulk.

12. Keep a supply of canned and other convenience foods for emergency meals.

13. Use of food in season. Preserving of such food will give supply when not so plentiful and save money. Use of glut of garden produce.

3. MEAT COOKERY

Meat is one of the most important of the animal protein foods. Because of the cost of meat and the need to produce meat dishes which are tender and tasty, it is necessary to appreciate that finished dishes depend upon the appropriate choice of meat cuts and cooking methods. Knowledge is required about the construction of meat related to choice, preparation and cooking.

NUTRITIVE VALUE OF MEAT

Protein
About 18% in lean meat – myosin, globulin (elastin, collagen).

Fat
About 3% although amount varies with the cut of meat – liver and kidney contain very little.

Carbohydrate
None in meat. Very little in liver (glycogen).

Water
Lean meat contains 75%. The more fat the less water.

Mineral elements
Iron. Liver, kidney and corned beef give a good supply. All meat provides some.
Phosphorus. Good supply especially in liver, sweetbread and kidney.
Sulphur. Some in all meat.

Vitamins
Vitamin A. Liver, heart and kidney give a good supply. Other meat a negligible supply.
Thiamin. Good suppy in pork, bacon and ham. Fair supply in other meat.

Riboflavin and *nicotinic acid*. Liver, heart and kidney give a good supply. Other meat a small supply.
Vitamin C. None in meat.
Vitamin D. A little in beef dripping. None in meat.

STRUCTURE OF MEAT
Lean

Lean meat is muscle tissue and consists of bundles of fibres which contain the meat and juices and protein. The length and thickness of the muscle fibres in lean meat vary according to the type of animal, the breed, the age, and the cut. Older animals have long coarse fibres; young animals have short, fine muscle fibres. Parts of the animal which have been more active, e.g. neck and lower leg, will also have coarser fibres. The fibres are held together by connective tissue.

Fat

There is fat under the skin, between the muscle bundles (marbling) and around the vital organs, e.g. suet around kidneys.

Connective Tissue (Gristle)

As already indicated, meat fibres are held together by connective tissue. The fibres are held in bundles and the bundles are held together by more connective tissue. The amount of connective tissue depends upon the type of animal, the age and the cut. As beef and mutton animals get older they develop more connective tissue which becomes less soluble and takes longer to soften in cooking. Lambs, pigs and calves which are young when slaughtered have less connective tissue, and it softens more readily during cooking. All animals have more gristle in the parts which have been more active, e.g. neck and leg.

Connective tissue contains two proteins, collagen and elastin. Both are insoluble in cold water but collagen can be changed to gelatin by slow, moist methods of cooking, e.g. stewing. Gelatin is more palatable and will provide setting for dishes such as brawn or pies. Elastin is not changed by cooking and remains tough and inedible.

Bone

The amount of bone is an important factor in the value of the meat which is obtained from a cut.

CHOICE OF MEAT

Particular cuts of meat recommended for various methods of cooking are listed on pages 41–46 and see table on page 48.

Colour

This varies according to the type of animal, the breed and age, and its feeding.
Lamb (and mutton). Cuts from young lamb are small. Smooth pinkish brown lean.
Creamy white fat. Mutton is darker with white fat.
Pork. Firm, smooth lean. Pinkish colour. White fat.
Veal. Pink lean. White fat.
Beef. The colour of uncooked beef is not a good guide to tenderness or taste but the
following is a general guide: Smooth and firm lean. Red to brownish red colour.
Creamy or pale yellow fat.

Many customers mistakenly look for bright red lean beef as an indication of
eating quality. In fact the colour can vary according to length of storage, handling
and packaging. A better guarantee of quality is to use a reliable butcher.

Fibres

The tender, lean cuts of meat with fine fibres, particularly beef, are the most
expensive. Tough cuts of meat which have long, coarse fibres and more gristle need
to be cooked by slow, moist methods of cooking to tenderise the fibres. Cutting
across the fibres for stewing or braising helps to make the meat more tender and
palatable. Breaking the fibres by mincing, passing the meat between sharp rollers,
or beating pieces of meat with a tenderiser enables the use of quicker methods of
cooking for tougher cuts.

Connective Tissue (Gristle)

Cuts of meat, particularly beef, with a lot of connective tissue should be cooked by
slow, moist methods of cooking to convert the collagen to gelatin.

Fat

The amount of fat present in a cut of meat can usually be seen, except for the
marbling within the cut. A high proportion of fat obviously reduces the amount of
lean, and thus protein provided by the meat. Some people are reluctant to eat fat.
However, fat can add flavour when cooking meat and some fat is necessary to keep
meat moist in dry methods of cooking such as roasting, grilling or frying.

CUTS OF MEAT

Lamb

Scrag and middle neck. Usually sold in slices or chops, on the bone, and used for
stewing or braising. Traditional cuts for Irish Stew or Lancashire Hotpot.

Best end of neck. Can be purchased as a roasting joint with a row of 6 or 7 rib
bones. The butcher will 'chine' (chop) through the back bone, to make carving

easier. Is also sold sliced as *cutlets*, with one rib bone on each. Recognisable by the dot of lean beneath the 'eye' of lean. Traditional cut for 'Crown Roast' or 'Guard of Honour'. Cutlets can be fried, grilled, stewed or braised.

Loin. Sold whole as roasting joint or cut into loin chops. Chops usually grilled or fried.

Chump. Usually sold as chump chops for grilling and frying. Recognisable by small round bone in centre.

Saddle of lamb. A large roasting joint which is the whole loin from both sides of the animal, left in one piece. Most often used for special-occasion entertaining.

Leg. Can be divided into fillet (tail) end or shank (foot) end. Usually roasted. Fillet end can be boned to provide cavity for stuffing.

Breast. Long cut, streaked with fat and lean (equivalent to belly pork and streaky bacon). Usually sold boned and rolled. Can be stuffed before braising or roasting.

Shoulder. Sold whole or halved into blade end and knuckle end. Very tender, succulent meat. Considerable amount of bone, which butcher will bone out, making carving easier. Roast or braise.

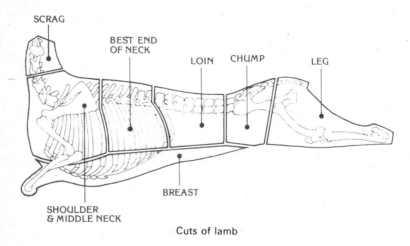

Cuts of lamb

Beef

Cuts suitable for stewing, braising and boiling

Shin (foreleg) ⎤ High proportion of connective tissue. Lean meat.
Leg (hindleg) ⎦ Suitable for stews, casseroles and soup.

Neck and clod. Usually minced or cubed and sold as 'stewing steak'. Needs slow, moist cooking. Often used as pie filling.

Chuck and blade steak. A large, fairly lean, high quality stewing cut. Usually cut into pieces for braising, stewing and for pie fillings.

Thick flank (also known as Top Rump). Lean cut with covering of fat, sold for roasting, pot-roasting, braising and frying.

Thin flank. Ideal cut for braising and stewing. Can be salted. Often sold as mince.

Brisket. Joint sold on or off the bone. Frequently boned and rolled. Requires slow, moist cooking such as braising or boiling. Often salted for pressed beef and served cold.

Thin and thick ribs. Usually sold boned and rolled. Ideal for braising and pot-roasting.

Silverside. Traditional for boiled beef and carrots, when it is purchased salted, ready for boiling. Today, usually sold for roasting. Very lean. No bone.

Cuts suitable for roasting, grilling and frying

Fore rib. Traditional cut for Roast Beef of Old England. Sold on the bone or boned and rolled. Equivalent to lamb cutlet, but joint size.

Sirloin. Equivalent to loin of lamb and pork. The most expensive roasting joint. Sold on the bone, or boned and rolled. The fillet is the smaller 'eye' on one side of the rib bone, which is usually removed and sold sliced 150–200 g fillet steaks. Large pieces of fillet also sold for Boeuf en Croûte. Sirloin steaks are slices of the larger 'eye' of lean.

Topside. Lean cut of meat with little or no fat. Often sold with layer of fat wrapped round it. Can be roasted or pot-roasted.

Silverside. In many parts of the country (especially Scotland) silverside is sold for roasting. Needs constant basting.

Thick flank (also known as Top Rump). A lean cut often sold for roasting or pot-roasting.

Rump. A large very lean, tender cut. Always sold as slices of rump steak for grilling and frying.

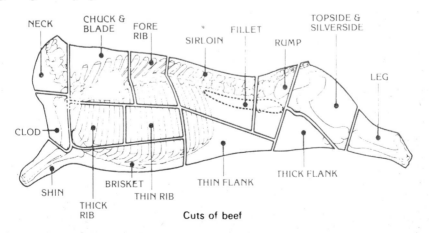

Cuts of beef

Steaks. The most common steaks served at home are rump, sirloin and fillet. Various other cutting methods are used to provide steaks for the restaurant trade such as tournedos, châteaubriand, T-bone, porterhouse, entrecôte and mignon.

'Flash Fry'. A term used for thin lean cuts which have been tenderised by passing the meat between knife-covered rollers. The knives puncture the meat, thus breaking it up into short lengths, 1–2 cm per fibre. This makes the meat more tender and reduces the cooking time, i.e. it can be flash (quickly) fried.

Veal

Most veal sold in this country is meat from young milk-fed calves which are slaughtered at about 16 weeks old. Bobby veal is produced from calves slaughtered at 1–2 weeks. Veal cuts are similar to lamb and pork. Veal is more popular in France and Italy than in this country where it is an expensive meat more commonly served in restaurants or hotels than at home.

Pork

All cuts of pork can be roasted.

Neck end (spare rib and blade bone). Either sold as roasting joints or cut into chops for braising or grilling.

Loin. Usually divided into fore loin and hind loin. May be sold as a piece for roasting, with the fillet (tenderloin) removed, or cut into chops for grilling and frying. Produces good crackling.

Tenderloin. Lean, tender cut found on the underneath of the backbone of the hind loin. Sometimes called pork fillet. Ideal for slicing and frying. Can be stuffed and rolled or covered with puff pastry, before roasting.

Chump. Usually cut into large, meaty chops suitable for grilling and frying.

Leg. Can be cut into 4 or more parts for roasting. The fillet end, nearest the tail, is

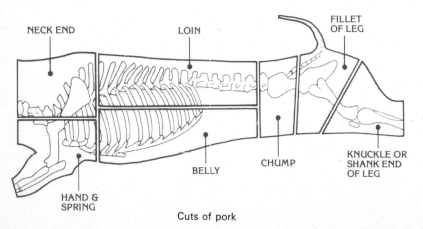

Cuts of pork

the prime roasting joint, which is often boned and stuffed. It is sometimes sold sliced for grilling or frying. The feet (trotters) are usually salted and boiled or used to make brawn.

Belly. Long fat cut, streaked with lean. Can be boned, stuffed and rolled for roasting or braising, or cut into slices for grilling. Sometimes salted for boiling.

Hand and spring. Large roasting joint, often divided into hand and shank. The hand (upper part) is often boned and stuffed for roasting. The shank (lower part) is sometimes salted for boiling or used for stews and casseroles.

Head. Usually used in manufactured pork products such as sausages, bath chaps, brawn and pies.

Bacon and ham

Bacon is the brine-cured flesh of pigs bred for bacon.

Green bacon is brine-cured but not smoked.

Smoked bacon is brine-cured and then wood-smoked.

Bacon curing

The head, trotters and organs are removed. The bristles are softened in scalding water, and taken off by a revolving drum. The carcase is singed to tenderise the rind, weighed and split lengthwise into two 'sides'. Brine is injected into the fleshy parts and the sides are then stacked in large brine tanks. They are clamped down and left to steep for at least four days. The brine is drained off to be used again. The salted sides are stacked in a maturing room and kept at a temperature of about 4°C for at least a week. This maturing period is most important as it gives the meat the characteristics of bacon. During smoking the cured sides are hung in the smoke from smouldering oak or deal sawdust for 36–60 hours, depending upon the degree of smoking required.

Storing bacon

Bacon will keep very well in an airy store-room or a household refrigerator where it should be wrapped in foil, polythene or grease-proof paper. If left unwrapped in the refrigerator, it will quickly become dry due to the evaporaton of liquid and concentration of salt on the surface.

Gammon. This is the hind leg of a bacon pig, which is brine-cured while still on the bacon side. It is cut off square and usually smoked.

Ham. This is the hind leg of a specially bred pig, cut off round on the bone and cured very slowly in dry salt. Hams are usually unsmoked.

Cuts of bacon and ham, and how to use them

Note: Names of cut vary from one district to another.

Gammon hock. A delicious cut for boiling, which is also excellent when braised (in water, stock or cider) After cooking, it can be skinned and pressed lightly. The hock can also be roasted.

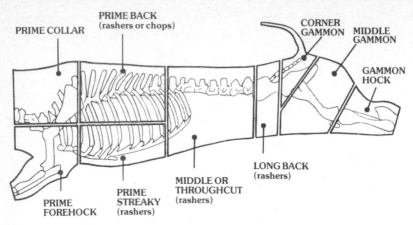

Cuts of bacon and ham

Middle gammon. Perfect for boiling or baking, and can also be baked in a crust. When cut into thick rashers (1 cm) it can be served as gammon steaks. See also the corner gammon joint.

Long back. Good and lean. Slice thinly to fry gently, or grill quickly. Makes generous servings.

Middle or Throughcut rashers. The back and streaky rashers cut together. An economical buy and perfect for cooking in the piece or rashered thinly.

Prime back. Should be grilled or fried in thin rashers, boiled or braised in the piece. Bacon chops are cut from here and these can be fried, grilled, or roasted. An excellent lean cut.

Prime streaky rashers. Lean, and streaky at the end of the rasher. Best sliced thin. Good for frying crisp.

Prime collar. Makes excellent rashers and equally good served hot or cold as a joint, though as a joint it needs to be well soaked before cooking.

Prime forehock. Makes an ideal basis for a lentil stew or can be cooked gently in a casserole with vegetables and split peas.

Reasons for cooking meat

To make meat tender and digestible.

To develop extractives and so the flavour.

To make meat more palatable by the changing of the red haemoglobin to brown to please the eye and palate.

To kill bacteria – to make meat safe to eat and to keep.

METHODS OF COOKING

1. *Dry heat*. Roasting or baking. Grilling.

2. *Moist heat.* Stewing. Boiling. Steaming. Frying.
3. *Combination of moist + dry.* Braising.

PRINCIPLES OF COOKING MEAT

Choice of cooking method will depend on the following:

1. Cuts with more connective tissue need long, moist cooking at a low temperature – stewing, boiling, braising or pot-roasting in liquid or steam at about 100°C.

2. Cuts with very little connective tissue can be cooked for a shorter time at higher temperatures and by drier methods – frying, grilling and roasting.

Protein coagulates and hardens when heated, so meat must never be overcooked, especially by dry heat, or by boiling instead of simmering. The flavour of meat is particularly well developed by dry cooking methods. As protein coagulates it shrinks, squeezing out liquids and flavouring extractives. Fat melts and runs away.

The table overleaf shows the choice of cut for each cooking method. The cut names are those generally used in the South of England.

There is no method of cutting a carcase which is common throughout the British Isles. There are variations between and within regions, so that not only are the cuts and joints different, but the names given to them change according to locality. Names for cuts of beef vary most of all.

General preparation of meat for cooking.

1. Trim and wipe with a clean cloth. Remove superfluous fat. Tie or skewer into shape if needed.

2. *Wash* all internal parts. Meat should be used as quickly as possible.
Salted meat. Soak if necessary to remove brine.

3. Frozen meat. Large cuts must be allowed to thaw completely before cooking. Allow several hours, longer if left in the refrigerator. Small cuts need not be thawed before cooking.

4. Boning may be an economy, as a joint may be stuffed. Will cut up without waste, bones may be used for stock.

STORAGE OF MEAT

Uncooked meat. Remove wrapping paper and leave joint on a plate, either covered with a large bowl or tightly wrapped in foil, in a cool place or in a refrigerator.

Cooked meat should be lightly wrapped in a plastic bag or aluminium foil and kept in a cool place or refrigerator. Remove from the refrigerator half an hour before carving or the meat will be hard.

Cooking methods and cuts of meat

Cooking Method	Beef	Pork	Lamb
Frying and Grilling	Rump ⎫ Fillet ⎬ Steaks Sirloin ⎭	Fillet (tenderloin) Loin chops Spare rib chops *Belly – sliced *Kidney *Liver	Best End of Neck cutlets Loin ⎫ Chump ⎬ Chops *Kidney *Liver
Roasting	Topside Sirloin Fore rib Silverside Thick flank	Neck end (spare rib and blade bone) Loin Leg Hand and Spring Belly	Loin Best End of Neck Leg Shoulder Breast
Braising	Chuck and Blade Brisket Thin flank Thick flank Topside Silverside Thick rib *Oxtail	Spare rib chops Belly *Liver *Heart *Kidney	Middle Neck Breast Shoulder Scrag *Sweetbreads *Heart *Liver *Kidney
Pot Roasting	Silverside Thick flank Topside Thick rib Thin rib Brisket *Heart	*Heart	*Heart
Boiling	Brisket (salted) Silverside (salted) *Tongue (can be salted)	Belly (can be salted) Hand and Spring (can be salted) Head *Cheek *Tongue (can be salted) *Trotters	*Tongue
Stewing	Thin flank Shin Leg Neck and Clod Chuck and Blade Skirt *Cheek *Oxtail *Liver *Kidney	Hands and Spring Shoulder *Kidney	Scrag Breast Middle Neck *Kidney *Tongue

N.B.: All cuts of Pork and most Lamb cuts can be roasted.   *Offal

ACCOMPANIMENTS

Roast meat

Beef – Yorkshire pudding. Horseradish sauce. Mustard. Thin gravy.

Lamb – Mint sauce. Redcurrant jelly. Onion suace. Rosemary. Thin gravy. Thick gravy with stuffed joint.

Mutton – Redcurrant or cranberry jelly. Onion sauce. Thin gravy *or* thick gravy with stuffed joint.

Veal – Bacon rolls. Lemon slices. Veal forcemeat. Thickened gravy.

Pork – Sage and onion stuffing. Apple sauce. Thickened gravy.

Ham – Sugar, mustard or cider glaze. Garnish of fruit – apricots, pineapple, etc., and cloves.

Boiled meat

Dumplings. Vegetables cooked with the meat. Strained cooking liquid. Caper sauce with mutton. Parsley sauce. Mustard sauce or onion sauce with ham or bacon.

Grilled or fried meat

Maître d'hôtel butter. Grilled tomatoes and mushrooms. Fried potatoes (game chips). Watercress. Worcestershire sauce. Pineapple or onion rings with pork or ham.

Braised meat

Cubes or balls of carrot or swede cooked separately.
Vegetables cooked with the meat (mirepoix). Reduced cooking liquid.

Stewed meat

Brown stews. Vegetables cooked with the meat. Vegetables cooked separately. Creamed or boiled potatoes or rice. Thickened cooking liquid. Parsley.

White stews (fricassée or blanquette). Mushrooms. Bacon rolls. Lemon butterflies. Parsley. Crescents of fried bread. Sauce made from the cooking liquid.

OFFAL

Name from 'off all entrails' – offal is any edible parts of the inside of an animal. Includes kidneys, tripe, liver, heart, sweetbread, brain and tongue. The small intestine is used for sausage casings or in the manufacture of pharmaceuticals. Lights or lungs are sometimes used in haggis.

It is very important that internal parts be absolutely fresh and free from any taint. They do not keep well, so cook as soon as possible after purchase. All organs which are connected with waste products of the body need very thorough cleaning before use. Some tripe may need blanching.

Much offal is constructed in the same way as lean meat with collagen between the fibres. If close textured, e.g. ox liver and kidney and heart, it will need long slow cooking to make it tender and prevent hardening.

Offal used to be despised, and was very cheap. But because of the realisation of its high nutritive value, it is now popular and relatively expensive, because there are only limited amounts of each type is every animal.

Nutritive value
Valuable source of protein.
Fat depends on organ – little in liver, more in tripe.
Iron – especially in liver and kidney.
Vitamin A – especially in ox liver.
Vitamin B group.

Liver

Valuable source of iron. Ox liver supplies vitamin A. Liver is largely protein with little fat. Protein present is different from that in lean meat and is liable to form uric acid on digestion so should be avoided by people with rheumatism, gout or kidney trouble. Allow 100 g per person.

Preparation. Wash well in cold water. Remove membrane and tubes especially from ox liver. Dry well.

Method of cooking. Fry, stew or braise depending on type and tenderness.

Lamb's liver. Most tender for frying, but not the most nutritious.

Calf's liver and pig's liver. Considered to have the most flavour.

Ox liver – is the best source of iron and vitamin A, but needs very gentle and prolonged cooking.

Kidney

Must be absolutely fresh. It is a good source of iron. Similar type of protein to liver. Should be a good colour – brown with no greenish tinge. Free from spots or unpleasant smell. Unbroken skin, plump, firm and dry.

Preparation. Skin. Remove hard core. Wash thoroughly in warm water and dry well. Ox kidney is traditionally used for steak and kidney pie.

Method of cooking. Fry or grill lamb's kidney and stew or braise kidney from pig or ox.

Tripe

Prepared from stomach and intestines of cattle and sheep. Cleaned and boiled for about 12 hours before use. It is valuable as protein food. It can supply calcium because of the lime used in preparation. It is easily digested because it contains large amounts of connective tissue – collagen which is changed to gelatine by the slow cooking. It contains no extractives so lacks flavour and is usually cooked with something, e.g. onions, to add flavour. The fat is usually in layers and is easily removed.

Types – Best is blanket or double with fat between the honeycomb. Monkshood is deeper in colour.

Heart

Lambs' hearts usually sold whole; ox heart is sold sliced.

Preparation of lamb's heart. Wash thoroughly in cold, salt water. Remove flaps, tubes and gristle. If the hearts are to be stuffed, cut through dividing walls of cavities.

Method of cooking. Stew or braise ox heart. Roast or pot-roast lambs' hearts. Stuffed hearts should be securely tied with string to retain the stuffing.

Sweetbreads

From the throat (thymus) and belly (pancreas) regions of animals, preferably calf. Sweetbreads are a delicacy – light in texture, easily digested protein.

Preparation. Soak in cold water for several hours. Blanch in water to which a little lemon juice has been added – skin and fat are then easily removed.

Method of cooking. Stew, steam, grill, fry.

Brain

Easily digested, but not very nutritious.

Sheep's pluck

Foundation of haggis. Consists of heart and liver and sometimes lights or lungs. Cheap and nourishing.

Tongue

Is usually prepared by the butcher who soaks and salts it before sale. The tongue should be blanched and cooked till tender, for 3–4 hours. After cooking, remove the skin and the lining of the gullet and windpipe and the small bones at the root. The tongue can then be placed in a suitable bowl or tin, covered, and pressed with weights until cold.

Calf's tongue (400–800 g) and sheep's tongue (200–300 g) are usually unsalted.

POULTRY

Poultry includes domestic birds suitable for food. Chickens, hen, duck, turkey, goose, pigeon, etc.

Structure. A similar composition to meat, but usually more easily digested, because the fibres are shorter and the flesh is not interlaced with fat. The fat is just beneath the skin and around the internal organs, particularly the kidneys.

The flesh is drier than some meat. Breast and wing, i.e. the white meat, are more digestible than the flesh of the legs, which is coarser and darker because of the greater muscular activity.

Food value. Chiefly eaten for easily digested animal protein, especially in an invalid diet. Duck and goose are not so easily digested because of higher percentage of fat. Gives a small supply of vitamin B group, iron and phosphorus.

Classification

Chickens are usually classified as follows:

Poussins. Very young birds 400–600 g in weight. Usually served whole or in halves.

Spring chickens. Young birds 600–1,200 g.

Broilers. Similar to spring chickens. This is a new method of production – birds are kept in batteries and sold about 10 weeks old. Tender but may lack flavour.

Roasting chickens. 1.2–2.4 kg.

Boiling fowls. 1.6–2.8 kg.

Capons. Neutered cockerels. 2.8–3.2 kg in weight.

Hens are older birds which have had one or two laying seasons and are more suitable for boiling or steaming. Considered a chicken until 9 months old.

Choice of poultry

Birds must be free from any unpleasant odour. The flesh must be firm and show no trace of blue or greenish tinge. The eyes clear and not sunken.

Frozen poultry may be affected by hard, white patches of 'freezer burn' if the wrapping has been torn or broken. This could affect taste and texture. Watch out for excess frozen moisture which will reduce the thawed weight of the bird. Allow plenty of time (12 to 24 hours at room temperature for a chicken and up to 48 hours for a 5–9 kg turkey) to thaw completely before cooking to avoid tough meat and danger of salmonella poisoning. Follow instructions on label.

It is recommended that very large birds, e.g. Christmas turkeys, should not be cooked with stuffing inside because this may prevent the temperature inside the bird becoming high enough to destroy salmonella bacteria.

Remove giblets from inside the bird as soon as possible and always before cooking.

Chickens. Breast bone and beak should be pliable. Breast should be plump. Should have smooth legs, short spurs and soft feet.

Turkeys. Flesh firm and white. Breast plump. Smooth legs, short spurs, soft feet. Norfolk-bred turkeys are considered to have the finest flavour. Medium-sized birds are more tender and have finer flesh and flavour than a large bird.

Geese and ducks. Skin is white and the breast is plump. Yellow bill and soft pliable yellow feet. Geese should be less than a year old.

Aylesbury ducks and ducklings are considered best. Ducklings are in season March to August. Ducks, August to March.

Hanging

To be tender and develop flavour, freshly killed poultry must be hung until the period of rigor mortis has passed. Hang by the feet in a cool, dry, well-ventilated larder. The time varies with the kind of bird and the weather. Fowl for at least 24 hours. Geese or ducks a day or two. Turkeys 3–5 days. The time also depends on the freshness of bird when purchased. Never overhang. Hang with all intestinal parts in.

Giblets. Gizzard, liver and heart. With the neck and feet, they are used to make stock for gravy.

Economical use of poultry

Because of intensive rearing, poultry is now often cheaper than other meat but there is a lot of wastage. It is frequently not used to the best advantage. Carcass bones, skin and trimmings may be made into stock which will give good flavour for soups or sauces. Remnants of cooked fowl with various additions will make good salads or light entrées. Scraps and trimmings and livers can be made into appetising savouries. A fowl may be divided into joints and made into an entrée. Accompaniments served with roast chicken, e.g. sausages, bacon rolls and stuffing, will supplement the meat.

Accompaniments to poultry

Roast chicken. Veal forcemeat. Bacon rolls. Bread sauce. Thin gravy.

Roast turkey. Stuffing of chestnuts, sausage-meat or veal forcemeat. Bacon rolls. Cranberry sauce. Thickened gravy.

Roast duck. Sage and onion stuffing. Apple sauce. Orange slices. Thin gravy or orange sauce.

Roast goose. Sage and onion stuffing. Apple sauce. Thickened gravy.

Boiled fowl. White coating sauce. Lemon slices. Parsley. Chopped egg white and sieved yolk.

GAME

Game includes partridge, pheasant, grouse, snipe, woodcock, and water game – mallard, teal and widgeon – which are in season usually in the autumn and winter. August 12th is the beginning of the season for grouse and snipe. Game includes pigeon, rabbit and hare for which there is no closed season. Game is usually hung to improve the flavour and tenderness. Hanging time varies according to the type of game, the time it has been dead, and the weather.

Cooking – may be roasted, braised, casseroled, and made into pies and patés.

4. FISH COOKERY

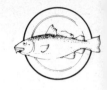

Oceans and inland waters contain vast resources of fish in both quantity and variety. With the increase in world population, it is necessary to use more of this food as an alternative to meat. The development of refrigeration and quick-freezing has made many varieties of fish available even to inland areas.

CLASSIFICATION OF FISH

a) *White fish*, e.g. sole, plaice, cod, whiting, coley.

The oil (fat) is stored in the liver only, thus leaving the flesh white and dry. The oil is used in vitamin capsules, cod-liver oil, halibut-liver oil.

b) *Oily fish*, e.g. herring, salmon, mackerel, eel.

The oil is distributed throughout the flesh, making it darker in colour but giving a higher nutritive value. It is more difficult to digest.

c) *Shell-fish*. Crustaceans – crabs, lobsters, shrimps, prawns, scampi.
                   Molluscs – mussels, cockles, etc.

Shell-fish supply protein and fat but are usually too expensive for everyday use. They must be cooked as soon as possible after leaving the water because they deteriorate rapidly.

Alternative classification

a) *Freshwater fish*, e.g. trout, salmon.

b) *Saltwater fish*.

Demersal. These fish live at the bottom of the sea and are caught by trawlers, e.g. cod, haddock, hake, plaice, whiting, sole.

Pelagic. This type swim near the surface of the sea and are caught by drifters, e.g. herring, mackerel, sprats, pilchards, mullet.

RECOGNITION OF FISH

Herring. Has a red eye. Diamond shaped markings with a silver underside and blue upperside. The gills are red and there are definite fins.

Haddock. Is a greyish bronze on the upperside and white below. There is a distinctive 'finger and thumb' mark behind the head and a definite black line along the body.

Cod. Has a cylindrical body of varying colour mostly greenish brown or olive grey, with or without mottling. A white line follows the line of the back.

Coley. Very nutritious fish, similar to cod in shape but flesh is pinkish grey colour and flavour stronger than cod. Use as for cod. Appearance improved by use of colourful sauce or garnish.

Hake. A very streamlined fish. Silver in colour and similar to cod in appearance but with a smaller head. It has a more delicate flavour and is more expensive.

Mackerel. Another long, cylindrical fish with dappled blue-black markings.

Halibut. A large, flat fish with a thick body, dark olive in colour marbled with lighter olive above and white below. Halibut flesh has a fine firm texture.

Plaice. A flat, oval fish. The skin is brown with orange-red spots above and white underside. The brightness of the spots is no indication of quality.

Lemon Sole. A long, oval flat fish with a smooth, yellow-brown skin marbled with darker and light blotches. The underside is white. Lemon sole has no scales.

Fillet from one side of round fish

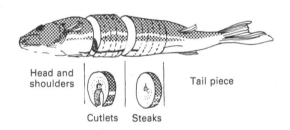

Head and shoulders   Tail piece

Cutlets   Steaks

How to buy fish

HOW TO BUY FISH

Small fish. 200–300 g weight are usually bought whole, e.g. herring, mackerel, whiting. The backbone may be removed before cooking. Grill, fry, bake or poach. Allow 1 fish per person.

Medium fish. 400 g–2 kg in weight. Whole fish are bought for stuffing and baking or poaching in a fish kettle. Allow 150 g per person.

Fillets. One fillet is cut from the whole length of the fish on either side. Allow 100 g per portion. Grill, steam, poach, fry or bake.

Not drawn to scale

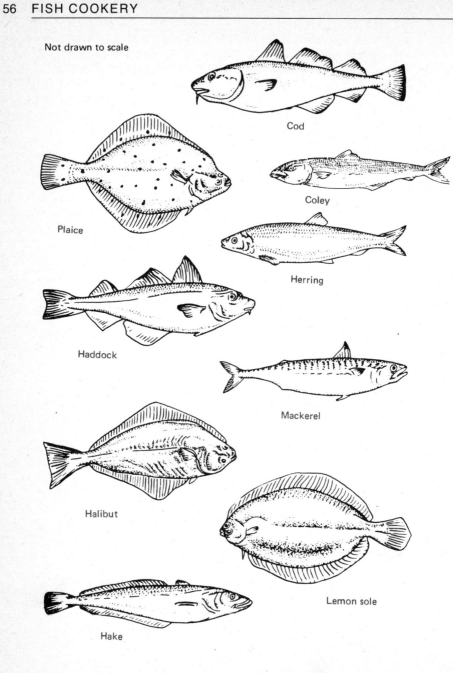

Cod

Plaice

Coley

Herring

Haddock

Mackerel

Halibut

Lemon sole

Hake

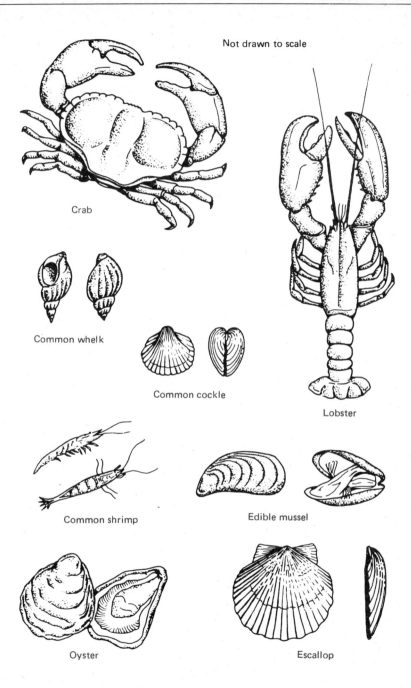

Not drawn to scale

Crab

Common whelk

Common cockle

Lobster

Common shrimp

Edible mussel

Oyster

Escallop

Large fish. 2 kg and over; can be divided into:

a) *Head piece*. Poach; use for fish soup, fish cakes, fish pie.

b) *Cutlet*. Allow 150 g per portion. Stuff and bake. Grill, fry or steam.

c) *Steak*. Allow 200 g per portion. Grill, bake, fry or steam. Sometimes bought as one large piece for baking.

d) *Tail piece*. Allow 150 g per portion. Bought as a piece for poaching or baking.

COMPOSITION OF FISH
Approximate percentage

White fish		*Oily fish*
17.5%	Protein	18.6%
0.5%	Fat	10.9%
80.0%	Water	67.5%
1.2%	Mineral elements	2.6%

Fish is a protein food which very closely resembles meat both in structure and composition, but is more easily digested and thus less satisfying.

The flesh is made up of muscle divided into flakes. The flakes or myotomes vary in size according to the fish. They are composed of the same type of protein amino-acid pattern as meat, but there is less connective tissue in fish and the flakes are therefore not held together as strongly as meat fibres. The connective tissue is collagen which is converted to gelatine by moist heat, thus causing the flakes to fall apart. For this reason fish is much more tender than meat and quicker to cook, but it is more liable to break up on serving. Fish is particularly suitable for invalids as it is easy to eat and digest if a suitable type and correctly cooked.

Some shell-fish have tough fibres, need more cooking and may be indigestible. They may be foul feeders and can cause food poisoning.

NUTRITIVE VALUE OF FISH

Edible portion.　App. 40% demersal (deep water) fish.
　　　　　　　　　　　55% pelagic (shallow)
　　　　　　　　　　　10.5% shell-fish

Waste material – skin, bones, head and shell.

Protein

The amount varies. White fish approximately 17.5%
　　　　　　　　　　Oily fish　　..　　18.6%
　　　　　　　　　　Shell-fish　　..　　10.2%

White fish is a valuable source of protein for invalids and children. Its lack of connective tissue makes it more easily digested.

Fat

White fish. Fat (oil) is present in the liver only. There is usually less than 1% but in halibut it is approximately 4%.

Oily fish. The oil is distributed throughout the flesh, the amount varying according to the time of year. It is high just before spawning and low afterwards. There is approximately 15% in herrings caught during the summer.

Shell-fish. Approximately 4%.

Carbohydrate

None in fish.

Energy value

White fish. 100 g – approximately 70 kcal.
Oily fish. 100 g – approximately 200 kcal.

Mineral elements

Iodine. In all sea fish.

Fluorine. In all sea fish. A little is found in freshwater fish.

Phosphorus. Present in all fish. Most is obtained from fish in which bones are eaten and from shell-fish.

Calcium. There is most in those fish eaten with bones, e.g. tinned sardines and salmon, but some is present in other fish.

Iron. A little in sprats, smelts and sardines.

Chlorine and Sodium. Obtained from sodium chloride, present in all fish.

Potassium. Found in all fish.

Vitamins

Vitamins A and D. Most oily fish contain the fat-soluble vitamins A and D. Eels are rich in vitamin A. Herrings, mackerel, sardines and tinned salmon are among the best fish sources of vitamin D. White fish contain no vitamin D and very little vitamin A in the flesh, but fish-liver oils contain large amounts of both vitamin A and vitamin D. Halibut-liver oil, cod-liver oil and tuna oil are very rich sources of vitamin D. Whale oil is a good commercial source of vitamin A.

Thiamin and riboflavin are present in small amounts in most fish. There is more in oily fish and fish roe is a good source of supply.

Nicotinic acid. The amount varies.

Vitamin C. Ascorbic acid. None in fish when sold.

Water. There is a high percentage of water, but this decreases according to the amount of fat present.

ECONOMIC VALUE

The price of fish is no indication of the nutritive value, but is regulated by the flavour, fashion and supply. The cheaper and more plentiful varieties of fish often supply the same nutrients as rarer and more expensive varieties. Compared with white fish, the oily fish, e.g. herrings, mackerel, supply most nutrients for a given sum of money. But fish may not be the most economical food because of the large percentage wastage in bone, head, etc. and in shell.

CHOICE OF FISH

It is essential to buy absolutely fresh fish as most types deteriorate very quickly, especially oily and shell-fish. Shell-fish may develop food-poisoning bacteria.

Fish is cheapest and at its best when in season and just before spawning. Fish of moderate size are superior in flavour and have finer flesh than large fish. Choose thick, plump fish. Shell-fish should not be faded and discoloured. Crab and lobster should be of medium size, preferably male.

Qualities to look for in fresh fish
1. Pleasant fishy smell.
2. Bright, prominent eyes.
3. Bright red gills.
4. Firm to the touch. Stiff tail (but this could be frozen).
5. Moist skin (could be wet).
6. Plentiful supply of scales on scaly fish, e.g. herring.

Use fish as quickly as possible, especially if it has been packed for transport in ice because it deteriorates on removal from ice. Shell-fish is usually sold cooked. If it is not it must be cooked as soon as possible as it deteriorates rapidly.

STORING FISH

Storage of fish in the home.
If possible, fish should be bought on the day it is to be used, and not stored. If storage is necessary, wrap loosely in fresh paper, plastic film or bag, and put in a refrigerator well away from odour-absorbing foods such as milk and butter. If you have no refrigerator sprinkle the fish with vinegar or lemon juice and put on a plate in a cool place and cover loosely.

Never soak fish in water or leave wrapped in tight layers of paper.

Do not store fresh fish for more than one day in a refrigerator.

Frozen fish should be stored according to the star marking on the packet and the frozen food locker/compartment of the household refrigerator or home freezer. If there are no star markings on the refrigerator frozen fish may be kept for up to 48 hours in the ice making compartment.

PRESERVATION OF FISH
Frozen fish

a) Fish may be frozen at sea for transport in ice lumps. Will keep for a short period.

b) Prepared fish (i.e. gutted and filleted or made, for example, into fish fingers) is quick frozen to a temperature of about −29°C. The ice crystals formed during quick freezing are very small and will not break up the fish. The fish will keep indefinitely in quick freeze conditions. Compared with fresh fish, frozen fish may be a little more expensive but it is convenient to buy and store, there is no waste, very little time is needed for preparation and it is very hygienic. 800 g fish yields approx. 400 g fillets.

Cured fish (smoked, salted)

Fish are smoked according to the taste in various districts.

Two methods of smoking are used. In *Cold Smoking* which is used for most fish cured in Britain the temperature of the smoke should not rise above 30°C or the fish will begin to cook. In *Hot Smoking* the fish is cooked as well as cured. The smoke reaches a temperature of approx. 120°C and the centre of the fish may reach 60°C. The smoke, obtained from fires of hardwood dust on top of white wood shavings, is blown across the fish under closely controlled conditions.

Herring may be cured in the following ways –

a) *Kippers* are herrings split open, washed, and soaked in brine. They are then impaled on hooks and smoked over a fire of hardwood chips and sawdust.

b) *Bloaters* are brined whole, threaded on to sharp wooden rods or speights and smoked over billets of burning wood.

c) *Bucklings* are beheaded herrings brined or dry-salted before being hot-smoked at 100°C which smokes and cooks them simultaneously.

d) *Roll mop* are filleted and washed before being marinaded in brine and vinegar. After maturing for ten days they are rolled and packed into containers with various spices.

e) *Salt herrings.* Freshly caught herrings are heavily salted, then gutted before being packed down in barrels in alternate layers of salt and fish.

f) *Red Herrings.* The whole herring is thoroughly salted and left in water for several weeks after which they are smoked for a further two weeks until they go dark reddish-brown in colour. They must be soaked in water to remove excess salt before eating, though small portions may be served raw in hors d'oeuvres. This is the oldest form of commercial smoking.

Haddock. Is preserved as smoked haddock, finnan haddock, Aberdeen fillets, golden cutlets. *Arbroath smokies* are small haddock which have been hot smoked.

Salted cod or ling. Is served more often in Scandinavian countries. It should be soaked overnight and then boiled.

Smoked mackerel. Whole mackerel are hot smoked which cooks and cures them at the same time. Use for hors d'oeuvres or as a main course.

Smoked salmon is hot smoked and ready to eat. Expensive, Scotch salmon is considered best. Canadian and Norwegian are cheaper but tend to be drier. Serve in thin pieces with brown bread and butter and lemon wedges.

Smoked trout. Whole rainbow trout are hot smoked to rich brown colour. Served as a starter or as a main course.

All these fish will keep for longer periods than fresh fish.

Canned fish

Salmon, tuna fish, sardines, pilchards, etc. Sardines are immature fish of the herring and pilchard family. They are a good source of calcium. Canned fish have little less nutritive value than fresh fish. There may be some loss of vitamin D. This may be made good by the use of animal oil in canning.

Roe

Fish offal. Hard roe – female fish. Soft roe – male fish. Large percentage of protein. Small percentage of fat. Caviare is the salted roe of the sturgeon.

PREPARATION OF FISH

Usually done by the fishmonger.

Cleaning. Scrape off all scales 'against the grain', using knife blade. Use a sharp knife to make an incision in the side or near the ear. Slit round the fish up the under side. Rinse it under the cold tap while removing the 'insides'. Remove the *dark skin* on *sole* by grasping the skin firmly in a clean cloth and pulling from the tail end towards the head.

Herring. Slit the fish along the belly. Clean. Place skin-side up, press firmly with thumbs down the backbone: this will loosen the bones. Turn the fish up and prise the backbone away from the flesh with the thumb and forefinger. This will also remove small bones.

Filleting. Cut the flesh along the line of the backbone and raise the fillet from the middle of the back to the sides, working from head to tail.

Note: Round fish and plaice should be filleted before skinning.

GENERAL EFFECTS OF COOKING

Cooking kills parasites and bacteria. Usually flavour is greatly improved as extractives are developed, but extractives in fish which are not strong are easily destroyed (note, oysters are eaten raw for flavour).

Chemical changes in cooking. (Similar to meat). Proteins begin to coagulate at about 60°C and shrinkage occurs at about 63°C. Collagen of the connective tissue turns to gelatine and myotomes gradually separate out as flakes. In oily fish, fat oozes away. Fish shrinks less than meat as there is less connective tissue. Cooking has little effect on vitamins A and D, but any vitamin C present would be destroyed. Thiamin is destroyed to some extent by heat. Soluble thiamin and riboflavin and nicotinic acid tend to be removed by moist methods of cooking because they dissolve in the cooking water; so the liquid should be kept for sauces.

Stewing is not the most conservative method of cooking. There is loss of protein, soluble mineral elements, extractives and vitamins – about 6% – due to shrinkage and leaching out. This is wasted unless cooking liquid is kept and used.

Boiling. Greater loss than stewing because more water is used.

Grilling or baking. No loss by diffusion and little loss by shrinkage of soluble mineral elements and extractives. Increased loss of water concentrates the flavour. About 50% thiamin lost by heat.

Frying. Most conservative method of cooking fish. More rapid evaporation of water. Very small loss of mineral elements, extractives and protein. Frying adds fat for flavour and nutritive value, but difficult to digest for invalids.

Pressure cooking. High temperatures tend to break up fish. Greater loss of nutritive material because of greater amount of shrinkage.

Cooking in vinegar, e.g. soused herrings. If vinegar is eaten with fish, there is a gain of calcium dissolved from bones. Softened bones may be eaten. Little other loss.

Serving fish

Many fish are rather tasteless, soft-textured and pale. Need strong flavoured, crisp, brightly coloured garnishes, e.g. tomato, caper, lemon, anchovy, etc. Sauces will add flavour, e.g. tartare sauce with fried fish. Parsley sauce with steamed or boiled fish.

For re-heated fish dishes see notes on réchauffés (page 120).

5. MILK COOKERY

Milk is the liquid produced by all female mammals for feeding their young, so it is an ideal food for the very young of each particular species. It is not an absolutely perfect food, but is the most complete single food known. Milk is a most valuable food at all stages of human life, particularly for children, old people, expectant and nursing mothers and invalids. Milk is obtained from cows, ewes, goats, mares, asses and reindeer. All these types of milk are very similar, but vary slightly in composition and proportions.

AVERAGE COMPOSITION AND NUTRITIVE VALUE OF COW'S MILK

Protein	3.3%
Fat	3.8%
Carbohydrate (lactose)	4.8%
Minerals	0.6%
Total solids	12.5%
Water	87.5%

Protein

The three principal milk proteins are caseinogen, lactalbumin and lactoglobulin. Caseinogen, combined with calcium, is present as tiny particles which, together with fat, give milk its colour. All the proteins are of high biological value in themselves, and can also supplement the biological value of some plant proteins, provided that these are eaten at the same time, e.g. cereal and milk. Milk proteins are easily digested.

Fat

Fat is present in the form of tiny globules of butterfat dispersed throughout the water of the milk in the form of emulsion. As the fat globules are the lightest part of milk they rise to the top when milk stands and form cream. If these globules are broken down to a smaller size (homogenised) they do not rise but remain evenly distributed throughout the milk. There are several fatty acids in milk, e.g. butyric and oleic acids.

The fat content of milk varies with the breed of cow. There is a legal minimum of 3% butterfat for all milk except that from the Channel Islands and South Devon breeds for which the minimum is 4%.

Carbohydrate

Milk contains sugar in the form of lactose which assists the absorption of calcium. There is no other carbohydrate in milk.

Water

Despite its excellent nutritional value, 87% of milk is water. Although an infant can obtain all his nutritional requirements from milk in the first few weeks, as his requirements increase solid food must be introduced into the diet. A moderately active adult would have about one quarter of the daily recommended intake of protein and all his calcium requirements supplied by ½ litre of milk.

Mineral elements

Milk is one of the best sources of calcium and phosphorus. The calcium is most valuable as there are very few good sources.

Energy value. Whole milk – 16 kcal to 25 ml, or 660 kcal to 1 litre.

Vitamins

Vitamin A is present in milk fats. The amount depends on the cow's food and is greater in summer when cows feed on green plants.

Vitamin D. The amount is small and variable. It is present in the butterfat. There is more in summer depending on the effect of sunlight on the cow. Milk does contain cholesterol, the precursor of vitamin D which could be converted to vitamin D by irradiating the milk – irradiated milk is sold in U.S.A.

Vitamin B group. Thiamin is present in small quantities.

Riboflavin – milk is quite a good source of supply. There is more in pasture-fed cows, and Jersey and Guernsey cows.

Nicotinic acid – very small amount supplied.

Vitamin C. There is a small amount when milk leaves the cow, but this decreases according to the treatment milk receives. Milk left on the doorstep, especially in direct sunlight, loses much ascorbic acid. The use of cartons or brown milk bottles would help to prevent this. Pasteurisation destroys some vitamin C and sterilisation or boiling destroys still more. Thus milk cannot be relied upon as a source of vitamin C. Babies need orange juice, fruit and vegetables to remedy this.

Deficiencies in milk

Milk is deficient in iron. Babies are born with a supply of iron sufficient for approximately six months. (It is important for expectant mothers to obtain a good supply of iron.) After six months babies need additional iron which may be supplied by egg yolk, finely minced liver or meat, fortified baby cereals and to a lesser extent, bread, sieved green vegetables and certain fruit, e.g. blackcurrants. The vitamin D supply is not good. Babies can be given vitamin A, C and D drops.

DIGESTION OF MILK

The digestion of milk by infants and young children is greatly assisted by rennin, an enzyme secreted by the stomach which clots milk. Rennin causes the protein caseinogen to be changed to casein which combines with calcium to form a clot. The clot is digested by gastric and pancreatic enzymes and shrinks to form a curd, expressing a liquid called whey.

Souring of milk

True souring only occurs in 'raw' milk, i.e. milk that has not been heat-treated. In raw milk there is a predominance of lactic acid producing bacteria and if temperature conditions are suitable for their growth they will convert the lactose into lactic acid, i.e. milk 'curdles'. This causes the caseinogen to be separated from the calcium, and the insoluble caseinogen is precipitated; unlike clotting in which the caseinogen is partially digested. Cream goes sour before the rest of the milk.

Note: Nowadays temperature conditions suitable for bacterial growth cause pasteurised milk to go bad or putrify rather than go sour. This is a result of the pasteurising process which destroys a high proportion of the acid forming bacteria. Of those that remain, proteolytic bacteria outnumber lactic acid bacteria and they break down the milk protein to produce compounds which give off the characteristic putrid smell.

PRODUCTION OF MILK

Milking is usually done by machine. The milk must be cooled immediately it leaves the cow to prevent souring by bacterial action.

Most milk produced in this country is sold to the Milk Marketing Board, a collective producers' association set up in the 1930s to sell from the farmers to the wholesalers and retailers. The collection and transport of milk from the farms to its destination is the responsibility of the Milk Marketing Board.

Under a bulk collecting system a farmer installs a tank on his farm which is a refrigerated container for holding milk. The tank cools the milk and holds it at a temperature of about 5°C until picked up by a collection tanker. This vehicle, which is insulated, keeps the milk in good condition and it can be transported long distances from the farm to the distributor's premises.

CONTAMINATION OF MILK

Because milk has such a high nutritional value it could become a breeding place for bacteria, introduced into the milk by the animal, milker, utensils or surroundings. In the past serious outbreaks of diseases such as scarlet fever, typhoid, diphtheria and dysentery have been traced to contaminated milk, but nowadays milk production is governed by strict hygiene rules and there is very little danger of infection from milk. Stringent testing is carried out on milk for hygiene, compositional quality and antibiotics, and carefully recorded for the Milk Marketing Board. Milk is tested at all stages from the farm to its arrival at the distributor. In the case of bulk collection the first sample is taken to the farm and tested at the dairy. Any milk which fails any tests is rejected. The Resazurin test (10 minute test) determines the level of bacterial activity in the milk and its keeping qualities. Resazurin is a violet dye when added to milk but can change to pink and finally through several shades to colourless if there is a high bacterial content. Each shade represents a standard of freshness.

If necessary, the milk is then cooled by brine to 4°C before being pasteurised. 85% of all milk sold today is pasteurised. Some of the remaining 15% is sterilised. Untreated milk may be sold under special licence.

METHODS OF ENSURING SAFE MILK

A pure supply of milk is vital to the health of a nation, especially now when so much milk is drunk. This may be achieved by:

1. Ensuring that all cows are perfectly healthy and kept under hygienic conditions. Milk from unhealthy cows might contain harmful bacteria which could be transmitted to humans causing diseases such as brucellosis (undulant fever), though there is little danger of this now because most milk is pasteurised or sterilised. All milking cattle in this country are regularly tested to maintain the present tuberculosis-free state of the national herd.

2. Making sure that milk is conveyed and kept under scrupulously clean conditions at all stages on its way to the consumer. It should be clean, cool and covered. No one suffering from infectious diseases should handle milk. There are laws enforcing this and laws governing the cleanliness of milk production and handling. All dairymen must be registered, and premises and milk may be inspected at any time. If the milk does not contain 3% fat and 8.5% of other solids when tested it is presumed to be adulterated.

3. Buying milk which has been processed to destroy harmful bacteria.

a) *Pasteurised milk* is named after Louis Pasteur (1822–95). About 97% of all milk sold retail in England and Wales is heat treated to kill any harmful bacteria and improve the keeping qualities. Most of this milk is pasteurised which means it is heated to not less than 72°C for at least 15 seconds, and then cooled rapidly. All pathogenic bacteria, and most of the lactic acid producing microbes which cause souring, are destroyed.

Pasteurisation has very little effect on the flavour of milk. Less than 10% of thiamin is destroyed, and 10% of vitamin C, but much vitamin C would be lost by exposure to light, and, in any case, milk is not a good source of this vitamin. The cream line may be slightly reduced or slow to form. There is very little other change.

Doctors favour pasteurisation because it produces safe milk and dairies favour it because the milk will keep longer. Pasteurised milk must pass the phosphatase test. Fresh milk contains an enzyme phosphatase which is destroyed by correct pasteurisation. Harmful bacteria are also destroyed by this so if no phosphatase is present, no bacteria of disease type will be present.

b) *Homogenised milk* is milk which has been warmed and forced through a fine apperture so that the fat globules are broken down into smaller particles which do not rise to the surface but remain evenly distributed throughout the milk. The milk is then pasteurised. Homogenised milk has no cream line and the milk tends to appear whiter in the bottle. It is claimed to taste richer and be more digestible due to the reduction in size of the fat globules.

c) *Sterilised milk* is homogenised milk which has been bottled, sealed and then heat-treated well above boiling point, under pressure, for 20–30 minutes. It should keep unopened for at least seven days and will usually keep for several weeks without refrigeration. The sterilising process alters the flavour of the milk slightly, but it is particularly popular in the Midlands and North of England. Its keeping qualities make it a useful emergency food. Sterilised milk is traditionally sold in crown-corked bottles (like beer).

d) *Ultra Heat Treated (UHT) milk* is often known as 'Long Life' milk. It has been available since October 1965 and is subjected to the most recent method of heat treatment. The milk is heated to at least 132°C for a second or two and then immediately cooled and packed in sterile containers. This process kills all bacteria including spores. UHT milk should keep without refrigeration for about four months if unopened, but an expiry date is shown on the pack as UHT milk of different lengths of shelf life is available. Once the pack is opened the milk should be treated and stored as other milk.

COLOUR CODE FOR MILK BOTTLE CAPS 1977

Regulations introduced in 1977 stipulated the colours to be used for milk bottle caps. This means that a standard colour indicates the type of milk in the bottle. The lettering on the cap is usually embossed in black or silver but where printed lettering is used the colour of this, too, is controlled.

Colour of cap	Description of milk
Silver	Pasteurised milk (min. 3% fat).
Gold	Pasteurised Channel Islands milk from Jersey, Guernsey and South Devon breeds of cow. It contains a minimum of 4% butterfat.
Red	Pasteurised homogenised milk (min. 3% fat).
Red and silver stripes	Semi-skimmed milk.
Blue and silver stripes	Pasteurised kosher milk for Jewish customers.
Green	Untreated milk, i.e. not heat treated. It is usually farm bottled by a licensed producer.
Green with single gold stripe	Untreated Channel Islands milk.
Blue	Sterilised milk.
Pink	Ultra Heat Treated milk.

At some supermarkets milk is also cold in non-returnable opaque plastic bottles or cartons. UHT milk is always sold in cartons. School milk for young pupils is often supplied in non-returnable 'tetra packs' (pyramid shaped cartons on a triangular base). These, being regular in shape, pack very economically in special milk crates. Care is needed when opening these packs, either by peeling off the special paper seal or by using scissors to cut a corner off a larger pack. (Similar small, tetra packs are also used for fresh cream served with coffee at some restaurants and coffee bars.)

In some areas, milk is delivered in plastic sachets which the user is advised to place unopened in the special jug supplied by the dairy. If a corner of the sachet is then cut off, the milk can be poured without spilling.

STORAGE OF MILK IN THE HOME

It is important to store milk carefully to avoid the growth of harmful bacteria and to prevent the development of an unpleasant flavour.

1. Never leave milk standing in sunlight.
2. Keep in a cool dark place – refrigerator or milk cooler.
3. Always use clean milk jugs. Never mix old and new milk in the same container. It is preferable to keep milk in the bottle or carton if possible.
4. Keep milk covered. Never allow strong smelling foods near milk.

Use of milk in the diet.
As much milk as possible should be included in the diet, especially for babies and children, invalids and old people, and expectant mothers. It may be served as milk drinks, with cereals, and in soups, sauces and puddings.

Effect of cooking

Cooking has little effect on the nutritive value of milk. Some B group vitamins are destroyed, and any vitamin C remaining after heat treatment and storage. Some doctors recommend that milk should be boiled for infants under nine months once they are weaned on to cow's milk. Boiling alters the flavour of milk, and, if left under certain conditions the milk will eventually putrify in the same way as unboiled milk.

PRESERVATION OF MILK

Evaporated milk (unsweetened condensed milk) is homogenised and then evaporated in a vacuum pan under reduced pressure at 66°C until the water content is reduced by 60–65%. The milk is finally sterilised. There is no loss of vitamins A and D but the amount of thiamin and vitamin C is reduced.

Condensed milk is evaporated to drive off water as above. 40% sugar is added which acts as a preservative. The product is then canned but need not be sterilised. Its use is limited by the high proportion of sugar it contains. It is unsuitable for babies.

Dried milk. The fresh milk, which may be whole or skimmed, is first homogenised, then is passed in a thin layer between two heated rollers or sprayed into a current of hot air in such a way that the water is removed, leaving a powder containing all the original milk solids. vitamins A and D may be added. Milk powder produced by the spray process is more easily reconstituted and is less likely to form lumps when mixed with water. Dried milk will keep up to six months in a sealed container under cool conditions. It is valuable as an economical source of additional protein, for emergency use and in low calorie diets.

MILK PRODUCTS

Cream

Cream consists of the fat of milk together with a smaller proportion of other milk constituents and water. It also contains some protein and is a relatively expensive but enjoyable source of energy and vitamin A.

The simplest and traditional way of separating cream from milk is to allow the milk to stand for 24 hours and then skim the cream from the top. Commercially produced cream is separated mechanically. The milk is heated to between 32°C and 49°C and fed into a rapidly rotating bowl. The heavier skim milk separates out from the cream and flows off. The fat content of the cream is regulated by a control valve and the cream is then cooled to 4.5°C.

The Cream Regulations specify the minimum fat content allowed in each type of cream, and stipulate that cream labels must show the type of heat treatment; whether the cream is 'untreated', 'pasteurised', 'sterilised' or 'ultra heat treated'.

The Regulations also permit controlled amounts of certain additives, e.g. sugar, stabilisers and emulsifiers, in specified types of cream.

Types of cream

a) *Half cream* (top of the milk). Thinner, pouring cream, suitable for fruit, cereal or coffee. Minimum fat content 12%. Available in cartons.

b) *Single cream* (Red cap). A pouring cream for coffee, used on fruit, cereals and in soups and sauces. Must contain at least 18% fat. It will not whip.

c) *Double cream* (Blue cap). A rich pouring cream which is slightly homogenised. It will float on soup or coffee. Must contain at least 48% fat. It can be whipped.

d) *Whipping cream* (Purple or Green cap). An economical substitute for double cream which can whip up to twice its original volume under the right conditions. Must contain at least 35% fat which is the minimum necessary for whipping.

e) *Clotted cream* (Gold cap). A thick cream with distinctive colour and flavour – served spread on scones or with fruit. Must contain at least 55% fat, e.g. Devonshire or Cornish cream.

f) *Soured cream* (Green or Turquoise cap). A single cream which has been soured by the use of specially cultured bacteria under controlled conditions. Soured cream enhances the flavour and creaminess of many dishes, particularly raw or cooked fruit and vegetables. It is used to make a piquant salad dressing, and in dishes such as Goulash.

Sterilised cream will keep for up to 2 years, if left unopened. It is sterilised in its container. It must have a minimum fat content of 23% (full cream) and 12% (half cream). The flavour is slightly different from that of fresh cream and the cream will not whip. It will thicken if left in a refrigerator overnight.

UHT (Long Life) cream is available in cartons. It is a pouring cream with 18% fat which has been ultra heat treated and has a long shelf life while unopened. As with all UHT products the carton is date stamped.

Imitation cream is made from an emulsion of refined vegetable oil, glucose, syrup, skimmed milk, solids, fat, flavouring and colouring.

Yogurt

Yogurt is an easily digested cultured milk which has been popular for centuries in Eastern Europe, the Near, Middle and Far East, but has only recently become popular in this country. The taste, texture and food value depend upon the type of milk and flavouring used. In this country, a semi-solid consistency and slightly acid flavour is preferred. Yogurt is a good source of protein, calcium and riboflavin (vitamin B). Home-made yogurt made from whole milk has much the same nutritive value as milk. Most commercially-made yogurt is made from skimmed milk and has a low fat content, usually no more than 1.5% fat. The addition of fruit and sugar increase the calorific value while slightly reducing the proportion of milk nutrients. Yogurt can be a particularly useful food for children who dislike milk. It can replace cream in sauces or soups and is used in some cooking, e.g. curry.

Manufacture of yogurt

The basis of yogurt is whole milk, skimmed milk, concentrated milk, dried milk or any mixture of these. The basic mixture is heated at about 88°C for, say, 30 minutes to destroy any harmful organisms. Then it is homogenised which brings out the flavour and improves the texture, making it smoother. After cooling, the mixture is inoculated with the yogurt culture. This consists of a mixture of lactobacillus bulgaricus and streptococcus thermophilus. Some natural yogurt is incubated in the retail packs which are filled, sealed and incubated at 42–45°C for 2½–3 hours until the required degree of acidity is reached and the yogurt is set. It is then cooled gradually to 4.5°C which arrests the growth of the culture but does not kill it. Yogurt should be stored at this temperature until consumed. It has a shelf life of about two weeks, and cartons are usually date stamped. Fruit for fruit yogurt is added after the natural yogurt has been incubated in large churns or vats. The fruit yogurt is put into containers and sealed and stored at 4.5°C.

Yogurt can easily be made at home using sterilised, UHT (Long Life) milk, or pasteurised milk which has been boiled and then cooled to 43°C. A tablespoon of bought natural yogurt is added to each pint of milk as a starter. Special equipment is available but is not essential as good results can be obtained using a wide neck vacuum flask or small glass jars, which can be incubated in an insulated cake tin. The convenience of the special yogurt maker accounts for its sale.

Method

1. Sterilise all equipment to be used by boiling or using Milton type solution.
2. Heat ½ litre of milk to 43°C.
3. Add a tablespoon of fresh natural yogurt.
4. Pour mixture into warmed, wide neck vacuum flask. Close securely and leave no longer than 8–10 hours to allow to set. OR pour mixture into small glass jars, leave in a warm place for 8–10 hours.
5. Remove from flask by shaking. Put in covered container in refrigerator or cool place until required.
6. Fruit yogurt can be made by stirring in fruit and jam after the yogurt has set.

Coffee Creamers

These are not a milk product but are used to replace milk or cream in coffee. They are made from glucose syrup solids and vegetable fat with a small percentage of sodium caseinate derived from milk. Available in powder or granulated form and when added to a cup of black coffee will produce white coffee without using milk or cream.

6. CHEESE COOKERY

Making cheese is a means of preserving the food value of milk in a condensed form which can be stored long after the milk itself would have soured. The process of cheese making has been used for centuries. It is a very valuable food. Cows' milk, or goats' milk or milk from other animals may be used. It takes approximately 4 litres of milk to make 400 g of cheese. It is a convenient way of utilising the surplus milk of summer throughout the year.

TYPES OF CHEESE

Each type of cheese is usually named after the place of origin, but it may be imported, e.g. Cheddar type made in America.

Hard cheeses. Contain less water, e.g. Cheddar, Cheshire, Double Gloucester, Leicester, Parmesan.

Soft cheeses. Contain a higher percentage of water and do not keep as well as hard cheeses. Caerphilly, White Wensleydale, Lancashire, Stilton, Gorgonzola, Camembert, Brie.

Processed cheese. Cheese spreads.

MANUFACTURE OF CHEESE

The manufacture varies according to the type of cheese being made, but basically the same process is used.

1. Milk which has been pasteurised has a 'starter' of pure lactic-acid organisms added to ripen or increase the acidity of the milk, i.e. begin to turn it sour. The milk is heated to 29–31°C, and rennet is added to produce a clot by turning the milk into curds and whey. This will give an acid curd which has more keeping qualities and is the most usual process, e.g. Cheddar.

or

Milk, whether pasteurised or not, may be directly treated with rennet. This produces a sweet curd, e.g. Roquefort.

or

Milk may be enriched by the addition of cream, e.g. Stilton.

or

Skimmed milk may be used – This gives a cheese where the fat content is low, but the protein percentage is increased, e.g. Dutch and German cheeses.

2. The curd is cut with special knives to separate the curd and whey. The curd is cut into small pieces about the size of a pea, and is gently heated to approximately 37–41°C. This helps to expel the whey. Whey is run off and the settled curd is put into blocks and drained. Whey is used as animal feeding stuff.

3. The cooled curd is cut by an electrically driven curd mill into small pieces.

4. Salt is added and curd is packed into moulds.

a) If the rest of the whey is squeezed out under pressure before the cheese is left to ripen, a hard cheese is produced.

b) If the remaining whey is allowed to drain out under the natural pressure of curd, a soft cheese results.

Blue-veined cheeses. Soft cheeses are open-textured and moulds from the air can enter. This process may be aided by injecting moulds into the cheese. The moulds give a veining effect, e.g. Stilton, Danish Blue, Gorgonzola.

5. Hot water may be sprayed on to the cheese mould; this produces a thin hard rind which helps to preserve it.

6. Cheese is allowed to ripen or cure until the correct flavour is obtained. This is brought about by the action of various bacterial organisms. The type of milk, amount of salt and when it is added, the amount of pressure on the curd, storage conditions and injection of various bacteria will all determine the type and flavour of the cheese.

Processed cheese

Processed cheese is popular as it is a convenient way to buy and store cheese. This type of cheese, however, rarely has such a good flavour as the original cheese and is more expensive than fresh cheese. The method of processing cheese was invented in Switzerland where processed Emmental, a type of Gruyère, was first sold in 1911. Cheese of the desired type has the rind removed. The cheese is ground and mixed with an emulsifying agent and perhaps additional flavouring, e.g. tomato. The cheese is heated in a steam-jacketed vat to melt and pasteurise it. Pasteurising destroys bacteria and enzymes, so preventing further ripening. The cheese is then poured into foil-lined containers, sealed and allowed to set. It is thus protected and will keep for a long time. Processed cheese can be blended to ensure uniform flavour and texture. It usually contains less fat and more moisture than fresh cheese, and is more easily digested.

Uses of processed cheese

Processed cheese has more limited uses than fresh cheese, but its property of melting quickly under the grill makes it useful for snack meals. It is easy to spread which makes it popular for use in sandwiches. Processed cheese may have additional flavouring added, e.g. butter, ham, celery, tomato.

Cottage cheese

A low-calorie almost pure white creamy acid curd cheese with a mild distinctive flavour. Bought cottage cheese is usually made from pasteurised skimmed milk which is inoculated with a special starter to develop flavour and texture. This produces a curd which is cut into small cubes and slowly heated until it reaches the required texture. The whey is drained off, the curd is washed and cooled, cream and salt are added and, if required, further flavourings such as chives or chopped pineapple are thoroughly blended in before the cheese is packed. Cottage cheese is easily digested and a valuable source of protein and riboflavin (vitamin B). It does not keep well and should be eaten while fresh.

Curd cheese

Made from skimmed or partially skimmed milk which has been soured naturally by lactic acid bacteria, by a special starter or, at home, lemon juice may be used. The resulting curds and whey are separated by straining. Salt and cream may be added. Curd cheese is rich in protein and easily digested but yeasts and moulds grow on the surface within a few days and the flavour becomes unpleasant. Cottage cheese and curd cheese are both popular in slimming diets because of their high protein and relatively low kilocalorie value.

Cream cheese

A soft cheese made by cultivating cream, rather than milk, with a 'starter' of lactic acid bacteria. When the curd has thickened sufficiently it is drained and salt is added if desired. It has a rather buttery texture and a high content of milk fat gives it a creamy appearance. There are two types, single cream cheese made from single cream with a maximum fat content of 20–25%, and double cream cheese made from cream containing about 50–55% butterfat. Carefully prepared single cream cheese will keep for about a week in a refrigerator but double cream cheese will not keep quite so long. The nutritive value of cream cheese is similar to that of cream but it contains more fat and less water.

NUTRITIVE VALUE OF CHEESE

Cheese has a very high nutritive value. Approximately 50 g of cheese is made from 500 ml milk.

Protein

Animal protein – caseinogen. Approximately 25–30%. The high biological value of cheese will increase the value of some plant proteins, provided they are eaten at the same meal, e.g. bread and cheese. There is almost twice as much protein in cheese as in the same weight of beef.

Fat

Cheese has a high fat content – it contains approximately 30–40% fat.

Mineral elements

Cheese is one of the best sources of calcium and phosphorus.

Vitamins

Cheese is a rich source of vitamin A, especially cheese made from summer milk. It is quite a good soure of riboflavin which is partly combined with the casein and so remains with the curd and is not removed entirely in the whey.

Water

There is approximately 35% of water in cheese depending on the amount of pressure during manufacture.

Carbohydrate

There is practically no carbohydrate in cheese, so cheese is usually eaten with carbohydrate food, e.g. bread, potatoes, or macaroni. Compared with meat, the moisture content is much lower; cheese supplies about three times more kilocalories than meat, as well as valuable calcium and phosphorus.

Energy value. 100 kcal per 25 g. This is more than twice the energy value of 25 g of lean beef.

The following is almost nutritionally complete:
100 g cheese
200 g bread
25 g butter or margarine
50 g watercress
More vitamin D may be needed, although cholesterol, its precursor, is present.

DIGESTIBILITY

Cheese can be difficult to digest because it is highly concentrated with a high percentage of fat. The fat forms a waterproof layer or coating round the protein, preventing the stomach juices from reaching the casein readily. The larger the lumps of cheese which reach the stomach, the more difficult the digestion will be. So it is important to divide cheese up or to chew it well before swallowing. Dry hard cheese is more easily broken up by the teeth than soft cheese and so is more easily digested. For people doing sedentary work, too much cheese in the diet is sometimes a source of too much fat which is not utilised. But in small quantities, e.g. savouries after meals, cheese encourages the flow of gastric juices because of its strong flavour.

RULES FOR COOKING CHEESE

a) *Reasons for care in cooking* (to render digestible)
  1. Cheese is highly concentrated.
  2. It contains a large percentage of fat.
  3. The fatty acids may be irritating to the digestive organs.
  4. If over-cooked, the protein becomes tough and stringy.
b) *Aids to digestibility*
  1. Fine division, e.g. grating or chopping.
  2. Mixing with starchy foods – potatoes, bread, cereal, cheese sauces, etc. When cheese is cooked, the fat melts and is absorbed by the starch.
  3. Application of heat melts the fat and exposes the protein to the digestive juices, *but* over-cooking will make cheese hard and stringy as the fat melts and heat makes the protein tough.
  4. Addition of high seasoning, e.g. mustard, stimulates the digestive juices.

Methods of cooking

Short, quick application of heat is best.
  1. *Grilling* – dishes au gratin.
  2. *Baking* – cheese pie, cheese pastry, etc.
  3. *Frying* – cheese aigrettes, etc.

Uses of cheese in the menu

As a main dish, e.g. cheese soufflé, cheese pudding, cheese and onion flan.
As a snack, e.g. Welsh rarebit, cheese omelet.
To flavour a sauce, e.g. fish mornay, macaroni cheese.
Cheese pastry – foundation for savoury flans and savouries.
Savoury after a meal – cheese and biscuits.
Cheese cakes.

7. EGG COOKERY

Eggs are pre-eminent among the high biological value protein foods. They contain minerals and vitamins, fat and protein to nourish the growing chicken and are a very valuable cooking ingredient because of their many uses.

COMPOSITION

Average weight. Whole egg – 50–65 g
Yolk – 30%
White – 58%
Shell – 12%

Shell consists almost entirely of carbonate of lime (chalk). As the process of hatching continues, the shell loses about 9% in weight by absorption of calcium for the formation of bones in the chick. The shell is pitted with tiny holes to allow entrance of air, but these also allow bacteria to enter, causing the egg to decay. There is a loss of moisture through the shell.

White is a solution in water of a protein known as egg-albumen or ovalbumen and some riboflavin. There are some mineral elements, e.g. sulphur.

Yolk is the chief storehouse of nutriment for the young chick and so is the most nourishing part of the egg. It contains much less water than the white and more solid matter, protein of high biological value, fat which is very highly emulsified and so easily digested, and contains with it a fat-like substance called lecithin which helps in nerve repair and stabilises emulsions. Iron, calcium, phosphorus and sulphur are present, and vitamins A and D. The colour of the yolk usually depends on the diet of the hen and does not affect the nutritive value. The colour of the shell bears no relation to the nutritive value either.

	Yolk	White
Protein	16.2%	12.6%
Fat	31.7%	None
Mineral elements	1.1%	0.6%
Water	51.0%	86.8%

Deficiency. There is no vitamin C in eggs, and very little carbohydrate. The energy value of an egg is 80–100 kilocalories.

Eggs are usually served with carbohydrate foods, e.g. bread or potatoes, and a food to supply vitamin C is needed, e.g. fresh fruit or green vegetables.

EFFECT OF COOKING AND PRINCIPLES IN USE

Egg albumin (protein) is soluble in cold liquid. It begins to coagulate immediately on application of heat, becoming opaque and firm. The degree of firmness depends on the degree of heat and length of cooking time. Egg yolk does not harden to the same extent or as quickly as the white due to the high percentage of fat.

Note: If egg is over-cooked or added too quickly to hot liquid, curdling will result. Heat does not have much effect on the nutritive value of the egg though a little vitamin B is destroyed.

Whisking of egg white

In this process, air is entangled. The larger the volume of air entrapped and the colder it is, the greater will be the consequent expansion when heated, and so the lighter the mixture.

1. Whisk under cold conditions.

2. There must be no fat present from the yolk or on the utensils used, as this has an adverse effect on the property of the albumen to hold air.

3. Fold egg white lightly into mixture to avoid expelling air.

4. Apply heat at once to coagulate the albumen and prevent the escape of air. Heat should be very slow to ensure complete and thorough drying, but a quick high-temperature 'flash' method may be used for lemon meringue pie, baked Alaska, etc. which are to be eaten at once.

Digestibility of eggs

Generally speaking, eggs cooked by almost any method are digestible. Lightly boiled eggs are more easily digested than raw eggs as a raw egg takes longer to leave the stomach. The difference in digestibility between soft and hard-boiled eggs depends to some extent upon the degree of sub-division of the latter. If finely divided, they are probably as easily disposed of as soft-boiled eggs. Some people have difficulty in eating even the smallest portion of egg without digestive upset, but this may be due to idiosyncrasy.

Absorption in the intestine seems to be very complete – there is very little residue left.

Uses in cookery

1. *As a main dish*. In combination with other foods or ingredients. Their animal protein which contains all the essential amino-acids makes them of great value in place of meat and fish. They are easily digested and so are suitable as invalid food. They are cooked very quickly and so are suitable as snacks.

2. *Thickening*. The coagulation of protein on heating (68°C) is responsible for their value as a thickening agent. This property is made use of in thickening of custards, sauces, soups, lemon cheese, etc.

3. *Binding*. The coagulating properties of an egg will give cohesiveness to a mixture containing dry ingredients, e.g. forcemeat, rissoles, croquettes, and icings.

4. *Coating*. Beaten egg forms a protective covering for fried foods – the albumen quickly hardens on heating and prevents the contents being saturated with fat while the heat penetrates. The use of an egg-and-breadcrumb coating helps to prevent fish breaking up during frying.

5. *Enriching*. The addition of whole eggs or yolks to a mixture is valuable, especially as a means of adding protein and fat, etc. Eggs improve nutritive value and flavour of cakes, etc. The fat has a moistening and shortening effect.

6. *Lightening*. By means of whisking either egg white or whole egg, air is entangled and lightness given to a mixture (see above). So they can be used as:
   a) raising agents in cakes, etc. A whole egg can aerate an equal weight of flour.
   b) Light fluffy dishes, e.g. soufflés, meringues.

7. *Emulsifying*, e.g. mayonnaise.

8. *Glaze*. Used on top of pastry, etc.

9. *Garnishes*. For most savoury dishes, e.g. dressed crab, savoury flans.

CHOICE, GRADING AND STORAGE

Eggs are graded according to weight. Since 1973 British egg packers have had to use the EEC classification of seven equally divided grades for eggs. The British system of five grades also stayed in use until January 1978 when it was replaced by the EEC system of seven sizes.

At the packing station eggs are candled, graded and packed in trays or cartons. Boxes containing 360 eggs are marked with date of packing, grade and packing station number.

EEC weight grades

Size 1
70 g or over

Size 2
65–70 g

Size 3
60–65 g

Size 4
55–60 g

Size 5
50–55 g

Size 6
45–50 g

Size 7
45 g and under

Candling test. Eggs are passed in front of a strong light which will show up any defects.

Quality

Extra means the eggs were packed within the last seven days and have passed stringent quality tests. The actual date of packing must be shown on the box.

Class A. The usual quality sold in the shops.

Class B eggs may be preserved or frozen, have dirty shells or have been washed.

Class C may be broken and beaten. These are used for food manufacture only, e.g. commercially produced cakes and puddings.

Egg boxes must have a date mark, i.e. the number of the week in which they were packed. E.g. week 3 is the third week in January. The box must also carry the name and address of the packing station or of the firm for whom they were packed.

Domestic tests for freshness

1. The shell of a newly laid egg should be slightly rough.
2. If held up to light an egg should be slightly translucent with no black specks showing.
3. The egg should feel heavy – loss of weight due to evaporation of moisture shows that the egg is stale.

Brine test. Place egg in saline solution 25 g salt – 250 ml water.

a) Fresh egg will sink.
b) Not so fresh egg is suspended.
c) Stale egg rises.

4. The white of a fresh egg is thick – the older the egg, the less thick white is present.

Effect of keeping

A natural layer of varnish protects the egg to some extent, but as the shell is porous, there is loss of moisture by evaporation, so that an older egg becomes less dense and lighter. The moisture is replaced by air which brings bacteria with it. The phosphoric acid of the yolk acts on the sulphur of the white and produces hydrogen sulphide, recognisable by the characteristic bad smell. The interior begins to decompose due to the growth of bacteria on fertile contents.

The green line produced when eggs are boiled for a long time is caused by the reaction of iron compounds in the yolk combining with the sulphide from the white. Very fresh eggs do not produce this. This tendency is lessened if the eggs are boiled for the minimum time, then cooled slightly in cold water.

Storage

Care must be taken of the yolk as it deteriorates quicker than the white. There are 9 protective coverings round the yolk but if the egg is kept pointed side up, the anchoring membranes are severed and the yolk rises against the shell to lose its freshness; so always keep eggs round side up, in a clean cool storage place that is not too dry. Normal refrigerator temperature is good.

Never wash eggs, or the protective varnish is removed. The porous shell allows penetration of odours, and so keep eggs away from strong-smelling foods – onions, fish, cheese, etc. Opened eggs: yolks will keep for several days if they are covered gently with water and kept in a cool place; whites can be kept in a covered jar in a refrigerator.

Duck eggs

Unless care is taken duck eggs may be the source of dangerous food-poisoning bacteria. They may be laid in dirty places, the edge of stagnant water, etc. They should come from a clean known source and must be thoroughly cooked.

PRESERVATION OF EGGS

Principle is to prevent the entry of air bringing bacteria in through the porous shell. This can be done by forming an impervious layer on the shell, and by keeping eggs under conditions where bacteria will not grow. Eggs can be separated and the whites and yolks frozen separately in a home freezer. They cannot be frozen whole successfully.

Commercial methods

1. *Chilling* at 2–4°C. Keep at least three months.
2. *Dehydration.* The moisture is removed by spraying the egg on to heated rollers. Egg solids in the form of a powder can be scraped off. Dried egg will keep almost indefinitely, in a cool dry place. Used in war and in catering trade. Disadvantage – albumen loses properties of holding air. Loss of flavour.
3. *Frozen eggs.* Shells removed. White and yolks separated or mixed.
4. *Pickling.* Eggs are immersed in odourless mineral oil, e.g. Chinese eggs pre-war for bakery trade. Cleaned by sand blasting before sale.

Preparation of eggs for preservation

Eggs should be fresh but not straight from the nest. Allow 24 hours so that air pressure and temperature in egg may reach equilibrium. Eggs which are more than 3 or 4 days old are not worth preserving as bacteria will have entered. Wipe clean but do not wash. Do not use cracked, dirty or rough-shelled eggs.

Duck eggs must not be preserved as they may be infected with bacteria at moment of laying.

Methods of cooking

1. *Simple methods.* Boiled, poached, scrambled.
2. *Custards.* Baked, steamed, boiled.
3. *Omelets and soufflés.* Savoury omelets, sweet puffed omelets, cold soufflés, hot soufflés baked or steamed.

8. FRUIT COOKERY

NUTRITIVE VALUE
Protein
There is a very small amount of vegetable protein. A little more is present in dried fruit.

Fat
A very small amount. More in olives – vegetable oil – and Avocado pears.

Carbohydrates
Ripe fruit contains sugar. Unripe contains more starch than sugar. As the fruit ripens, the enzymes and acids in fruit change the starch into sucrose and this is changed into glucose and fructose. So the carbohydrate available will be mixture of sucrose, glucose and fructose (and perhaps a little starch).

Unavailable carbohydrate is present in pith, skins, seeds, cell walls, etc. and pectin. A good supply given by fruit.

Vitamins
Vitamin C. Fruit is an important source.

Richest – rose hip.

Rich – blackcurrant.

Good – orange, strawberry, redcurrant, gooseberry, grapefruit, tomato, raspberry, loganberry, lemon.

Fairly good – cherry, damson, peach, banana, apple, apricot, rhubarb.

Vitamin C is only present in a very small amount in dried fruit, but is in approximately full supply in frozen fruit and only a small amount is destroyed by cooking in tinned fruit.

Vitamin A (as carotene). Fairly good supply in apricots.

Very small supply from other fruits. None in lemons.

Vitamin D. None.

Vitamin B group. Very little.

Mineral elements

Iron. Small supply.

Calcium. Small supply.

There is a good supply of fruit acids – tartaric, citric and malic acids. The supply decreases as the fruit ripens. Citrus fruits have a good supply. Acids help the laxative action of fruit by stimulating the action of the intestines. They also help in the setting of jams, etc. together with pectin. If unripe fruit is eaten, excess acids may upset the digestion.

Water

There is a large amount of water in fruit – 85–90%. This gives fruit its refreshing quality.

CHOICE OF FRUIT

Fruit should be eaten just ripe. Under-ripe fruit may be difficult to digest, especially if eaten raw, because of excess fruit acids. Over-ripe fruit may contain bacteria which will upset the digestive system.

Fruit in the diet. Fruit is eaten for vitamin C content, fibre, water content and flavour. Raw fruit provides the most vitamin C.

EFFECT OF COOKING

1. May increase the digestibility by softening the fibre.
2. Will destroy some of the bacteria present.
3. Fruit containing a lot of seeds may be made less irritating to the digestion by cooking and sieving.
4. Vitamin C is destroyed by heat, but not quite so quickly as in vegetables. The presence of fruit acids helps to retain the vitamin.

USES OF FRUIT

Fruit drinks. Fresh fruit drinks as well as being refreshing provide a good supply of vitamin C. The zest or outer part of the rind as well as juice should be used, but the pith would give a bitter flavour.

Fruit may be served as a starter to a meal, e.g. grapefruit, and also in pies, puddings, fruit fool, salad, etc. and as stewed fruit.

9. VEGETABLE COOKERY

There is much scope for the wide use of vegetables in our diet. Because of increased home production and imports of more unusual vegetables there has been more interest in them in the last few years. Improved techniques in freezing have contributed to the popularity of vegetables. But vegetables are still more widely used on the Continent. More attention is needed in vegetable cookery in order to use vegetables to the best advantage.

Vegetables are important for the essential vitamins and mineral elements they contain, for fibre, for flavour and for the colour they add to the diet. Vegetables can be served as an accompaniment to a dinner, or as a separate course. They may be used as a substitute for meat in the diet (see Vegetarian Cookery pages 36–37).

Parts of plants used as vegetables

Roots. Carrot, parsnip, horse-radish, beetroot, celeriac.
Bulbous roots. Onion, shallot, leek.
Tubers. Potato, Jerusalem artichoke.
Flowers or head. Cauliflower, broccoli, globe artichoke.
Leaves. Cabbage, spinach, lettuce, curly kale, sprouts.
Fruit. Cucumber, tomato, bean (pod), pulse (seeds).
Blanched stem. Celery, seakale, chicory.

CLASSIFICATION OF VEGETABLES

1. Green vegetables.
2. Roots and tubers.
3. Blanched stems.
4. Seed or pulse vegetables (fresh or dried).
5. Fruits.

NUTRITIVE VALUE
Protein

Pulse vegetables – a fair supply of vegetable protein.
Root vegetables – a small supply of vegetable protein.
Green vegetables – a trace of vegetable protein.

Fat

There is no fat in most vegetables, but soya beans contain a good supply of vegetable fat and so do nuts.

Carbohydrate

Available

May be starch or sugar or both.

Starch. In potatoes.

Starch and sugar. Peas, beans, lentils, carrots.

Sugar. Beetroots, onions, radishes, tomatoes, leeks, marrows.

Unavailable (fibre)

Skins, seeds, pith, fibres, cell walls of vegetables.

Water

A high percentage of water is present in all fresh vegetables. Many contain 90% or more.

Potatoes 76%.

Dried pulses 8%.

Mineral elements

Iron. A moderate source in spinach, watercress, cabbage, peas, beans, lentils, parsley, but it may be unavailable because of the oxalic acid present. Other vegetables a trace.

Calcium. Green vegetables give a supply but most may be unavailable because it is in the form of calcium oxalate.

Sulphur. In green vegetables.

Phosphorus. A small supply.

Vitamins

Vitamin A. Present in the form of carotene. Rich sources – carrots, green vegetables, especially the darker coloured varieties, tomatoes. None in turnip, onion, cauliflower, potato, beetroot, haricot bean.

Vitamin B group. Thiamin (B_1) – Pulse vegetables are especially rich, but all vegetables contain a little. Riboflavin and nicotinic acid – a very small supply in all vegetables.

Vitamin C. Vegetables are a most important source. Very rich supply – brussels sprouts, kale, turnip tops. Rich supply – cabbage, spinach, watercress, cauliflower, asparagus, tomato. A fair amount is present in other vegetables, especially in potatoes, important because of the amount eaten. Normal supply in frozen vegetables. None in most dried vegetables or soups.

Vitamin D. None.
Vitamin E. A little in green vegetables.
Vitamin K. Green vegetables and peas.

Energy value of vegetables
Not very high because many have no fat. Most kilocalories are supplied by pulse vegetables and potatoes from the carbohydrate present.

Reasons for cooking
1. They may be difficult to digest because of the starch present.
2. The bulk may be reduced, enabling more to be eaten, e.g. spinach.
But, eat vegetables raw if possible to get the full value of vitamins, mineral elements and fibre.

Aims in cooking
1. To soften the fibre and make the starch digestible.
2. To preserve colour, flavour and shape.
3. To prevent unnecessary absorption of water.
4. Most important – to minimise the loss of vitamins, mineral elements and extractives.

Effect of cooking
1. Softening of the fibre.
2. Gelatinisation of the starch.
3. Extraction of the soluble mineral elements, extractives and vitamins.
4. Lowering of the vitamin value, especially vitamin C, by heat destruction.
5. Absorption of water which adds to the bulk in some cases, e.g. potatoes.

To preserve vitamins and mineral elements
1. Use fresh when there is most food value.
2. Peel thinly – most vitamins and minerals are just below the skins. Use a sharp knife to avoid cell damage.
3. Prepare just before cooking – or vitamins will be destroyed by the action of the enzymes.
4. Do not soak – to avoid vitamin and mineral loss by solubility.
5. Cook in a small amount of boiling water. This reduces the loss by solubility. The enzymes which destroy vitamin C are themselves destroyed by boiling water. Cooking is quicker and so there is less loss of vitamins by heat. Keep a lid on the pan to avoid oxidisation.
6. Never use bicarbonate of soda as this destroys vitamin C.
7. Serve immediately to avoid vitamin loss by oxidisation.

PURCHASE AND CHOICE

Freshness is important. Wilted or damaged vegetables, although cheaper, have lost water and vitamins and mineral elements. Freshly picked vegetables are best for nutritive value and flavour.

Green vegetables. A good green colour, of medium size according to the species, firm and crisp. Vegetables stripped of outer leaves should be avoided as these leaves have most nutritive value and vegetables must have been wilted to need stripping.

Root vegetables. As free from soil as possible. No spade marks, as firm as possible. No sign of sprouting.

STORAGE

Storage destroys some vitamin C.

Green vegetables. Do not store if possible as there will be loss of flavour and vitamin content. If necessary to store, keep wrapped in a refrigerator (after washing and drying) or place in a covered dish or saucepan.

Root vegetables. Will lose a little vitamin C in storage. Store in a well-ventilated rack in a cool, dry place. To store large quantities in the winter, keep in a dry, dark, frost-proof place in layers of sand or dry soil.

Tubers. Potatoes should be stored in a cool, dark, dry place. Warmth causes sprouting, light turns them green, damp causes rot. Do not store near strong smelling foods because potatoes easily absorb flavours. Handle carefully, potatoes bruise easily.

METHODS OF COOKING

Boiling. Suitable for all vegetables.

Baking. Potatoes in their jackets. Most vegetables, except some of the green leaf variety, may be baked in a casserole (see Conservative Method below). Marrows, tomatoes, etc. may be stuffed and baked. Some vegetables, e.g. cauliflower, courgettes, may be served au gratin.

Roasting. Potatoes and other root vegetables may be roasted in fat or round the joint.

Frying. In deep fat – potatoes, sprigs of cauliflower, onion rings, parsley; in shallow fat – sauté potatoes (usually partially cooked first), onions, tomatoes, mushrooms.

Braising. Celery, chicory, onions, lentils.

Grilling. Tomatoes, mushrooms.

Stewing. Mushrooms, celery (usually stewed in milk).

Conservative method

This is a suitable method of cooking most vegetables except the green leaf varieties. The vegetables, cut finely, are sauté'd in fat. Then they are cooked with a small amount of liquid in a covered casserole, by gentle heat in the oven or on top of the stove. This method retains much of the flavour and shape of the vegetables. The liquid should be used as a base for sauces or gravy.

SERVING VEGETABLES

Serve hot vegetables in hot dishes as soon as possible after cooking. If kept they will lose flavour and vitamin C content.

Flavour and nutritive value may be improved by the method of serving.

Tossed in butter. French beans, cabbage, sprouts, carrots, potatoes.

Served with melted butter. Asparagus, corn on the cob.

Served with a sauce, e.g. parsley, cheese, tomato sauce. Butter beans, beetroot, cauliflower, celery, chicory, leeks, marrow, onions.

Chopped parsley. Potatoes, carrots.

Paprika. Green vegetables.

Main faults in vegetable cookery

1. Monotony of choice.
2. Waste before cooking.
3. Bad cooking methods – the English method of boiling is the worst method as it destroys by heat or loses by solubility many of the vitamins and mineral elements.
4. Slovenly dishing and serving.

PULSE VEGETABLES

The dried seeds of leguminous plants, e.g. lentils, peas – split or whole – butter beans, haricot beans, are called pulse vegetables. Pulses contain a high percentage of carbohydrate in the form of starch and some sugar, a fairly good supply of vegetable protein, a rich supply of thiamin (vitamin B_1) and a good supply of iron. There is no fat in pulses and very little water.

Pulses need careful cooking as they may be difficult to digest because of the tough outer skins. Steeping is necessary to soften the skins. A little bicarbonate of soda may be added to the steeping water to soften it. Cook very slowly and thoroughly. The pulses may be liquidised or sieved after cooking to make a purée which is easier to digest. A little fat may be added for flavour and nutritive value.

Uses of pulse vegetables. Soups, curries and stews, cutlets for vegetarian cookery. As a vegetable, e.g. butter beans in parsley sauce.

MORE UNUSUAL VEGETABLES

Most people do not take full advantage of the wide range of vegetables which is available. The use of some of the less well-known vegetables could add variety to the diet. They may sometimes be a little more expensive, but this is not always the case.

Globe artichokes. The leaves and bottom of this vegetable are eaten. The choke, or fibrous part, is not edible and is removed. Artichokes should be young and a fresh green colour. They may be boiled in salted water when the fibre may be removed and the leaves pulled out and served with melted butter or Hollandaise sauce.

Jerusalem artichokes. These vegetables are tubers. They are prepared and boiled in a similar way to potatoes, usually with lemon juice or vinegar to keep them white. They may be boiled and served with white sauce or served au gratin or baked in fat.

Asparagus. Has thick white stalks and green tips. The tips are the edible part. Asparagus must be fresh or it will be bitter. Wash the vegetable and tie into bundles of equal size. Boil in salted water, with the bundles standing upright, until the tips are tender. The white stalks are kept on for easy handling Serve with melted butter. Asparagus makes a delicious cream soup. Sprew is the name given to thin asparagus.

Aubergine or egg plants. Aubergines are actually a fruit with a deep purplish-green skin. They are prepared and served rather like marrows. They may be served whole – stuffed and baked, or cut into cubes or slices or dipped in flour and fried.

Avocado pear. Avocado pears are also fruits, about the size and shape of a large pear. They have a dark green skin with a 'buttery' textured flesh. To test for the ripeness handle very gently – the ripe flesh should 'give' to gentle pressure. To prepare, use a stainless steel knife to make a level cut encircling the fruit lengthwise. Remove stone and fill cavity with French dressing or shrimp or egg mayonnaise as an appetiser. Avocado may be served in a salad, blended in a dip or in ice cream, or served with fruit. Avocado have a high vegetable oil content (up to 25%), are rich in vitamins and minerals but have no starch and very little sugar.

Beanshoots (bean sprouts). Young shoots of mung beans. Can be fresh or tinned. Use quick (stir) fried or raw.

Chicory. Often used as a salad plant. It resembles a very tight, crisp white lettuce heart, but has more bitter flavour than lettuce. Chicory is often incorrectly called endive in this country. It may be cooked by boiling whole in salted water and served with melted butter, lemon juice or white sauce. The leaves may be shredded and used in salads with French dressing.

Chinese leaves (Chinese cabbage). Looks like a long, crisp lettuce. Use quick (stir) fried or raw.

Corn cobs (sweet corn or maize). Must be young or will be tough to eat. Remove the husks and silky threads and boil in salted water. Serve on the cob with melted butter or remove the grains from the cob and toss in butter or cream. Corn may be made into fritters.

Marrow. Young marrows about 17–20 cm long may be boiled whole without peeling. Older marrows must be peeled, cut into cubes or slices and boiled in salted water, stewed in fat or baked. They are served with butter, white sauce or au gratin. Marrows may be stuffed with a savoury filling and baked.

Courgettes (Zucchini). Courgettes are a member of the marrow family, 10–15 cm long with a dark green skin and delicately flavoured flesh. To prepare, wash, cut off top and tail, do not peel. May be cooked whole, sliced lengthwise, or cut into rings. Boil, bake, sauté or fry. Can be stuffed like marrow with savoury fillings.

Sweet peppers (Pimentos or Capsicums). These are a very attractive looking vegetable – green, red or yellow in colour, with a mild flavour. The stem, seeds and white pith must be removed before or after cooking. Peppers may be cut into rings and boiled, or the tops may be cut off and the peppers stuffed and baked. Thin strips or rings of peppers are used as a colourful garnish.

Sweet Potato. These are not related to the British potato. They are imported throughout the year. They may be globular in appearance, similar to turnips, or elongated. The outer skin is white, pink, red or purple with white/yellow firm sweet flesh inside. To prepare, scrub well, peel if necessary, boil in salted water. May be used in same ways as potatoes.

PRESERVATION OF VEGETABLES

Preserved vegetables are convenience foods. They may be more expensive than fresh vegetables but are sometimes cheaper; there is no waste and preparation time is saved. Only good quality vegetables are worth preserving. Specially selected varieties are grown, harvested and preserved at the peak of perfection. Frozen and canned vegetables may have as much vitamin and mineral content as fresh vegetables. Vegetables dried by the old methods contained little vitamin C but modern methods of accelerated freeze drying are claimed to retain most of the vitamin content.

Potatoes may be cooked and mashed to give a powder which may be reconstituted as mashed potato.

The flavour of dried vegetables may not be quite as good as the fresh variety. Monosodium glutamate is usually added to retain the flavour.

10. CEREALS

Cereals are the seeds or grain of cultivated grasses. They are staple foods in the diet of most human beings. Wheat, barley, rice, oats, maize, etc. are eaten according to the area lived in, although transport has now made their use universal.

Cereals are an important food. They are easily grown, are convenient to transport, quite cheap, can be stored for long periods, and are easily prepared and cooked.

NUTRITIVE VALUE OF CEREALS

Carbohydrate

Large percentage of starch. Farinaceous foods, e.g. cornflour (from maize), sago, tapioca, arrowroot, are practically pure starch. Other cereals contain approximately 70%.

Protein

Some vegetable protein, depending on type of cereal.

Fat

A very small quantity. Germ of wheat contains more.

Mineral elements

A small supply of calcium, iron and phosphorus, especially in the outer skins and germ. These elements may not be available because of the presence of phytic acid which makes them insoluble and so unavailable.

Vitamins

Good source of vitamin B (thiamin, riboflavin and nicotinic acid), especially in the germ and outer layers.

Moisture

Cereals are deficient in moisture – they are dry stores and will keep well.

WHEAT

The wheat grain

The grain is the fruit of the wheat plant; approximately 84% of the grain is endosperm, 2% is germ, 14% the outer layers – aleurone layers and bran. It is necessary to soften or penetrate the outer skins of the grain in order to digest it. This is done by crushing and sieving the grain by a series of processes called milling.

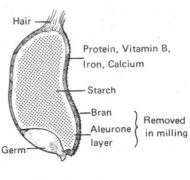

A wheat grain

Nutritive value of wheat

The nutritive value depends on the degree of milling. More milling means a higher percentage of starch, a smaller inclusion of bran and germ and thus a reduction in nutritive value.

The milling of wheat

1. The wheat is cleaned to remove dust, stones, etc. and it is washed and dried.
2. Different varieties of wheat are blended for the particular flour to be produced.
3. *To produce white flour.* The wheat is passed through roller mills which split the grain, release the endosperm and crush up the outer layers into flakes.
4. The mixture is sieved and the endosperm is separated from the bran and the germ. The endosperm at this stage is called semolina.
5. The endosperm is crushed and passed through increasingly fine sieves to produce flour.
6. The germ is separated out and used to make germ flours, e.g. Hovis, and germ extracts, e.g. wheatgerm products.
7. The bran is used for cereals, biscuits and animal food.

The old method of producing flour from wheat was to crush the grain between heavy millstones. This flour is wholemeal flour which contains the whole of the wheat grain. It is coarse, dark in colour and does not keep well because of the fat and enzymes in the germ. Some stone-ground flour is still produced, but most wholemeal flour is now processed by modern milling methods.

TYPES OF FLOUR

White flour is heavily milled and sieved to remove the outer skins and germ. It will store better without the germ which contains fat and enzymes. It is about 70% extraction.

Wholemeal flour is the whole grain crushed into flour (the bran is not digested by humans – acts as fibre). Stone-ground flour is ground by stones, and is said to have a superior flavour.

Germ flour (e.g. Hovis) is a mixture of 75% white flour + 25% cooked germ – the germ is cooked to delay the onset of rancidity in the fat. Cooking gives a malted flavour.

Starch-reduced flour. Prepared for commercial products. Much of the starch is washed out, leaving the gluten and other proteins.

Self-raising flour. This is white flour usually of medium to soft strength with the correct proportion of raising agent, e.g. cream of tartar and acid calcium phosphate to give sufficient raising action for plain cake making.

STRENGTH OF FLOUR

Flour contains a protein substance called gluten which, when combined with liquid, has elastic or stretching properties. When cake, pastry or bread doughs, etc. are formed, the gluten is able to stretch during the rising processes in cooking. On further heating the protein sets to give the mixture its structure.

Wheat contains a large quantity of this protein substance. Other cereals do not contain so much, so they are not so suitable for making cakes, bread, etc. Spring wheat (usually Canadian) contains more gluten. Winter wheat (e.g. British, Australian) contains less gluten.

Strong flours. These are milled from a mixture of wheat, in which spring wheat predominates, and contain 10–16% of strong glutens. They give a strong structure to a mixture. Used for plain breads, rolls and yeast buns.

Medium or general-purpose flour. This contains a less strong and elastic gluten. It is used for plain cakes, scones, rich yeast mixtures, most pastries.

Soft flour (cake flour). This contains a small percentage of gluten to give a soft structure to a cake. Used for most cakes, especially sponge cakes and biscuits.

CEREAL PRODUCTS MADE FROM WHEAT

Semolina. This is produced from the middlings of hard wheat, i.e. the endosperm. It is sieved to produce three grades – coarse, medium and fine, but is not as fine as flour. It is used to make milk puddings.

Pasta. These are made from the middlings of hard wheat, made into a paste with water and sometimes egg. Various shapes are produced by passing the paste through tubes or by moulding it. The products are dried and partly baked. They are made into savoury dishes with the addition of milk, cheese, meat, tomatoes, etc.

1. *Spaghetti*. 'Little strings', the most familiar pasta, long, round, holeless.
2. *Vermicelli*. Long, thin, round pasta, used in soups, e.g. chicken noodle soup.
3. *Macaroni*. Generic term for larger pasta varieties, generally tubular, available in many shapes, e.g. elbows, shells, stars, etc.
4. *Ravioli*. Stuffed pasta squares.
5. *Tagliatelle*. 'Noodles'. Flat, noodle-shaped ribbons.
6. *Gnocchi*. Small semolina dumplings eaten with cheese.
7. *Lasagne*. Wide ribbon-shaped noodles. May sometimes be coloured green using spinach or vegetable colouring in manufacture.

OTHER CEREALS

Rice. The staple food of the Far Eastern countries. It contains a higher percentage of starch than most cereals. When highly milled to remove the outer husks, polished rice is produced. This lacks vitamin B_1 (thiamin). If the diet consists mainly of polished rice the deficiency disease beriberi might result.

The rice eaten in this country is usually of the polished variety and is of two types:

Carolina rice. A round type of rice which is used for puddings. It produces a soft gelatinous mass when cooked with milk. Japan-type rice which is similar but cheaper than Carolina rice is now more widely used. This type is grown in many countries, e.g. Australia, Italy.

Patna rice. This is usually grown in Asia. It has long, thin grains which have the property of remaining separate when they are cooked. This rice is served with savoury dishes, particularly those of Eastern origin, Chinese dishes, curry, etc.

Ground rice. Rice is ground and used in puddings, cakes and biscuits, and for thickening soups.

Flaked rice. Used in milk puddings.

Note: *Rice paper*, which is edible and used as a base when cooking certain biscuits, e.g. macaroons, is not made from rice but from the pith of a tree grown in China.

Oats. A very hardy cereal which can be grown in cool climates. It has more fat and protein than other cereals. Oatmeal may be obtained in several grades – coarse, medium, fine and extra fine. It is used for porridge, muesli and oatcakes and used to thicken soups and stews. Rolled oats have been processed for quick cooking and are used for porridge and in flapjacks and parkin. Oatmeal does not keep for very long because of its fat content.

Barley. This is a very hardy cereal, but its use in cooking has declined over the years. It is now used mainly as a thickening agent in soups and stews, to make barley water, as cattle food and in the brewing of beer and whisky. It is sold as pearl barley which is polished to remove the husk, the Scotch barley which retains some husk.

Rye. Another hardy cereal which is eaten in some parts of Europe in the form of rye bread (black bread) or in rye biscuits.

Maize. Originates from America where it is called corn or Indian corn. Corn on the cob is eaten as a vegetable.

Cornflour which is produced by crushing and sieving corn is practically pure starch. It is used for thickening soups and stews and for making milk puddings. Commercial custard powders are principally cornflour with colouring and flavouring added.

Breakfast cereals

These are prepared from various cereals, e.g. wheat, oats and rice, which have been treated in some way, such as shredding or 'puffing' and then cooking so that they are ready to eat with milk and sugar. Bran is used for cereals to add fibre to the diet.

Arrowroot, sago, tapioca

Although not strictly cereals, these are usually grouped with cereals for convenience. They are practically 100% starch, and contain few other nutrients. They are prepared from the roots or stems of tropical plants.

Arrowroot. Prepared from the pulped rhizomes (underground stems) of the maranta plant. It is used to thicken milk puddings, in glazes for flans and to make cakes and biscuits. Because it is easily digested and has a delicate flavour, it is used for invalid dishes.

Sago. Prepared from the pith of the sago palm and shaped into small round pellets. It is used to make milk puddings.

Tapioca. The tubers of the cassava plant are used to prepare tapioca. It is sold in various sizes – seed pearl, medium pearl and pearl, and also as flake tapioca. It is used to make milk puddings or to thicken soups and stews.

STORAGE OF CEREALS

Store in a cool, dry place. If exposed to damp air they take up moisture and go mouldy. Mould may develop in a warm place. Flours containing germ do not keep well because of the fat in the germ. Protect against pests and examine periodically for insects. Use up older stores first.

Addition of nutrients

Cereals are usually cooked with, or eaten with, protein and fat-rich foods to add nutritive value, e.g. bread and butter milk puddings.

Milk puddings. See notes on Puddings (page 146).

Effect of heat on starch. See notes on the effect of heat on foodstuffs (pages 107–108).

METHODS OF COOKING

Cooking of rice

(for savoury dishes)

>   1 cup Patna rice (long grain)
>   1 teaspoon oil
>   2 cups boiling water or stock
>   ½ level teaspoon salt

1. Gently heat oil in pan. Add rice and stir.
2. Add boiling water or stock and salt. Stir.
3. Adjust heat to maintain a steady boil.
   Put lid on pan. The oil helps to prevent boiling over.
4. Patna rice should be cooked in 12 minutes, and no liquid left in the pan.
5. Stir with a fork and serve.

Note: Brown rice – use 3 cups of water to 1 cup of rice.
>   Cook approximately 30 minutes.
>   Quick-cook rice – follow instructions.

Cooking of pasta

Allow 100 g per portion
Method 400 g spaghetti
>   2 litres water
>   4 level teaspoons salt
>   2 teaspoons oil

1. Bring water to the boil in a large pan.
2. Add salt and oil.
3. Hold spaghetti at one end and lower into the water.
4. Stir until the mixture reboils.
5. Lower heat to maintain a steady boil. Do not use lid on the pan.
6. Stir occasionally.
7. Cook for 12 minutes. (Until 'al dente' or firm when bitten.)
8. Strain and serve.

Note: Cooking time will vary according to the thickness of the pasta.

11. SUGAR

Sugar is obtained both from sugar cane grown in hot countries and sugar beet grown in temperate climates such as in Britain. Both types of sugar are chemically identical and are used in exactly the same ways but brown sugar can only be obtained from cane sugar.

Sugar cane is processed by crushing and squeezing it to extract the liquid or 'juice'. The juice is clarified then concentrated by boiling it until crystals of raw sugar are formed. The raw sugar is sent to refineries to be purified, bleached and recrystallised to form granulated, castor and other familiar types of sugar.

Sugar beet is processed by pulping and squeezing out the juice which is then processed in the same way as juice from the sugar cane.

TYPES OF SUGAR

Granulated sugar is 99.9% pure sucrose and it has a medium sized white sparkling crystal. It is the cheapest and most widely used refined sugar. It is used for sweetening drinks and fruit, rubbed-in cake mixtures and in sweet making.

Castor sugar has smaller, finer crystals than granulated sugar. It is a pure white free-flowing sugar which dissolves quickly giving a fine texture when used in cake making. It may be sprinkled on fresh fruit, fruit pies, cereals and cakes.

Icing sugar is made by grinding sugar crystals to a fine powder. It dissolves very easily and so appears (wrongly) to be sweeter than other sugars. It is used mainly for cake icing and decorating, in sweet making and in some biscuits.

Preserving sugar is specially made for jelly and marmalade making. The large crystals dissolve slowly so sugar does not settle at the bottom of the pan and the jam thus needs less stirring to prevent burning. It is also said to produce less scum.

Cube sugar is produced from granulated sugar which is moistened, moulded and then cut to shape. The regular cubes are a convenient way of measuring an exact amount of sugar for hot drinks.

Soft brown sugars (sand sugar) are fine-grain, refined sugars which range in colour from creamy beige ('pieces') to dark brown ('Barbados'). They sweeten, add flavour, and may add colour to dishes, e.g. Christmas cake.

Demerara sugar (brown sugar) was originally a large crystal, raw (unrefined) sugar but may nowadays be a coarse grained refined sugar mingled with molasses which give its characteristic flavour and colour. Used in baked apples, flapjacks and coffee.

Coffee crystals (candy sugar) can be white or brown. The large crystals take longer to dissolve than other sugars. They were originally intended for the coffee connoisseur who likes the first sips of his coffee to be bitter and the sweetness to increase gradually. Multicoloured 'rainbow' coffee crystals are also available.

Glucose may be bought in powder or liquid form (usually from a chemist). It is used in invalid cookery because it is quickly and easily absorbed, in sweet making and in making fondant icing where it retards the rate of crystallisation of cane sugar (sucrose).

Syrup is made from selected refinery liquor after the refined sugar has been crystallised. Used in light-coloured melted cake mixtures, e.g. flapjack, gingerbread.

Treacle is a dark brown full-flavoured liquid used in baking and confectionery where a strong flavour is required, e.g. dark gingerbread, treacle toffee.

USES OF SUGAR

1. As a valuable source of energy because it is quickly and easily assimilated by the body.

2. As sweetening agent for drinks, fruit, biscuits, cakes and sweets.

3. As a preservative in jam, marmalade, crystallised fruit, condensed milk, etc. because in high concentrations (60%) it prevents the growth of yeast and mould which cause decay.

4. For improving the keeping qualities of some frozen goods, e.g. frozen whipped cream keeps better if sweetened.

5. A small amount of sugar added in the early stages of bread making supplies the yeast with food and so speeds up the bread making process.

6. For a lightening effect in cake making because when sugar is creamed with butter or margarine air is trapped in the mixture by the fat-covered sugar crystals.

7. If fine sugar is added carefully to stiffly beaten white of egg, it can give the protein in the egg an adhesive quality which enables the mixture to retain a very high proportion of air, e.g. in making meringues.

8. For decorative finishes, e.g. cake icings and for sweet making.

9. A useful 'dry store' which will keep in good condition for several years under normal atmospheric conditions.

10. Caramel, the final stage in sugar boiling is used in the manufacture of gravy browning.

Note: Doctors, dentists and experts in nutrition advocate a reduction in sugar intake.

12. FATS AND OILS

Fats and oils must be selected for specific cooking needs if the best possible results are to be obtained. A wide choice is available. Only animal and vegetable fats are edible. Mineral oils cannot be digested and could be dangerous if swallowed.

COMPOSITION OF FATS AND OILS

Fats and oils are composed of fatty acids and glycerine. Fatty acids may be *saturated* or *unsaturated*.

Saturated fatty acids
A saturated fat has each carbon atom in the fatty acids combined with two hydrogen atoms, e.g. palmitic and stearic acid. Saturated fats are solid at room temperature and predominate in fats of animal origin, e.g. butter, cream, hard cheese, egg yolks, lard and suet. They are also present in hard margarines.

Unsaturated fatty acids
Monounsaturated fatty acids have an adjacent pair of carbon atoms, each with only one hydrogen atom attached, so they are capable of taking up more hydrogen atoms. Monounsaturated fats are soft at room temperature but will solidify when in the coldest part of the refrigerator. They are present in many animal and vegetable fats. Oleic acid found in olive oil is an example of a monounsaturated fatty acid.

Polyunsaturated fatty acids have two or more pairs of carbon atoms which are capable of taking up more hydrogen atoms. Polyunsaturated fats are very soft or even oily at room temperature and will not solidify even in a refrigerator. They are present in soya bean, corn and sunflower seed oils.

Polyunsaturated fats are thought to be particularly valuable in the diet of people suffering from heart disease, or who are overweight, because they help to avoid the build up of cholesterol in the blood (saturated fats raise the cholesterol). Too much cholesterol may contribute to heart disease. Some fats, such as Flora margarine which is made up of at least 50% polyunsaturated fats, are claimed to be particularly suitable for people who need a low cholesterol diet. Unsaturated fatty acids tend to break down at high temperatures.

ANIMAL FATS

Butter

Butter is composed of the fat of milk, traces of curd (casein) and milk sugar (lactose), water and mineral matter which includes salt added to improve flavour and help preservation.

Average composition	%
Fat	85.0
Curd	0.6
Milk sugar (lactose)	0.5
Mineral elements	2.0 (salt, calcium, sulphur)
Water	11.9 (limited by law to 16% in Great Britain)

Butter owes its flavour to its fatty acid – butyric – but this acid can cause butter to go rancid fairly quickly by separating from the glycerine. A good butter is sweet and nutty, not excessively salty, and free from oiliness, acidity and excessive moisture. Can be unsalted.

Good butter adds flavour to cakes, biscuits and pastry. A soft butter is needed for cake making. For puff pastries, a tough waxy butter is needed – usually butter is blended with some pastry margarine to toughen it.

To clarify butter – melt it gently and sieve or skim it to remove curd and impurities.

Note: A blend of cream, vegetable oil, salt, colour and an emulsifier is available which gives a 'butter' flavour with easy spreading.

Lard

This is fat derived from a pig. The best lard is leaf lard obtained by rendering fat from the fatty tissues surrounding the kidney and intestines. Poorer qualities are obtained from other fatty parts. Good lard is pure white fat with practically no flavour. It is a tough plastic fat, with no creaming properties but excellent shortening properties. It is usually mixed with margarine or butter for cakes, etc. to add flavour and colour. It is suitable for frying as it is fairly stable at high temperatures.

Suet

This is prepared beef fat. The best suet is obtained from around the kidneys of the beast. Suet is a hard fat and cannot be rubbed into flour or creamed. It is added by chopping finely and stirring into a mixture.

It is used to make steamed and boiled puddings and in stuffings. Moist methods of cooking – steaming or boiling – should be used. Baking would give a hard, dry result. Prepared suet is purified fat which has been shredded and mixed with wheat or rice flour to stop the pieces sticking together.

VEGETABLE FATS AND OILS

Soya beans, sunflower seeds, cottonseeds, groundnuts, sesame seeds, coconuts, palm, palm kernels, olives and tea seeds all yield oils which are used in cooking fats and oils, margarine and salad oils and creams.

Margarine

Margarine was developed as a substitute for butter but is now accepted in its own right because it is easy to spread when cold, can be used in 'quick' methods for cakes and pastries, and has a bland flavour. Brands are produced for the table, for cakes and pastry.

The selected oils and fats – a choice of groundnut, cottonseed, palm, palm kernel, coconut, soya and whale oils, oleo (beef tallow) and stearin (mutton tallow) – are extracted, refined to remove strong colours and flavours, and blended together. The prepared oils, fat-free pasteurised milk, salt, and colouring agents are mixed and churned in a Votator machine. A thicker liquid is produced which is refrigerated to solidify it and then it is moulded and packed.

Table Margarine. This is blended to give the best possible flavour. A percentage of butter may be added.

Cake Margarine. Developed to have good creaming properties. Some butter may be included.

Pastry Margarine. Blended to produce a tough plastic margarine which has a fairly high melting point. May contain a high percentage of stearin or be hydrogenated to harden it. Used for puff pastries.

COMPOUND FATS AND OILS

These are practically 100 per cent fat, salt-free, and with no flavour. They are made by refining extracted vegetable oils. The blend of oils is hydrogenated to produce the consistency desired, processed by creaming and chilling, and then packed.

All-purpose fats. These are produced to give fats which may be used for cooking purposes – cakes, pastries and frying. If an all-purpose oil is used to make a cake, the oil, sugar and eggs are beaten together before the dry ingredients are added.

For pastry and scones the oil is mixed with a little cold water or milk, then the sieved flour is gradually mixed in using a fork. (See also quick mix pastry page 125 and quick mix cakes page 136.)

Frying oils and fats. These contain oils and fats which do not break down at the high temperatures needed for frying. They have a smoking point of about 220°C.

Note: the danger of overheating to the point of ignition.

PROPERTIES OF FATS

Fat, when rubbed into flour, coats groups of flour particles with a waterproof layer. Lard, cooking fats and oils make the shortest pastry because of their high shortening power.

> Lard – very short but lacks flavour and colour.
> Cooking fats – very short but lack flavour and colour.
> Butter – fairly short, good flavour and colour.
> Margarine – less short, quite good flavour and colour.

Frying properties

Fats for frying must not break down at high temperatures. This breakdown causes smoking, bad flavour and appearance of food, and indigestion.

Vegetable cooking oils which are rich in unsaturated fatty acids are often preferable to animal fats for frying because higher temperatures can be reached without decomposition. Stabilisers are added to reduce the chance of fat breakdowns. Fats used should contain no water, salt or non-fat solids. They should be tasteless or well flavoured at high temperatures and should not begin to decompose until after they reach the required temperature for frying food. The smoking point should be about 220°C.

Repeated heating or heating to a temperature higher than that required for frying purposes will encourage the various forms of breakdown with the development of off flavours in the fat or any food cooked in it.

Suitable fats
> Oils and fats specially produced for the purpose – best.
> Good-quality lard – quite good.
> Bulk lard and clarified dripping – fairly good.
> Butter – good flavour but browns too quickly. May be used with oils.
> Margarine – not suitable. Causes food to stick.

Creaming properties

Fats for some types of cakes must cream well, i.e. mix with sugar enclosing air. To do this they must possess a plastic, waxy consistency and have a good flavour. Fats may be plasticised and precreamed for easier working.

Suitable fats

Cooking fats – very easy to cream, but extra flavour needed.

Margarine – good, some variation in different brands.

Butter – fairly good, but adds good flavour to rich cakes.

13. THE COOKING OF FOODS

Although many foods may be eaten raw, especially fruit and vegetables, it is usual, and in many cases essential, for food to be cooked in order to be digested and absorbed.

REASONS FOR COOKING FOOD

1. To assist digestion and absorption, e.g. uncooked starch granules in potatoes, flour, etc. are less fully digested and therefore less fully absorbed.
2. To make the food more attractive to the eye and palate, e.g. the changing of the red haemoglobin in meat to brown.
3. To develop the extractives and therefore the flavour of foods, e.g. grilled steak.
4. To give variety.
5. To kill harmful bacteria.
6. To preserve the food.
7. To stimulate the digestive juices by the smell of food cooking.
8. To reduce bulk and thus increase intake.
9. To provide hot food in cold weather.

THE EFFECT OF HEAT ON FOOD

Protein

Is coagulatd by heat. The process is gradual, e.g. white of egg thickens, becomes opaque and firm. Over-heating will harden the protein, making it tough, unpalatable and shrunken. This characteristic coagulation of protein when heated can be observed in its use as a coating for fried foods and the development of crust in bread formed by the protein gluten in wheat.

Fats and oils

Fat melts to oil when heated. Water is given off with a bubbling noise as heating continues. When all the water has been driven off, a faint blue haze appears and further heating will result in smoking and burning. The unpleasant smell of burning fat is caused by the presence of fatty acids.

Cooking oil when heated does not produce a haze so there is a danger of overheating and spontaneous ignition.

Carbohydrates

Effect of moist heat on starch. Moist heat causes the molecular structure of starch grains to separate, releasing the starch which will thicken liquids.

Blending the uncooked starch with a little cold liquid helps to avoid lumps during cooking, e.g. cornflour mould.

Stirring is necessary during cooking to prevent the starch grains settling and sticking together at the bottom of a pan, forming lumps and burning.

Effect of dry heat on starch. The starch will change colour from pale cream to shades of brown, and will eventually carbonise if heated long enough. Water is given off during heating and the starch on the surface is reduced to dextrin, a form of sugar, e.g. toast and the brown surface of cakes.

Effect of moist heat on sugar. Sugar dissolves in water – more rapidly in hot water than in cold. On heating it becomes a syrup, colours, caramelises, and will eventually burn to carbon and ash.

Effect of dry heat. Sugar will quickly caramelise and burn.

For effect of heat on vitamins and mineral elements see the chapter on nutrition.

TRANSFERENCE OF HEAT

Heat is essential for cooking. It may be transferred by radiation, conduction and convection.

Radiation. Heat passes from its source in direct rays until it falls on an object in its path, e.g. grilling.

Conduction. This is a means of transferring heat through a solid object by contact. Some materials, e.g. metals used for pans, transfer heat more quickly than the wood used for wooden spoons. Conduction is the principle involved in the use of a solid electric hot plate.

Convection. This is the movement of heated particles of gases and liquids. On heating, the particles expand, become less dense and rise. The colder particles sink to take their place, thus causing convection currents which distribute heat. This principle is used in heating a gas oven and in the heating of liquids.

All methods of cooking depend upon one or more of these principles.

STEWING

Stewing is a slow, moist method of cooking in a covered pan or slow cooker. It can be carried out on top of the stove or in a covered casserole in the oven. The container must have a tight fitting lid to reduce the loss of moisture by evaporation and prevent drying up or burning. This cooking method is most commonly applied to mixtures of meat and vegetables, or fruit.

When stewing meat for long periods, the soluble meat extracts are dissolved in the cooking liquid, which may be water, stock, wine or cider. It is important that the amount of liquid used should not be more than that which can conveniently be served with the stew. It is usually not more than 250 mls of liquid to each 500 g of meat. Cooking must be slow in order to give time for the connective tissue in tough meat to be changed in to soluble gelatine, so releasing the fibres and making the meat tender. The ideal cooking temperature for stewing on top of the stove is approximately 82°C, i.e. simmering. In the oven, a stew should be cooked at Gas mark 3, or 170°C. Too rapid cooking will harden the protein fibres. If the connective tissue gelatinises too quickly, the meat fibres will fall apart and the stew will be tough and stringy. 'A stew boiled is a stew spoiled.' Gentle heat will ensure coagulation of the protein without hardening. Stewing is an ideal method of producing appetising dishes from the cheaper, tougher cuts of meat.

Suitable cuts of meat

Beef. Thin flank, shin, leg, neck and clod, chuck and blade, skirt.
Lamb. Scrag, breast, middle neck.
Pork. Hand and spring, neck end.
Veal. Breast, knuckle, neck.

Advantages of stewing

1. Economy. Tough cheap cuts of meat may be rendered tender and palatable.
2. There is little loss of flavour and nutritive value because the extractives are served in the gravy.
3. Economy of labour – a stew needs little attention.
4. Economy of fuel – very little fuel is used.
5. The large amount of vegetables used in some stews will form a cheap vegetable supplement to meat protein.
6. Economy of washing up. The whole dish may be cooked and served in one vessel.
7. A wide variety of stews may be served depending on the ingredients.

Disadvantages

1. It is a slow method of cooking; tough meat may need 3–4 hours. But stews cooked in a pressure cooker will be cooked in one third of the normal time.
2. A stew may tend to lack bite.

Types of stew

Simple stews are those in which the cooked meat and vegetables are served together, e.g. hot pot, Irish stew.

Brown stew is a simple stew, but the meat and vegetables are browned in hot fat and a brown roux is made from the fat and flour which will colour the stew.

Richer stews – better quality meat is generally used. After cooling, the liquid is strained to remove the flavouring vegetables and is made into a sauce. The stew is garnished or served with fresh vegetables.

Brown stews, e.g. beef olives.

White stew, e.g. fricassée of veal or chicken.

Note: Some fruits are also stewed, e.g. apples, rhubarb.

BOILING

This is a moist method of cooking where the food is wholly or almost covered with liquid. The pan should have a well-fitting lid to reduce evaporation. 'Boiling' is a misnomer as the food should be simmered after the initial cooking. See Stewing.

Suitable foods

Beef. Silverside (salted), brisket (salted).
Pork. Cheek, belly, ham, hand and spring.
Meat loaf or galantine. In foil or a cloth.
Fish. Whole or large pieces.
Vegetables. Most.
Puddings. In a basin or cloth.

STEAMING

Steaming is a moist method of cooking food in the steam which rises from boiling water. The food may be cooked by direct or indirect contact with the steam.
Direct. In a steamer.
  In a pan of boiling water.
Indirect. Between two plates over a pan of boiling water.

Advantages of steaming

1. There is less loss of soluble nutrients from the food than by other moist methods of cooking.

2. Steamed food is lighter and more digestible and so more suitable for invalids, e.g. fish. Sponge and suet puddings are lighter if steamed rather than baked.

3. Steaming is economical on fuel.

Disadvantages

1. It is a slow method of cooking but there is little risk of the food being overcooked.

2. There is little development of flavour.

Methods of steaming

1. *In a steamer over boiling water*. The steam is in direct contact with the food, e.g. puddings enclosed in a basin, joints of meat or poultry, larger pieces of fish which are wrapped in cooking parchment or foil to prevent breaking up and to retain some of the soluble extractives and nutrients. Some vegetables, e.g. potatoes, can be steamed, but this method of cooking is not recommended for green vegetables as it makes them unpalatable.

A two- or even three-tiered steamer may be used and some food, e.g. potatoes, cooked in the boiling water at the same time.

2. *In a pan of boiling water*. The food is placed in a covered receptacle in the pan with water one-third to half way up the side of the receptacle, e.g. suet puddings.

3. *Between two plates over boiling water*. The steam does not come in contact with the food, which cooks in its own juices. But this method will take a little longer because of the indirect contact with the steam, e.g. thin fillets of fish.

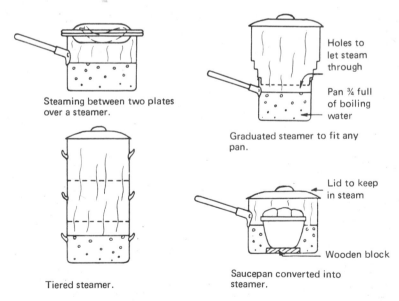

Steaming between two plates over a steamer.

Holes to let steam through

Pan ¾ full of boiling water

Graduated steamer to fit any pan.

Tiered steamer.

Lid to keep in steam

Wooden block

Saucepan converted into steamer.

Methods of steaming

Rules for steaming

1. The lid must fit tightly and a steamer must fit the pan to prevent steam escaping.

2. Food, e.g. pudding, must be protected from condensed steam which would make it soggy. Use vegetable parchment, cooking foil, etc.

3. The water in the pan must be boiling before the food is put in or the cooking timed from when the water boils. The water must be kept boiling steadily throughout the cooking time.

4. A supply of boiling water must be available to replenish the water in the pan.

ROASTING

This is a dry method of cooking. Correctly speaking, roasting is cooking by means of radiant heat, i.e. meat on a rotating spit in front of an intense heat. Nowadays oven roasting, which is actually baking (a combination of convection and radiation) is carried out. The food is put in a hot oven which will coagulate the surface protein, thus sealing it and preventing the escape of too many extractives. When the food becomes slightly browned the temperature must be reduced to cook the inside without hardening the surface too much.

Cuts of meat suitable for roasting

Beef. Topside, sirloin, fore rib, silverside, thick flank.
Lamb. Loin, best end of neck, leg, shoulder, breast (usually rolled).
Pork. Neck end (spare rib and blade bone), loin, leg, hand and spring, belly.
Veal. Fillet, loin, breast.
Poultry.

Note: Some slightly tougher cuts of meat, e.g. topside of beef, may be pot-roasted in a pan on top of the stove, or in the oven.

Basting is necessary when roasting in an open oven tin, to prevent the meat becoming too dry, to give it flavour and reduce shrinkage. The exception is pork with crackling which should never be basted.

The use of roastabags enables meat to brown without basting, and helps to keep the oven clean.

BRAISING

A moist method of cooking combining stewing and pot roasting. It is suitable for slightly tougher cuts of meat which are not tender enough for roasting. A mirepoix is prepared of vegetables, herbs and sometimes bacon, in a strong saucepan. The meat is browned all over in hot fat and placed on top of the mirepoix. Stock is added to come half way up the meat. The meat, which cooks in the steam, should be basted frequently with the hot liquid. The lid of the saucepan must fit tightly to prevent evaporation. Simmer until tender allowing 30 minutes to 400 g and 30 minutes over. Cook on top of the stove or in the oven. The meat may be browned under a hot grill after cooking.

GRILLING

This is a very quick method of cooking by radiant heat from a metal fret (gas) or open electric element. Because the heat is intense and the food is very close to the source of heat, it must be moistened with melted butter or oil before cooking. Grilling is only suitable for small tender pieces of food. The surface of the food is quickly sealed and the flavour is retained.

In a barbecue, grilling is done over charcoal.

Suitable foods for grilling

Beef. Rump, fillet and sirloin steaks, sausages.
Lamb. Best end of neck cutlets, loin chops, chump chops, kidney, liver.
Pork. Fillet (tenderloin), loin chops, spare rib chops, belly (sliced), kidney, liver, sausages.
Bacon. Chips, rasher, gammon steaks.
Fish. Fillets, steaks.
Vegetables. Mushrooms, tomatoes.
Mixed grill consists of a selection of the following: steak, pork chops, lamb chops, cutlets, kidneys, liver, sausages, bacon, tomatoes, mushrooms. It is accompanied by watercress, potato crisps or game chips and maître d'hotel butter.

Important points in grilling

1. Food must be brushed with fat to prevent drying.
2. The grill must be pre-heated to a red heat, then reduced after initial cooking.
3. Cooking time will vary according to the type of food, thickness, quality, etc.
4. Food must be turned frequently using spoons or tongs to avoid pricking the surface resulting in loss of juices.

FRYING

Frying is a quick method of cooking food in hot fat or oil, but it requires constant attention and care in both preparation and cooking of the foods. The surface of the food is sealed as soon as it comes in contact with the hot fat, so the full flavour is retained.

Fat. The fat used should have a high 'smoking temperature', i.e. it can be heated to a very high temperature without burning, at least 182°C (compare with boiling point of water 100°C). Most fats and oils smoke at 180–200°C, but some vegetable cooking fats smoke at 215°C; therefore smoke is not always a good guide to the temperature of the fat. (See Fats and Oils, page 105.) The cooking temperature of the fat will depend upon the nature of the food to be cooked, e.g. doughnuts should be cooked at 182°C, fish cakes at 200°C.

Test for temperature. Drop a cube of bread into the hot fat:

    180°C – bread will brown in 60 sec
    193°C – bread will brown in 40 sec
    200°C – bread will brown in 20 sec

Note: the danger in overheating fat and oils with a high smoking point.

Methods of frying

Deep fat frying

The food is totally immersed in hot fat. The pan must be heavy and at least 16 cm deep, and only half filled with fat because the moisture in the food will cause the fat to bubble up. It is essential that most foods to be deep fried should be coated to protect the surface from the intense heat and prevent the food breaking up. The protein in the coating, e.g. egg or milk, will coagulate rapidly on heating, thus sealing and protecting the surface of the food.

Foods suitable for deep fat frying

Potato chips, fish fillets or steaks, fish cakes, Scotch eggs, croquette mixtures, doughnuts, fritters, choux pastry, etc.

Note: Frying baskets may be used for chipped potatoes, fish, etc. *but* certain foods, e.g. doughnuts and fish in batter, would stick to the basket. These should be removed from the pan with a perforated spoon.

Coatings for fried foods

  1. Egg and breadcrumbs for fish cakes, croquettes, Scotch eggs, etc.
  2. Batters used for fish and fritters (see Batters page 158).
  3. Pastry or pasta, e.g. rissoles.
  4. Economical coatings can be made from milk and flour or oatmeal. Fat used for frying and ingredients used in coating will add nutritive value.

Shallow frying

Dry frying. This method is used for foods naturally rich in fat; this fat is extracted during cooking and will prevent the food sticking to the pan, e.g. bacon, sausage. Adding extra fat would tend to make these foods greasy and unappetising.

Frying in shallow fat. Use sufficient fat just to cover the bottom of the pan when sauté'ing vegetables, e.g. onions or mushrooms. Foods such as eggs, fish cakes, liver, steak, chops, etc will need more fat to come half way up the food being cooked to ensure thorough cooking.

Stir frying. This is the quick cooking of small pieces of tender meat or fish, or vegetables, in a small amount of fat.

Rules for frying

1. Use good quality, clean fat which is free from moisture.

2. A strong pan must be used, large enough to hold fat, food and basket if used. A cheap frying pan is false economy.

3. The fat must be heated to the required temperature.

4. The food should be prepared according to type, divided into portions suitable for this quick cooking method, and coated if necessary.

5. Add the food to the hot fat in quantities small enough to avoid cooling the fat and raising its level to danger point. If the fat is too cool the food will not be sealed – it will absorb the fat and will be greasy and indigestible. If the fat is too hot the outside of the food will be burned and the flavour bitter while the inside might be raw.

6. Allow sufficient time for cooking and turn the food if necessary, taking care not to puncture the surface.

7. Most fried food must be drained on absorbent paper to remove excess grease.

8. Some fried foods, e.g. fried fillet of plaice, are served on dish papers to absorb more grease.

9. After use, the fat should be strained to remove crumbs, etc, which would give the next food to be fried a bitter flavour and black specks.

10. Care during frying is essential because of the very high temperature used and the danger of fire. Keep a lid or metal cover, e.g. a baking sheet, at hand to use to cover a pan in case of fire.

11. NEVER leave a frying pan in use unattended. Keep children away.

PRESSURE COOKING

The modern domestic pressure cooker now forms part of the basic equipment in many kitchens. It is an economical method of cooking because it saves time and fuel.

Principles of pressure cooking

Under ordinary kitchen conditions most cooking liquids boil at 100°C at normal atmospheric pressure and the temperature cannot be raised beyond this. However, if the atmospheric pressure can be increased, the temperature can be raised and the food cooked more quickly. This is the principle on which pressure cooking is based. The pressure cooker is designed to retain the steam which escapes from a normal saucepan, thus causing pressure to build up and the temperature inside the cooker to rise above normal boiling point. The steam is forced through the food, cooking it very quickly. By this method even tough meat can be made tender, and foods can be cooked in a fraction of the normal cooking time. Because of the short cooking time, little liquid needs to be added to the food, and it can all be used for sauces, gravy, etc. to serve with meat or fish, or added to soups.

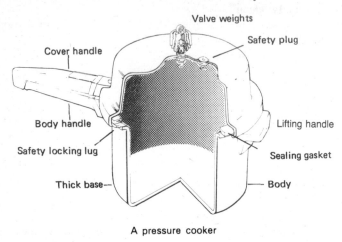

A pressure cooker

Types of pressure cooker

There are two types available in this country:

1. *Saucepan* type. More versatile since it is fitted with a variable pressure control and available in various sizes.

2. *Casserole* type. Suitable for ordinary everyday cooking. Has a 15 lb (fixed) pressure control valve.

Most household models are made from aluminium or stainless steel and it is now possible to buy non-stick pressure cookers and models with automatic timing and pressure reduction. All models may be used on any source of heat – gas, electricity, solid fuel or oil, with a substantial saving of time and fuel.

Types of pressure controls

Every pressure cooker is fitted with a pressure control. There are two main types. Pressure levels are now usually known as High (15 lb), Medium (10 lb) or Low (5 lb).

1. *Lever* type. Non-variable control valve fitted with a spring, loaded to take 15 lb (High) pressure only.

2. *Variable control type*. Enables three different pressures to be used in cooking. Consists of an inner 5 lb (Low) weight, a ring which screws on to give 10 lb (Medium) pressure, and an outer ring which can be added to complete the maximum 15 lb (High) pressure.

Safety devices

Every pressure cooker must be fitted with a safety device which comes into action automatically if the pressure control should become blocked, e.g. through overloading the cooker. One of the most common types is:

Dual Safety Rubber Plug. Has a movable metal centre pin which will pop up to release excessive pressure, and can be reset for further use. Should the temperature inside the cooker become excessive, or it starts to boil dry, the pin will melt.

Most pressure cookers also require a gasket or sealing ring to ensure there is no leakage of steam at the join between the cover and the base of the cooker.

A locking device ensures that the cover cannot be removed from the base during cooking or while there is still pressure inside.

These safety devices are designed to protect the cooker from damage if misused, but they should not be needed if the manufacturers' instructions are followed.

Water or cooking liquid

The amount of liquid used in a pressure cooker depends on the length of the cooking time and not on the quantity of food being cooked. The liquid should always be added to the cooker first to avoid omission. Any liquid can be used, provided that it will give off steam when boiled, e.g. water, stock, thin gravy, soup, wine, fruit juice or milk. Melted fat is not suitable as it does not give off steam which is required to build up pressure. As a general rule, a minimum 250 ml of liquid is needed for the first 15 mins. or part of 15 mins. cooking time, plus a further 125 ml for every subsequent 15 mins. or part of 15 mins. cooking, but the manufacturers' recipes will give the exact quantity for each food and *must* be followed.

Steamed puddings. These contain a raising agent so a period of pre-steaming is necessary before pressure is built up so that the pudding will rise. The amount of liquid required will vary with the type of pudding and the cooking time, e.g. Christmas pudding requires a longer cooking time and more liquid than a much lighter sponge pudding.

Milk puddings. These may be cooked 'loose' in the pressure cooker. Rice pudding requires the same amount of liquid as in normal cooking, i.e. 500 ml milk to 50 g rice, but cooking time is considerably less, about 12 mins. at High pressure. Tapioca, Sago or Semolina require 500 ml milk to two large heaped tablespoons of the cereal and about 7 mins. cooking at High pressure.

Soups or Stews. Only the quantity of liquid to be served in the finished dish should be added, as long as this is not less than the minimum required for the type of cooker being used. There is little or no loss of liquid from the cooker by evaporation.

Seasoning. Small quantities of seasoning are needed. They should be sprinkled on the prepared, washed and drained vegetables before they are placed in the cooker. Do NOT place salt in the water as it is not volatile and cannot possibly come in contact with the vegetables. Where foods to be pressure cooked contain liquid, seasoning should be added in the normal way but a reduced quantity may be needed.

Bringing the cooker to pressure

The cooker is first put on a high heat with the vent pipe open. The liquid will boil and turn into steam which pushes the air out of the cooker through the open vent pipe. It is necessary to wait for a steady flow of steam from the vent pipe before putting on the pressure weight or closing the control lever. When this is done the cooker must be kept on the recommended heat until it has reached pressure which is indicated by a loud hissing, a further escape of steam and a few drops of water around the pressure control. At this point timing can begin and the heat should be adjusted so there is a continuous hissing and escape of steam throughout the cooking time.

Incomplete exhaustion of air causes:

1. Oxidation of light-coloured vegetables, darkening of potatoes and cauliflower.

2. Greater destruction of vitamin C due to oxidation.

Controlling pressure

High heat is required until pressure is reached, then very low heat. If using a modern electric hotplate, and the cooking time is less than 10 mins. the control should be switched to Low or Simmer, and *not* turned off, as the cooker would lose pressure and the food take longer to cook.

Note: Older type, solid electric hotplates were less easy to control and it was suggested that they should be turned off if the cooking time was less than 10 minutes.

Loading

The pan should not be more than two thirds full, or half full for soups or stews, to allow adequate clearance between food and lid. If over-filled, the food may bubble up and clog the vent pipe, bringing the safety device into action. If using basins or moulds inside the cooker, make sure that these fit easily, allowing at least 2 cm between basin and lid. The basin should only be two thirds full so that the pudding can rise and still be clear of the vent pipe.

Steamed puddings should be put into well greased containers and the covering should be a double thickness of greaseproof paper, tied down securely.

Timing

Usually one-fifth to one-third of the normal cooking time but follow manufacturers' instructions. If in doubt allow less time. The lid can be replaced and the cooker brought to pressure again quickly, but some food, e.g. vegetables will be spoiled by over-cooking.

Recipes

Supplied by the manufacturer of the pressure cooker and *must* be followed. Several foods may be cooked together in a pressure cooker as flavours do not mingle because
  a) food does not come into contact with the water.
  b) no air should be present.
Do not use a rack or trivet for stews as the flavours need to blend so the ingredients should be in liquid.

Reducing pressure

There are two methods, depending on the type of food being cooked.

Reducing pressure immediately with cold water

Cold water is allowed to run over the lid and sides of the cooker for approximately 30 seconds, or the cooker may be stood in a bowl of cold water until pressure is reduced to normal boiling point, 100°C. This does not make the food cold or unpalatable.

Reducing pressure at room temperature

Turn off the heat, and allow the cooker to cool slowly to reduce the temperature and pressure gradually (not more than 5–10 mins.). This method can be used for milk puddings, dried vegetables, egg custards, sponge puddings, stews, fruits and vegetable bottling, soups, etc. but recipe instructions should be followed.

Opening the cooker

No pressure cooker can be opened while it contains pressure as there is force against the pan and lid. It must *never* be forced open. Handles should slide apart easily. Resistance indicates that there is still pressure and further cooling is needed.

After use

Wash and dry all parts carefully, making sure there is no blockage in the vent pipe.

Nutritive value

There is no evidence that food which is cooked in a pressure cooker loses any more vitamin C than food cooked in an ordinary saucepan. With some vegetables, e.g. cauliflower and cabbage, the vitamin C retention has been found to be slightly better than in normal cooking.

RÉCHAUFFÉS (RE-HEATED DISHES)

In the average household it is inevitable that there will be left-over food, e.g. meat left on a joint. If possible, this food should be used up to avoid waste.

It could prove to be dull and unappetising, but if care is taken to re-dish and re-dress it, left-over food can make quite attractive dishes. The food should be well seasoned and garnished, and served attractively, perhaps with a good sauce which will also enhance the nutritive value and appearance of the re-heated dish.

Rules for preparation

1. Left-over food must be absolutely fresh. (See notes on food poisoning, pages 188–191.)

To store. Food should be put into clean, covered containers and protected from dust and flies. Cool the food as quickly as possible and put in a refrigerator or a cool place. If a home freezer is available the re-heated dish can be prepared ready for cooking, e.g. shepherd's pie, potato croquettes; then frozen until required.

2. Food must be finely divided for quick penetration of heat.

Meat. Remove excess fat, gristle or bone and mince or chop the meat.

Fish. Remove skin and bone and flake finely.

Potatoes. Mash or put through a sieve. The food is more easily divided up while it is still warm.

3. Avoid over-cooking which will harden the protein fibres of meat and fish and make the food indigestible.

4. Additional ingredients, e.g. onion or potato, must be cooked, as re-heating does not allow time for cooking.

5. Additional moisture is needed to replace that which is lost in cooking. Moisture may be added in the form of accompanying sauces, or the food may be bound with a well-cooked panada. Stock or gravy may also be used. Care must be taken to ensure that gravy is free from taint as thickened gravies in particular deteriorate rapidly. Sauces may add nutritive value in the form of milk, eggs, etc., and they are also important as a means of supplying flavour and colour.

6. Re-heated dishes could be insipid, and so flavouring and seasoning are important.

With *beef, pork and lamb* use onion, tomato, parsley and other herbs.

With *veal, poultry and rabbit* use lemon, mushroom, bacon, parsley and other herbs.

With *fish* use lemon, parsley, mushroom and anchovy essence.

7. Food must be protected from heat to prevent re-cooking. This may be achieved by:
   a) Coating with egg and breadcrumbs, e.g. fish cakes and croquettes.
   b) Coating with potatoes, e.g. fish pie or shepherd's pie.
   c) Dipping in batter, e.g. meat and fish fritters and kromeskies.
   d) Sealing in pastry, e.g. in rissoles.

8. Serving. Care should be taken with serving and garnishing to make re-heated dishes look attractive. Small individual dishes, e.g. scallop shells, may be used for fish.

Small pieces of crisp toast or fried bread may be used as garnishes in some savoury dishes and will give bite to dishes in which it would otherwise be lacking, e.g. mince or kedgeree.

9. Fresh vegetables or fruit to supply vitamin C should be served with a re-heated dish as re-heated food could lack this vitamin.

Methods of re-heating

1. *Frying*, e.g. croquettes or rissoles. This is quick, and the heat penetrates rapidly. Frying adds flavour and fat.

2. *Baking*, e.g. shepherd's pie, fish pie. These may also be grilled.

3. *Heating in a sauce or gravy*, e.g. curry or mince.

Use of left-over food

Meat. Shepherd's pie, rissoles, hamburgers, savoury mince (on toast or with borders of potatoes or rice). Curry, fricassée, hash, croquettes, fritters, kromeskies, meat roll, meat mould.

Fish. Fish pie, fish cakes, kedgeree, scalloped fish.

Potatoes. Croquettes, cakes or sauté potatoes. Scones. Used in shepherd's pie, fish pie, etc.

Bread. Bread puddings – queen of puddings, cheese pudding. Also used for raspings. Fresh breadcrumbs freeze very well.

Stale cakes. Can be made into trifles (if not too stale) or used in puddings in the place of breadcrumbs.

Biscuits. Some types of plain biscuits may be used in refrigerator cakes, flan cases, etc.

14. PASTRY MAKING

The ingredients used in pastry are flour, fat, water and salt. The proportion and method of incorporating these will determine the variety and texture of finished pastry. (Richer types may have sugar, eggs or cheese added.)

Good pastry should be light, flaky, crisp and not hard, and should crumble easily.

Ingredients

Flour. Soft flour is advisable for short crust pastry, but a stronger flour could be used for flaky pastry. Always use plain flour (except for suet pastry, when S.R. flour or plain flour and baking powder are used because of the hardness of the suet, or in economical short crust if the amount of fat is less than half the weight of the flour). The flour should be good quality, fresh and dry. It is sieved to introduce air and to remove lumps.

Fat. Lard, margarine, butter, cooking fats and dripping are all used, but dripping is not recommended for sweet dishes. Suet is used for suet crust pastry; cooking oils may be used in some cases. Lard alone, although it makes pastry short, makes it rather soft and lacking in flavour and colour. Margarine makes rather hard pastry, but gives a good colour and flavour. A mixture is best – half lard, half margarine. Butter, even a small percentage, gives a better flavour. Fat must be cold and fresh.

Liquid. Usually cold water (milk is used only in hot water pastry). In richer pastries a little egg yolk is used. The amount depends on the type of pastry, temperature of weather, etc.

Raising agent. Air is usually the raising agent, so the more air which can be incorporated and kept in the pastry the lighter and flakier the pastry will be. Air is incorporated by sieving flour and by rubbing in, and is retained by handling lightly. Some is incorporated by folding for flaky pastry, rough puff and puff pastry. Air, being a gas, expands on heating and pushes up the layers of pastry.

In suet pastry baking powder is used because suet takes longer to melt than other fats, and the pastry might be heavy if extra raising power is not given.

Water vapour from liquid used gives some raising power.

Salt. Added to bring out the flavour.

Methods of incorporating the fat

1. Shredding or finely chopping and mixing with the flour, as in suet pastry.
2. Rubbing into the flour – short crust.
3. Adding in small flakes to the paste and rolling in as in flaky pastry.
4. Adding in small lumps to the flour, then rolling in as in puff pastry.
5. Enclosing a block of fat in the paste and rolling in as in puff pastry.
6. Melting fat with milk or water and mixing with the flour as in hot water crust pastry.
7. Putting all the ingredients into a bowl and mixing with a fork, as in quick-mix or fork-mix methods used with compound fats for short crust.

GENERAL RULES FOR PASTRY MAKING

1. Keep everything as cool as possible – utensils, ingredients, hands, etc. Cold air has more capacity to expand than warm.
2. Introduce as much air as possible in sieving, mixing, etc.
3. Handle lightly and roll lightly to avoid pressing out air. Do not turn the pastry over and avoid re-rolling if possible.
4. Use only enough water to bind pastry together – too much makes pastry hard. (Note that in flaky pastry more water is used to make an elastic dough.)
5. Use as little flour as possible for rolling out. Too much makes pastry hard.
6. Do not stretch the pastry during rolling or it will shrink during cooking.
7. Pastry may be improved by leaving it to relax in a cool place before cooking. If it is to be kept for any length of time it must be covered to prevent the surface drying out.
8. Cook in a hot oven until pastry is set. If the oven is not ready leave the pastry in a cool place.
9. Cool after cooking.

Cooking pastry

The oven must be hot when pastry is put in so that:

a) The pastry will rise when the air it contains expands on heating. The gluten in the flour absorbs water, stretches entangling air with it, and rises as the air expands. Then the heat of the oven sets the gluten (protein) in its risen shape.

b) The starch grains on heating will absorb fat. If the oven is too cool the fat will melt and run out while flour remains uncooked and the resulting pastry will be moist, heavy, and greasy. After pastry is set (in 10–15 mins.) oven temperature may be lowered to cook fillings of pies, e.g. meat, fish.

TYPES OF PASTRY

Suet crust pastry

Proportions:
¼–½ suet to flour (S.R. flour, or plain flour plus 3 level teaspoonfuls baking powder per 400 g flour)
Approx. 250 ml water per 400 g flour
1 level teaspoon salt per 400 g flour

The fat used is beef suet which may be bought ready prepared, i.e. shredded suet coated with starch to prevent its forming lumps. Beef suet surrounding the kidneys is best, as it is softer, easier to prepare and has a better flavour. If suet is not available, hard, clarified dripping may be grated and used in its place.

Suet is too hard to rub in. It is mixed with the flour and raising agent and enough water is added to form an elastic dough which must only be rolled once to avoid hard pastry.

The raising agent is important as it helps to produce a light open pastry which may otherwise be difficult to achieve, because the high melting point of suet makes it possible for the starch grains to be cooked before the fat melts. A moist method of cooking, e.g. steaming, also helps to overcome this. In some cases breadcrumbs may replace up to half the weight of flour to give a light suet pudding.

Uses of suet pastry
Steak and kidney pudding, dumplings, jam roly-poly.

Short crust pastry

Proportions:
½ fat to flour
Approx. 100 ml water per 400 g flour
1 level teaspoon salt per 400 g flour

It is advisable to blend margarine and lard for making short crust pastry, as lard, being soft, tends to melt during rubbing in. With some compound fats less than half fat to flour will be needed. Refer to label for use.

After sieving the flour and salt to remove lumps and incorporate air, the fat and flour are rubbed in, using the finger-tips only until the mixture resembles fine breadcrumbs. If the hands are lifted, air will be incorporated.

The liquid should be as cold as possible and preferably added all at once, but care should be taken not to add too much water. Wet pastry will be hard and tough when cooked because the flour will absorb water rather than fat. Use a round-ended knife to mix in the liquid and draw the pastry together with the finger-tips. This will keep the mixture cool.

The pastry is pressed *very lightly* with the finger-tips before turning on to a *lightly floured* board. It is important to use as little extra flour for rolling as possible or the proportions will be wrong (no extra fat being added).

Rolling must be done using short, sharp strokes in a forward direction only to maintain *even*, *light pressure*. Turn the pastry as necessary, but *do not* turn the rolling pin. *Do not* turn the pastry over or re-roll as this causes tough, heavy pastry by absorbing more flour.

Allow the pastry to relax for a short time in a cool place before cooking. This will allow the elastic protein substance, gluten, to relax, and thus reduce shrinkage.

Bake in a hot oven at 220°C until set. The temperature may then be reduced.

Uses of short crust pastry
Pies, tarts, etc.

Short crust pastry may be eaten hot or cold. It will keep a day or two.

The pastry itself may be frozen or dishes made from the pastry may be frozen, cooked or uncooked.

Varieties of short crust pastry

Cheese pastry is made like short crust pastry with the addition of half to equal finely grated cheese to flour. It may be mixed with yolk of egg. Cheese pastry is used for savoury flans, cheese straws, etc.

Biscuit pastry. This is made with the addition of 25–50 g castor sugar per 400 g flour and bound with yolk of egg. In some cases it is made by the creamed method and the fat used is all margarine. Half the flour is beaten into the creamed fat and sugar, the liquid beaten in and the remaining flour beaten in. This pastry is very short, difficult to shape and is used for sweet flans.

Quick Mix Pastry is made by sieving the dry ingredients into a bowl, adding a soft margarine or soft cooking fat and the exact amounts of liquid stated in the recipe. The ingredients are mixed together using a fork. As the pastry may stick to the pastry board, more flour may be needed when rolling out. Although the texture is not as good as pastry made by the traditional method, the results are reasonable. This method can also be used for scones and biscuits. Can be made in a food processor or food mixer.

Flaky pastry

Proportions:
⅔–¾ fat to flour
Approx. 200 ml water per 400 g flour
1 level teaspoon salt per 400 g flour

It is advisable to use a strong, plain flour for flaky pastry and the fat should be all margarine to give a hard, crisp result. A quarter of the fat is rubbed in, then the liquid added all at once and mixed with a knife to a soft dough. The mixture is drawn together and kneaded to develop the elasticity of the gluten, resulting in an elastic dough which will rise easily. Lemon juice helps to develop elasticity and counteract the richness of the pastry.

When smooth and even in texture the pastry is rolled to an oblong three times as long as wide. A third of the remaining fat is flaked or 'dotted' on to the top two-thirds of the pastry in rough lumps and the pastry folded envelope-style, forming a double sandwich of dough and fat which also incorporates some air. The edges of the dough are sealed by pressing with the rolling pin to enclose the air and to prevent the fat oozing out and sticking to the rolling pin. The folded dough is given a half turn to the right and re-rolled, the remaining fat being added half at a time as above. In warm conditions, cool before re-rolling.

During this process the gluten will have been stretched and must be allowed to relax in a cool place so that it will have regained its full elasticity before being put in the oven. After relaxing, the pastry is rolled and folded three times more, taking care to keep the corners square to ensure even thickness when rolling. Careless rolling will result in uneven rising. The pastry is then cut to shape; removal of the folded edges will assist rising. If a glaze is to be used, e.g. on meat pie, care must be taken not to seal the cut edges of the pastry as this will prevent rising.

It is advisable to let the pastry relax again in a cool place before baking to reduce the loss of shape during cooking.

Bake in a hot oven so that the flour will absorb the fat, the air and water vapour will expand, and the mixture will rise in flakes. Continued heat will set it in the risen position after which the temperature may be reduced to ensure thorough cooking without burning. Refer to recipe baking instructions.

Once cooked, flaky pastry will not keep long, unless frozen for storage, but if desired it may be prepared as far as the final rolling, then the uncooked pastry may be wrapped in aluminium foil and stored in a cool place for up to 48 hours, or it may be sealed and frozen.

Making flaky pastry

Rough puff pastry

In most respects rough puff pastry is like flaky pastry, but all the fat is added to the flour at once in soft lumps the size of a walnut. The water is added and the dough drawn together, kneaded very lightly and rolled in the same way as flaky pastry (but no fat is flaked on). It has the disadvantage of being sticky to handle at first. If equal fat to flour is used, more flour can be used to roll out.

Puff pastry

Proportions:
Equal fat to flour
Approx. 200 ml water per 400 g flour
1 level teaspoon salt per 400 g flour

This pastry may be difficult to handle because of the high proportion of fat. A quarter of the fat is rubbed into the flour and salt. Water is added to make a soft dough. Cake margarine or butter may be used. For the block of fat to be rolled in it is advisable to use the fat at the same consistency as the dough and to cool as necessary during making.

Roll the dough as in the diagram. Fold the thin outer edges over the thick centre block and margarine block ensuring that all corners are completely covered. The dough is then rolled as for flaky pastry. It should rise in flakes to 6 to 8 times its original height if it is allowed to stand at least 30 minutes before baking at 232°C.

Uses. Vol au vent, palmiers, vanilla slices.

Commercially frozen puff pastry is widely available and gives satisfactory results.

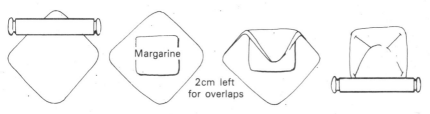

Making puff pastry

Hot water crust pastry

Proportions:
125 g lard per 400 g flour
175 ml mixture of milk and water per 400 g flour
1 level teaspoon salt per 400 g flour

Success in this pastry depends on warmth of utensils, flour and salt throughout the process of making and shaping, or it will be difficult to handle and mould.

The fat and water are heated together. They are then poured immediately into a well in the centre of the flour where the heat partially cooks the starch grains and a glutinous dough is formed which is kneaded till smooth.

The pastry should be raised or moulded while still warm and pliable. It is important to make a hole in the top of pies to allow steam to escape. This is used later to fill the pie with jelly.

Bake at 220°C for 10 mins, then reduce.

Uses. Pork pie, veal and ham pie.

Choux pastry

Proportions:

3 eggs
125 g flour
75 g butter or margarine
200 ml water
½ level teaspoon salt
1 level tablespoon sugar

The fat and liquid are brought to boiling point. The flour, salt and sugar are added. Cook like a roux over gentle heat until the mixture leaves the sides of the pan, and then cool. The eggs are added gradually and beaten in until the mixture is smooth and elastic. The more the mixture is beaten, the better the result will be, because of the air which is incorporated. The pastry is shaped by forcing it through a plain meringue pipe.

Bake at 200°C.

Uses. Eclairs, cream puffs. Cheese puffs (omit sugar).

REASONS FOR COMMON FAULTS IN PASTRY MAKING

Tough and hard pastry
  a) Conditions for preparation of the pastry were not cool enough.
  b) Insufficient air introduced to act as a raising agent.
  c) Heavy handling of the pastry which pressed out the air.
  d) Incorrect proportion of water used.
      i) Too much in short crust pastry, or
      ii) Too little in flaky, rough puff or puff.
  e) Too much flour used in rolling out, or turning the pastry over during rolling or re-rolling.
  f) Wrong type of fat used and wrong proportions.
  g) Too cool an oven
Short and crumbly pastry
  Too much fat used and probably too little water.
Crisp outside but underdone inside
  Too hot an oven or too short a cooking time.

Shrinkage after cooking
The pastry was stretched during preparation and not allowed to relax before baking.

Faults in suet pastry

Tough and hard pastry
a) Insufficient raising agent used.
b) Insufficient liquid.
c) Wrong cooking method – moist heat is desirable.

Heavy wet pastry
a) Insufficient raising agent.
b) Condensed steam allowed to come into contact with the pastry.

Faults in short crust pastry

Blistered pastry
a) Uneven rubbing in.
b) Water added too slowly and unevenly.
c) Cooking too high in the oven.

Soggy pastry (This may occur in fruit or meat pies.)
a) Steam not allowed to escape during cooking.
b) Presence of sugar on top of fruit.

Sunken pie crust
Insufficient filling. Non-use of pie funnel.

Speckled appearance in flan pastry
Too much or too coarse a sugar used.

Faults in flaky and rough puff pastry

Uneven rising
a) Uneven distribution of the fat.
b) Uneven shaping, folding, rolling and turning.
c) Uneven baking position.
d) Insufficient time allowed for the pastry to relax.

Lacking in flakiness
a) Too dry a mixture.
b) Careless blending and placing of the fat.
c) Fat allowed to melt during preparation.
d) Edges sealed by careless rolling.
e) Insufficient time allowed for relaxation.
f) Too cool an oven.

Faults in puff pastry

As above.

Poor shape – e.g. vol au vent cases.
   a) Uneven rolling.
   b) Poor cutting or cutting too near the edge of the pastry.
   c) Insufficient time for pastry to relax after shaping.
   d) Uneven baking position.
   e) Opening oven door too soon, causing draught.

Faults in hot water crust pastry

Cracking
   a) Insufficient fat used.
   b) Fat and liquid not hot enough when added to the flour.
   c) Dough allowed to cool too much before shaping.

Poor shape
   a) Insufficient filling.
   b) Pastry too thin.
   c) Edges not sealed before cooking.

Faults in choux pastry

Close, heavy texture
   a) Too much flour used.
   b) Insufficient beating, so less air incorporated.
   c) Wrong oven temperature.

Cracked éclairs
   Too hot an oven.

15. CAKE MAKING

Main ingredients. Flour, fat, sugar, eggs, fruit, raising agent. The higher the proportion of fat to flour, the richer the cake. The proportion of fat to flour will influence the method of mixing:

half or less fat to flour – method used is rubbing-in.

half or more fat to flour – method used is creaming.

CLASSIFICATION OF CAKES

a) *Plain* – Half or less fat to flour (rubbed-in method).

b) *Rich* – More than half fat to flour (creamed method).

c) *Sponges* – Contain no fat (whisked method).

d) *Gingerbread* – (Melted method).

e) *Quick mix* – (One stage method).

METHODS

Whatever the method used, it is essential for a good result that there is a carefully balanced proportion of ingredients.

Rubbed-in cake mixtures

(e.g. rock cakes, plain fruit loaf, raspberry buns.)

Cakes made by this method are quick to prepare, but are rather dry and will not keep long. It is not practical to rub in more than half fat to flour – the mixture might become rather sticky and difficult to handle.

General proportions to 400 g flour

Fat – 100–200 g

Sugar – 100–200 g

Fruit – 100–200 g

Eggs – 1–4

Baking powder – 3 level teaspoons, or use self-raising flour

Fat. Margarine is most often used, but lard and clarified fat will give good results. Use of even a small proportion of butter to other fat gives a better flavour.

Sugar. Granulated sugar is quite satisfactory. For fruit or spice cakes, soft brown sugar may be used.

Flavouring. Dry powders, e.g. spice, may be sieved with the flour, but ingredients which might making rubbing-in difficult, e.g. fruit or coconut, should be added later.

Fruit. Must be clean and dry – wet fruit will sink. Glacé cherries in syrup should be washed, dried and dusted in a little flour.

Liquid. The amount needed depends on the number of eggs used and the proportion of fat and sugar, which act as liquids when heat is applied, and on the consistency of the cake being made. Milk or water or a mixture may be used. A quick addition of liquid ensures smooth mixing and a more even texture.

Raising agent. Incorporated air, carbon dioxide produced by the baking powder, and water vapour from the liquid, push up the gluten in the flour (which is elastic by nature). Application of further heat causes the cake to set while still in the 'risen' position.

Method

a) Sieve the flour (with baking powder, spice, etc.)

b) Rub in the fat until the mixture looks like fine breadcrumbs. Air is introduced during this process to act as a raising agent. The finer the division of fat, the more readily it is absorbed by the flour. This should give a cake with a more even texture.

c) Stir in the sugar and the fruit, or any other dry ingredient used, e.g. coconut.

d) Stir in the egg or other liquid to make the required consistency, e.g. stiff for raspberry buns, a soft dropping mixture for larger cakes. Use a knife or fork to mix stiff mixtures, a wooden spoon for softer mixtures.

Baking. Small cakes – two-thirds of the way up at 200°C.

Large cakes – just below half-way up at 180–190°C.

Test for cooking. Evenly brown, slightly shrunk, no bubbling noise, firm to the touch.

Storage. Rubbed-in cakes should not be kept for more than 3 days as they tend to become dry. Can be frozen.

Creamed cake mixtures

(e.g. Victoria sandwich, rich fruit cakes, Madeira cake.)

Cakes made by this method should be light and even textured. The higher the proportion of fat, sugar and eggs to flour the richer the cake will be.

General proportions to 400 g flour

Fat – 200–400 g

Sugar – 200–400 g

Fruit – 200 g–1.2 kg

Eggs – 4–8

Baking powder – 0–3 level teaspoons

If equal quantities of fat, sugar, eggs and flour are used, no extra liquid or baking powder should be required.

Fat. Margarine is often used, but butter will give a better flavour – even a small proportion of butter will improve the flavour and keeping qualities. If quick-creaming fat is used, the basic ingredients may be placed in a bowl and mixed in one stage.

Sugar. Castor sugar should be used as the larger crystals of granulated sugar do not blend easily with the fat. Soft brown sugar may be used in fruit cakes, but Demerara sugar crystals may be too large.

Eggs. Eggs should be fresh and at room temperature.

Flavouring. Dry powder should be sieved with the flour, fruit, etc. added with the flour to ensure even distribution. Essences, etc. should be beaten in with the eggs.

Method

a) *Cream the fat and sugar* very thoroughly until light, fluffy and white. The creamed fat and sugar can hold air. The more thoroughly it is creamed, the more air the mixture will retain to act as a raising agent. Creaming also breaks down the sugar crystals and ensures a smoother texture.

b) *Addition of eggs.* Eggs should be beaten in a basin. If cold, leave to stand at room temperature for an hour. They must be added *slowly* and well beaten to hold air, or curdling might occur, especially if egg is cold.

Curdling in cake mixture. The fat, cooled by the addition of cold egg liquid, separates out from the sugar and eggs. The fat globules become surrounded by water from the egg, causing the appearance of curdling. A curdled mixture will hold less air and give a closer textured cake. A very small quantity of the flour (in the recipe), well stirred in, will sometimes remedy curdling, as will warming the bowl before re-beating. It is better to avoid curdling, so care must be taken while adding egg.

The above type of curdling is not the 'true' type, but is used to describe a condition when foods separate and lose their smooth even texture. Curds are actually the substance formed when milk separates into curds and whey.

c) *Flour and other powders.* Thorough incorporation of the flour is necessary to ensure even distribution. Sieve the flour to remove lumps and to incorporate air. Fold lightly into the mixture with a metal spoon to keep in as much air as possible.

d) *Consistency.* A soft dropping mixture which will just drop off the spoon is the correct consistency. Because of the high proportion of fat and sugar the mixture will become more liquid in the heat of the oven.

Preparation of tins. Because of the high proportion of fat and sugar, these cakes tend to burn. Use thick tins carefully greased, and evenly lined with greased paper. Very rich fruit cakes need brown paper or several thicknesses of newspaper tied round the outside to protect them during the long cooking time. Sandwich cake tins are greased and dusted with flour.

Baking Small cakes – two-thirds of the way up, 190°C.

Large cakes – half-way up, 180°C–190°C.

Large fruit cakes – 150°C–180°C (depending on size). Reduce temperature to finish. Cook in the lower half of the oven.

Test. As for rubbed-in cakes. Rich fruit cakes are difficult to test because of their size – a fine skewer stuck into the centre will come out clean if the cake is cooked. Shrinkage from the sides of the tin indicates cooking is complete.

Cooling. Cakes should be removed from the tin as soon as this is practicable, and stood on a cake tray to avoid 'sad' cake as a result of condensation.

Storage. Depending on the ingredients. Creamed cakes will keep for days – or months – in an airtight tin. Rich fruit cakes may be brushed with spirit before storage to improve their keeping qualities.

Undecorated cakes freeze well. Rich fruit cakes will keep without freezing but the desired moist texture and the development of flavour may be speeded up by freezing for a short time.

Sponge cake mixtures
(e.g. Swiss roll, sponge drops.)

Fatless sponge. General proportions to each egg (standard)
25 g castor sugar
20 g plain flour

If 3 or more eggs are used, one tablespoon of hot water may be added to each group of 3 eggs.

Eggs should be fresh, as these will whisk more readily and hold more air.

Sugar. The castor sugar gives a smooth, even texture.

Flour should be a 'soft' flour, and must be dry. Cornflour may be used to soften a hard flour – approximately 1 part cornflour to 2 parts flour.

Flavourings, e.g. essences. Liquids must be concentrated to avoid a wet mixture. If cocoa is used, take out the same weight of flour.

Raising agent. No chemical raising agent is usually added. Air, incorporated during whisking, and water vapour from the liquid cause the cake to rise.

Method

a) Eggs and sugar are whisked together over hot water until pale and thick. Air will become entangled with the albumen in egg white. Whisk until the whisk leaves an impression on the surface. Heat from the water helps to dissolve the sugar and the mixture will hold more air. Water must not come in contact with mixture or the egg might set.

b) Remove from the water and whisk until cool.

(A food mixer will whisk successfully without the use of hot water.)

c) Fold in the flour very lightly with a metal spoon to avoid crushing out the air. The characteristic texture of this sponge, an open, even-sized, cell-like structure, is due to an even distribution of air in whisking and of flour in folding-in. Lightness depends on the amount of air included.

Note i) Eggs may be separated – the yolks whisked with the sugar and the stiffly whisked whites folded in before the flour.

Note ii) Genoese sponge. This is not a true sponge as fat is used. 1 tablespoon melted butter or oil is added to each 25 g flour.

Preparation of tins. Swiss rolls – grease the tin carefully, line with greaseproof paper and grease. Sandwich cakes – grease the tin and shake in it a mixture of half castor sugar and half flour to coat the tin. Dredge the top of the cake mixture in the tin with castor sugar before cooking if a crispy crust is required.

Baking. Swiss rolls – two-thirds of the way up, 220°C (7–8 mins.).

Sponge sandwich or flans – half to two-thirds of the way up, 190°C. Reduce to 180°C or 170°C if necessary.

Sponge drops – two-thirds of the way up, 200°C (5–6 mins.).

Test. After light pressure the surface will spring back. The sides will be shrunk a little. A pale golden colour. No sound of bubbling.

Storing. Use the day of cooking. These cakes go very dry after 2–3 days. Genoese sponge will keep 3–7 days in an airtight tin because of the fat content. Undecorated sponge cakes freeze well, with or without cream filling.

Melted method

(gingerbread, parkin, etc.)
Fat is melted usually with sugar and/or syrup and added to the flour in liquid form.

General proportions to 400 g flour

Fat – 150–200 g

Sugar – 150–200 g

Syrup – 150–300 g

Eggs – 0–2

1½ level teaspoons ginger or spice

1 level teaspoon bicarbonate of soda, *or* 1½ level teaspoons baking powder

Liquid. Approximately 250 ml in total liquids.

Fat. Lard, margarine or clarified dripping may be used.

Sugar. Moist brown or Demerara sugar preferable. It gives a darker colour. Black treacle might give a bitter flavour but this is disguised by the ginger.

Raising agent. Bicarbonate of soda gives a darker colour. The residue of sodium carbonate left after carbon dioxide is given off might flavour the cake, but this flavour is disguised by spices.

Flour. Sometimes (in parkin) oatmeal or rolled oats are used to replace part of the flour.

Method

a) Sieve the flour together with raising agent and spices.

b) Melt the fat, sugar and syrup or treacle by warming gently in a pan. *Do not overheat* or the cake would be hard. Stir carefully.

c) Add the melted mixture to the sieved flour together with any liquid used. Stir with a metal spoon to help blend the sticky ingredients thoroughly.

d) The consistency is a batter and should pour easily into the tin.

Preparation of the tins. Tins may be greased for a plainer type of gingerbread, but the richer types will need a tin lined with greased paper to prevent the syrupy mixture sticking and burning. A shallow, square or oblong tin is usually used so that the cake may be cut into squares.

Baking. One-third to half-way up the oven. 170–180°C. Reduce temperature to finish.

Test for cooking. Shrunk a little from the side of the tin. Evenly brown. Firm when pressed lightly. No sound of bubbling. Remove from the tin and take off the paper while still hot and place to cool.

Storing. Store when cool in a tin. The cake should be kept for at least 1 day to let it become moist. It will freeze successfully and the texture may be improved by the moisture.

Success in cake mixing depends upon using the correct proportion of ingredients, careful mixing, and cooking for the required length of time at the right temperature.

Quick mix or 'one stage' method

Cakes and puddings can be made using soft margarine or soft cooking fat. All the basic ingredients are put together in the mixing bowl and stirred for 1–2 minutes until the mixture is smooth and creamy. Dried fruit and nuts, if used, are added at this stage because it would be difficult to get a smooth texture quickly if they were added earlier. The quick mix method is not recommended for rich cakes, such as Christmas cakes, which are to be kept for some time.

REASONS FOR COMMON FAULTS IN CAKE MAKING

A close, heavy texture

a) Caused by too slow an oven.

b) Insufficient cooking.

c) The mixture was too wet.

d) Insufficient raising agent used.

Coarse, open texture

a) Too much raising agent.

b) Uneven mixing-in of flour.

Sunken cake
   a) Excess raising agent resulting in overstretching and collapse of the gluten, or too much sugar.
   b) Too slow an oven or under-baking.
   c) Moving the cake tin or allowing cold air to enter the oven before the cake was set.
Badly shaped
   a) Uneven lining of the tin.
   b) Careless filling of the tin.
   c) Wrong consistency.
Cracked top or a peak
   a) Too small a tin used.
   b) Too hot an oven.
   c) Cake placed too high in the oven.
Dry cake
   a) Caused by insufficient liquid.
   b) Too much chemical raising agent.
Hard, sugary, speckled crust
   a) Too high a proportion of sugar used.
   b) Too slow an oven.
   c) Too coarse sugar used.
Uneven rising
   a) Tilted in the oven.
   b) Tin put unevenly near the source of heat.
The above faults apply to all types of mixtures, but faults relating to a specific type of mixture are shown below.

Faults in rubbed-in mixtures

Uneven texture
   a) Insufficient, i.e. uneven, rubbing-in.
   b) Too vigorous mixing after adding the liquid.
   c) Too much baking powder used.
Close heavy texture
   Too high a proportion of fat or hot hands causing the mixture to become sticky.
Dry cake
   Insufficient liquid where the proportion of fat is low.
Loss of shape in rock buns, etc.
   a) Too wet a mixture.
   b) Too cool an oven.

Faults in creamed mixtures

Close heavy texture

a) Insufficient creaming or beating-in of the egg, resulting in less air being incorporated.

b) Allowing the mixture to curdle. It will then hold less air.

Note: It is possible to over-beat a cake when using a mixing machine. This will cause curdling, resulting in a close, heavy texture, sometimes sunk in the middle or excess air beaten in can cause sinking.

Large holes may be produced in a close mixture by uneven distribution of the raising agent or by over-beating during the addition of the flour.

Streaky appearance

a) Bowl not scraped round while creaming, resulting in uneven mixing.

b) Flour unevenly folded in – this may be very obvious in chocolate cakes.

Faults in melted mixtures

In addition to the general faults listed above, melted mixtures may be spoiled by the use of too much syrup or treacle, resulting in a close, heavy texture often sunk in the middle.

Over-beating after adding the liquid will give a close texture with a shiny surface.

Faults in whisked mixtures

Close heavy texture

a) Insufficient whisking or over-beating while whisking.

b) Careless folding-in of the flour, pressing out the air.

Hard lumps may be caused by pockets of unsieved flour left in the dough.

Cracked Swiss roll

a) Use of too hard a flour.

b) Too cool an oven.

c) Too dry a mixture.

d) Insufficient trimming of edges.

Faults in fruit cakes

Sunken fruit

a) Wet fruit.

b) Wet mixture.

c) Too much raising agent.

d) Moving the cake in the oven before it is set.

e) Too hot an oven.

Burnt crust
   a) Too hot an oven or too long cooking time.
   b) Thin cake tin.
   c) Insufficient outer protection of the tin, e.g. brown paper or newspaper used to protect Christmas cake tin.

MERINGUE

Meringue is a sweet mixture used for cakes and puddings. The ingredients used are white of egg, castor sugar (granulated sugar is too coarse) 40–50 g to each egg white, a pinch of salt and flavouring or colouring if required. Fresh eggs, two to three days old, give the best results. Preserved eggs are unsatisfactory because the white becomes too thin and watery for good results. Do *not* use duck eggs because the amount of heat needed to dry out meringues is insufficient to make duck eggs safe. The increase in volume of whisked white of egg is due to the property of albumen to stretch and hold air. This property is not stable and is readily altered as a result of:
   a) The presence of any fat or grease in the white of egg – this could be caused by the inclusion of particles of yolk or by using greasy dishes.
   b) Intermittent whisking.
   c) Lack of uniformity in the rate of whisking, particularly if some mixture is splashed round the bowl.
   Once the property of the albumen to hold air is lost it is *not* regained, and no matter how much more it is whisked the volume will decrease. This may happen if the meringue is over-whisked. If it is left to stand for too long before cooking it will collapse.

Points for success when whisking white of egg

   1. Have a wide bowl with space for the whisk to rotate.
   2. Keep it free from grease.
   3. Separate the eggs carefully – keeping out all traces of yolk of egg.
   4. Work in a cool atmosphere. A pinch of salt will tend to reduce the temperature of the mixture.
   5. Thorough preparation is important. Have ready the sugar, palette knife, teaspoon, tablespoon, etc.
   Three stages in whisking white of egg
  i) Frothy.
 ii) Smooth.
iii) Rocky.
During whisking the rate of work should be even, the whole egg should rotate round the beater which can be used to gather the mixture together.

Making meringue

Castor sugar is preferable. Granulated sugar gives a gritty texture.

a) Whisk in half the sugar in small quantities; this gives smooth results and hard meringue.

b) Fold in the remainder in three stages. This makes for a light open texture. If the meringue has a tendency to go smooth avoid further friction and fold in the remaining sugar.

Drying meringue 95°C or gas – Low. Gentle warmth is essential. If correctly dried, meringue shells will keep for some time in an airtight tin.

Note: For meringue shells the use of a 75 g sugar per egg white may give better results.

Heat causes browning due to caramelisation of the sugar. The protein hardens, toughens and shrinks, and the meringue will lack crispness. Once it goes tough it will not regain its crispness. On standing, tough meringue will exude beads of moisture.

But the 'flash' method of cooking may be used for puddings, e.g. lemon meringue pie or baked Alaska, which are to be eaten immediately. In the case of baked Alaska the heat sets the egg protein on the surface and the enclosed air acts as an insulator keeping the ice-cream cold.

CAKE ICINGS AND DECORATIONS

Almost all cakes, large or small, can be iced to improve their appearance and make them appeal to both children and adults. Icings and fillings will add flavour and give variety to an otherwise plain sandwich cake, and can transform a rich fruit cake into an elaborate celebration cake.

Types of icings. The type of icing chosen will depend upon the cake to be iced, the occasion for which it is to be served and whether it is intended to keep the cake for a longer time than is normal, e.g. wedding cake.

Special points for success in making icings

1. Always sieve icing sugar before use.
2. The consistency is very important especially in glacé or royal icing.
3. The flavour should be appropriate and delicate.
4. Add colour very slowly. Strong colour usually looks synthetic and unattractive.

Butter icing

Butter icing is very simply made by creaming butter and icing sugar in the proportion 25 g butter to 50 g sugar, and adding colouring and flavour as desired. It is a sweet, rich, creamy-textured icing used for coating, filling and decorating cakes. This type of icing can be piped easily in a variety of simple shapes.

Glacé icing

This is a quickly made icing used to coat sponge and sandwich cakes which are to be eaten within a day or two. (It is not suitable for freezing.) It is a glossy, soft, easily cut mixture of icing sugar and water, using approximately 250 g sugar to 3 tablespoons water. The water used may be cold or warm, but heating will give a dull surface. Glacé icing should be carefully coloured and flavoured, e.g. for an orange cake the icing should be coloured pale orange and flavoured with orange juice. The consistency should be such that the icing will coat the back of a spoon and flow over the cake and down the sides, covering the cake evenly so that it will set level without the use of a palette knife. If the top of the cake only is to be iced, the consistency should be slightly stiffer. Decorations should be put on before the icing sets.

Note: The cake to be iced may be first coated with an *apricot glaze* or 'crumb coating' made from 400 g apricot jam and 75 ml cold water, heated till the sugar dissolves, sieved and then boiled gently until clear. This will prevent loose crumbs spoiling the surface and will help the icing to run smoothly over the cake.

Fondant icing

Fondant icing, like glacé icing, is used to coat light sponge cakes. It is made by boiling sugar and water to 114°C and adding cream of tartar or glucose (glucose gives a less firm crystal), which will reduce the rate at which the sugar re-crystallises, so producing small crystals which reflect the light well. The mixture is cooled slightly, then beaten and kneaded until smooth, fine and glossy. In this form fondant icing may be stored in a covered jar until required. For use it is warmed gently with a little stock syrup to a smooth pouring consistency, flavoured and coloured.

Proportions:
200 g granulated sugar
250 ml water
½ teaspoon cream of tartar
or 1½ teaspoons glucose

Stock Syrup is made by boiling together without stirring 400 g lump or granulated sugar and 250 ml water until it reaches 104°C. Cool and store in a clean jar with a lid.

American frosting (Fudge icing)

American frosting sets firm and crisp on the surface, but remains soft underneath. It can be used on almost any type of cake from sponge cake to fruit cake and is particularly suitable for children's birthday cakes.

To make American frosting, dissolve the sugar in water without boiling, then boil the dissolved sugar and water to 114°C. Pour on the stiffly beaten white of egg and whisk until it has a coating consistency, and pour immediately onto the cake where it will set quickly.

Proportions:
600 g granulated sugar
250 ml water
2 whites of egg

Almond paste

Almond paste is the traditional icing for Simnel cake. It is used to coat cakes which are to be covered with royal icing, as it can be made quite level, thus forming a smooth foundation and preventing crumbs spoiling the icing.

Proportions to 1 egg + 1 yolk
300 g ground almonds
150 g castor sugar
150 g icing sugar
½ teaspoon vanilla essence
1 tablespoon lemon juice

A smooth, easily moulded almond paste can be made by whisking sieved sugar and eggs together over hot water until light and creamy as for a whisked sponge cake. Cool slightly and stir in ground almonds and flavouring, knead a little and wrap in waxed paper until required. It will keep a day or two before use. Good quality dry almonds must be used or the oil will discolour the royal icing. Almond paste is sometimes brushed with white of egg to prevent possible discoloration.

Marzipan

Marzipan is used for making cake decorations such as fruit, flowers and small crackers, Christmas trees, etc.

Proportions to each egg white
200 g granulated or castor sugar
150 g ground almonds
75 ml water
½ teaspoon glucose
or pinch of cream of tartar
½ teaspoon vanilla essence
½ teaspoon lemon juice

The sugar is dissolved in water without boiling, glucose or cream of tartar are added and it is boiled to 114°C. The ground almonds are added, unbeaten white of egg stirred in and the marzipan cooked for 2–3 minutes over a gentle heat. Flavouring is added, and when cool enough the marzipan is worked to a smooth consistency. It will keep a short time if stored in waxed paper or aluminium foil.

Royal icing

Royal icing is a firm icing used to cover wedding cakes. It may be firm enough to support the weight of two or more tiers and will form a protective coating for a cake which may be expected to keep for several months. Royal icing is the only type that can be used for elaborate piped decorations such as flowers and intricate trellis work.

Proportions:
200 g icing sugar
1 white of egg
1 teaspoon lemon juice

White of egg and lemon juice are whisked slightly before the sieved sugar is beaten in very thoroughly, until it will stand in peaks for piping. The peaks should bend over for correct coating consistency. It is impossible to over-beat royal icing by hand, but if an electric mixer is used, over-beating will produce a rough bubbly surface on the cake.

If the cake is to be kept for some time, the egg white will cause a yellow colouring to appear. This may be counteracted by the use of one or two drops of blue food colouring dissolved in water, *BUT* care must be taken not to add too much or the icing will appear grey and unattractive.

In some cases the hardness of royal icing makes it difficult to eat. The addition of a drop of glycerine will keep the icing soft, but it may not then support the weight of tiers above.

Chocolate icing

Chocolate icing can be made by melting broken chocolate to 36°C and adding stock syrup until the desired consistency is achieved. It should be used like glacé icing. It will not lose its gloss if made carefully.

Specially prepared chocolate is available for home baking. It can be melted, moulded, grated, and piped. It is easy to use and may be convenient for quick results.

Confectioner's custard

This is a type of cake filling used in vanilla slices, etc. It is a blended custard mixture thickened with cornflour and egg yolk.

Proportions:
250 ml milk
2 yolks of egg
20 g cornflour
25 g castor sugar
Few drops of vanilla essence

Other fillings

Lemon curd, jam, cream and fresh soft fruits may all be used as cake fillings. For suitable cake decorations see section on Garnishing and Decorating. Most iced decorations and some fillings are easier to apply if a forcing bag is used. These are cone-shaped bags made from folded paper, or from shaped nylon or closely woven cotton, into which an icing pipe is fitted.

SCONE MAKING

Scones are a plain mixture usually made by the rubbed-in method. The proportion of fat to flour is low, so scones have a low fat content. They are usually eaten with butter on the day they are made. A high proportion of chemical raising agent is used, which gives an open, light texture, but makes the scones rather dry. The consistency of the scone dough must be soft and elastic; so a high proportion of liquid is used to mix the dough. The liquid may be milk or milk and water. A small proportion of egg may be used to add nutritive value and flavour, but too much would make the scones heavy. Sour milk will help the raising action (see notes on raising agents) but the amount of cream of tartar must be halved. Add the liquid all at once and mix in with a round-ended knife. When the mixture forms large lumps, press gently together. Turn onto a lightly floured board and knead *lightly* with the *finger-tips* for a few minutes to develop elasticity. Roll or pat the dough into shape, making it at least 2 cm thick or the width of a table-knife blade. Scones should be made quickly and cooked quickly. They should be baked in the top of a hot oven – 230°C to ensure quick, even rising. Scones may be brushed with milk or egg glaze before baking to make them brown, but are traditionally served dusted with flour.

Proportions to 400 g plain flour
Fat 50–75 g (margarine, butter, lard, cooking fat, dripping)
Sugar 0–50 g
Salt – 1 level teaspoon
Milk – 250 ml
5 level teaspoons baking powder
or 1½ level teaspoons bicarbonate of soda + 3 level teaspoons cream of tartar
or 1½ level teaspoons cream of tartar + 1½ level teaspoons bicarbonate of soda + sour milk to mix.

Variations. Afternoon-tea scones, cheese scones, potato scones, treacle scones, girdle scones.

Dropped scones – made by the batter method.

Scones freeze very well. They are usually allowed to thaw gradually before being crisped up in the oven but cheese scones grill well from frozen.

BISCUITS

Biscuits are classified according to the basic methods used which are similar to those for making cakes.

They do not usually contain chemical raising agents. Less moisture is used than in cake making because stiffer mixtures are required.

Biscuits are usually pricked to prevent rising and ensure crispness. They are dried out rather than baked to give a crisp or short result.

Biscuits must be stored in air-tight tins to prevent crispness being lost because moisture is absorbed from the air. Never store biscuits in the same tin as cakes because they will absorb moisture from the cakes.

16. PUDDINGS AND SWEETS

Puddings must be chosen carefully as they are an important part of a meal. They should balance or round off the meal. Texture, colour, flavour and nutritive value should all be considered.

CLASSIFICATION OF PUDDINGS

Puddings are usually classified according to the basic recipes.
See appropriate chapters for details.
1. *Suet mixtures*, e.g. jam roly-poly, Christmas pudding.
2. *Rubbed-in mixtures*, e.g. apple crumble, ginger crunch.
3. *Creamed mixtures*, e.g. castle puddings, sultana sponge.
4. *Milk puddings*
   a) Whole or flaked grain – rice, tapioca, etc.
   b) Small grain – semolina, sago.
   c) Powdered grain – cornflour, arrowroot, ground rice.

   Proportions to 500 ml milk
   Whole grain – 50 g
   Small or powdered grain – 40 g
   Sugar – 25 g
      Flavouring – lemon or orange rind, vanilla essence, cocoa, nutmeg, cinnamon, etc.
   Eggs may be added to give food value, flavour and colour.
   d) Custard puddings, e.g. caramel custard, queen of puddings.

   Proportions to 500 ml milk
   Cooked over
gentle heat 2–4 eggs	
baked 2–4 eggs	+ 25 g sugar
steamed 4–6 eggs	

   Extra egg yolks may be used to give a smoother, stiffer texture.
5. *Batters*, e.g. pancakes, fritters.
6. *Pastry dishes*, e.g. flans, fruit pies, choux pastry, profiteroles.
7. *Apple dishes*, e.g. baked apples, apple charlotte.

8. *Hot soufflés*, e.g. vanilla soufflé, chocolate soufflé.
9. *Cold sweets*
   Fruit mixtures, e.g. fruit fool.
   Milk sweets, e.g. custards, junkets, instant desserts.
   Jellies.
   Creams.
   Soufflés and mousses.
   Trifles.
   Cheese cakes.
   Ice cream and sorbets.
   Yogurt.

17. RAISING AGENTS

A raising agent is added to a cake or bread mixture, etc. to give lightness to the mixture. This lightness is based upon the principle that gases expand when heated. The gases used are air, carbon dioxide or water vapour. These gases are introduced before baking or are produced by substances added to the mixture before baking.

When a mixture is cooked, the cold gases expand. In flour, especially wheat flour, is a protein substance called gluten, the elasticity of which is developed with warmth and moisture. Gluten stretches when pushed up by the expansion of the gases. Upon further heating, the mixture, because of the presence of the protein gluten, rises and sets, so giving a risen cake or bread, etc.

TYPES OF RAISING AGENTS AND THEIR USES

Air

Expands very quickly.

May be introduced by:

a) Sieving the flour – all mixtures.

b) Rubbing in the fat – short crust pastry, rubbed-in mixtures.

c) Creaming of fat and sugar – creamed cake mixtures.

d) Beating the mixtures – batters.

e) Folding and rolling – flaky pastry.

f) Adding whisked white of eggs which have the property of holding air, e.g. soufflés, meringues, or adding whole eggs to a cake mixture. Whole eggs do not hold air as easily because of the fat in the yolk.

Dishes almost entirely dependend upon air as a raising agent

Short crust pastry.

Whisked sponges, some creamed mixtures – rich fruit cakes.

Soufflés, meringues.

Carbon dioxide (CO_2)

May be introduced by:

A. *Bicarbonate of soda (sodium bicarbonate) used alone* – as in gingerbread.

$$2NaHCO_3 \text{ on heating} \rightarrow Na_2CO_3 + H_2O + CO_2$$

bicarbonate   washing   water   carbon
of soda   soda   dioxide
(sodium bicarbonate)   (sodium carbonate)

A strong flavour of washing soda is produced and a dark colour, but the flavour and colour are disguised by the use of spices, e.g. ginger, and by treacle.

B. *Bicarbonate of soda + acid*
 i) *Bicarbonate of soda + cream of tartar (potassium hydrogen tartrate)*
 Use 2 of acid + 1 of alkali.

$$KHC_4H_4O_6 + NaHCO_3 \rightarrow NaKC_4H_4O_6 + H_2O + CO_2$$

cream of   + bicarbonate → sodium   + water + carbon
tartar   of soda   potassium   dioxide
                                           tartrate

Residue is colourless and almost tasteless.

ii) *Bicarbonate of soda + tartaric acid*
 Yields 25 times its own volume. Use equal quantities.
 Residue formed is tartrate of soda, which is slightly bitter.
iii) *Bicarbonate of soda + sour milk*
 Less accurate. Use in scones, etc. Sour milk is acid (lactic acid bacteria).
iv) *Bicarbonate of soda + vinegar or lemon juice*
 Less accurate. Vinegar – acetic acid. Lemon – citric acid.
 The strength of the acids in i) and ii) is constant, but the strength of the acids in iii) and iv) will vary, making the result less accurate.

C. *Baking powder*
 This is usually a commercial preparation of bicarbonate of soda + cream of tartar or tartaric acid, with rice flour or a similar substance added to absorb any moisture and prevent lumps. The quality of commercial baking powder is controlled by law and it is of standard strength.

Recipe
25 g bicarbonate of soda
25 g rice flour
50 g cream of tartar

Proportions of baking powder used
   a) Rubbed-in cakes – 3 level teaspoons to 400 g flour.
   b) Scones – 5 level teaspoons to 400 g flour.
   c) Creamed mixture cakes (rich cakes) – amount depends on the proportion of eggs, fat and sugar to flour and the time given to creaming to incorporate air.

D. *Self-raising flour*

This is a prepared mixture of a soft cake flour and raising agent. The dryness, strength of flour and amount of carbon dioxide which will be produced have been tested. This flour is not suitable for all mixtures. It will give good results for plain cakes, but there is too much raising agent for rich cakes and whisked sponges and too little for scones.
Never use for bread, pastries, biscuits and batters.

E. *Baking ammonia (bicarbonate of ammonia)*

$$NH_4HCO_3 \rightarrow NH_3 + H_2O + CO_2.$$

Reaction gives carbon dioxide and ammonia which leaves a strong, unpleasant taste and a yellow colour. Used commercially – taste and colour may be disguised by jams, icings, etc. Reaction is very quick and rising is very good but may give a coarse texture.

F. *Yeast*

When the yeast is given the right conditions – food, warmth, moisture and time – it can break down sugar by a process known as fermentation, producing alcohol and carbon dioxide. (See Yeast Cookery pages 152–157.)

Use of water vapour

This is produced, during cooking, from the liquids used in mixing. Water vapour has approximately 1,600 times the original volume of the water. The raising power is slower than that of a gas and its use is limited to certain mixtures – batters, éclairs, and other choux pastry dishes. It has some use in pastry, particularly flaky and puff pastry, and in cakes.

Addition of raising agent

   1. Buy a reliable brand.
   2. Store in an air-tight tin in a cool dry place to prevent reaction and loss of strength before use in mixture.
   3. Use the correct proportion for the type of mixture, or under- or over-rising may result.
   4. Sieve raising agent with flour and/or dry ingredients to mix evenly and give an even reaction.

5. Distribute moisture evenly into mixtures to ensure even action of raising agent.

6. If a large proportion of raising agent has been added to a mixture, e.g. scones, and it is not possible to cook them at once, keep them in a cool place to avoid too much reaction before cooking.

Results of incorrect proportion of raising agent

Too little raising agent used:

    lack of volume

    close texture

    insufficient rising

    shrinking

Too much raising agent used:

    over-risen mixture which may collapse, resulting in:

    a sunken cake

    coarse texture

    poor colour and flavour

    sinking of fruit

Comparative proportions of raising agents for plain cakes or scones

The following have the equivalent raising action of 400 g self-raising flour:

To 400 g plain flour

1 level tablespoon (4 level teaspoons) baking powder

1 level teaspoon bicarbonate of soda + 1½ level teaspoons cream of tartar

1 level teaspoon bicarbonate of soda + 1 level teaspoon tartaric acid

1 level teaspoon bicarbonate of soda + 250 ml sour milk

1 level teaspoon bicarbonate of soda + 3 tablespoons vinegar

18. YEAST COOKERY

Introduction. Bread made without yeast or 'leaven' is hard and unpalatable. The old method of leavening bread was to leave a piece of dough to ferment by the action of 'wild' yeasts from air and then use the dough in baking. Today yeast is specially grown.

Yeast. Yeast is a living organism. It is a plant of the fungi group. It is unicellular. There are many types both of cultivated and wild, e.g. yeasts on the skins of grapes used in wine making. Yeast has the power of producing carbon dioxide by fermentation. This occurs when it is given food in the form of sugar, warmth, 25°C–29°C, and moisture, usually water or milk. Yeast reproduces rapidly by budding.

TYPES OF YEAST

1. *Compressed yeast* (German yeast or barm). This is the most widely used. It is a very pure form of yeast, packed and sold in cakes. It crumbles easily and has a fresh, fruity smell. It keeps in a cold place for 2–3 days.

2. *Brewers' yeast*. This is taken from the tops of the vats during brewing. It has a rather strong taste and will not keep well.

3. *Dried yeast*. This is usually dried brewers' yeast. It can be stored indefinitely if dry and sealed. It takes longer to cream and is more concentrated – use approximately half the amount. Sprinkle it into a teacupful of the measured tepid water, to which a level teaspoonful of sugar has been added; stand till softened and the liquid goes frothy. 'Easy blend' dried yeast is mixed with dry flour and is not fermented in liquid before being added to the flour.

CHOICE OF YEAST

Fresh yeast has a pleasant characteristic smell, is a putty colour, crumbles easily, and creams readily with sugar.

If the yeast is stale, fermentation is not so rapid and the flavour of the bread will be unpleasant. Yeast is destroyed by heat or will die if kept too long. Cold retards its activity, as does excess sugar. Large quantities of salt would damage the yeast but it is important for flavour.

Conditions for fermentation of yeast

The following must be supplied:
1. Food, usually in the form of sugar.
2. Moisture, milk or water. Milk improves the nutritive value; water acts more quickly.
3. Warmth, supplied by the liquid and surroundings.

The ideal temperature for the growth of yeast is 25°C–29°C. It is destroyed at higher temperatures and its activity is retarded at lower temperatures. Yeast can be destroyed during the mixing or rising processes if it is put in a very hot place.

Fermentation is brought about by a number of enzymes present in yeast, but before these can be effective, diastase present in the flour converts some starch to dextrin and maltose.

The yeast enzymes include:
1. *Maltase* acts upon maltose to form glucose.
2. *Invertase* acts upon sucrose, producing glucose and fructose.
3. *The zymase group* of enzymes changes simple sugars, i.e. glucose and fructose, to carbon dioxide and alcohol.

In bread making, alcohol is driven off with steam during cooking and the carbon dioxide collects in small bubbles throughout the dough. Together these raise the dough.

CHOICE OF FLOUR FOR BREAD MAKING

For bread a strong flour is needed. A mixture of wheats where spring wheat predominates produces a strong flour containing a good supply of gluten, a strong, elastic protein substance capable of absorbing water. When the proteins in wheat flour are mixed with water during bread making, the gluten becomes elastic and can be pushed up by the carbon dioxide produced by the yeast. The gluten entangles the bubbles of carbon dioxide, and when heated, sets, giving bread its typical open texture.

Soft flour is unsuitable for bread because it contains less gluten.

Whole wheat flour. The whole grain is crushed into flour. The bran is not digested by humans, but is valuable for fibre.

Germ flours, e.g. Hovis. 75% white flour + 25% cooked germ (cooked to kill enzymes and stop fat going rancid). Contains naturally more thiamin and nicotinic acid than other flours.

Starch-reduced flour. For sugar-diabetes sufferers. Much of the starch is washed out, leaving a higher proportion of gluten, e.g. flour used for Energen rolls and biscuits.

Self-raising flour is unsuitable for bread.

Proportions of yeast to flour
Under 500 g flour – 15 g yeast
500 g–1.5 kg flour – 25 g yeast
1.5–3.0 kg flour – 50 g yeast
More yeast is needed for quick fermentation methods.

Steps in the traditional process of bread making

1. Creaming
2. Sponging
3. Mixing
4. Kneading
5. Rising
6. Kneading
7. Shaping
8. Proving
9. Baking

Throughout the process the dough must be kept warm, i.e. at approximately blood heat, but it must not be overheated. Flour and utensils should be warm before starting. Dough can, however, be stored if necessary for up to 24 hours in mild refrigeration. It must then be allowed to soften in a warm place, and be shaped and proved before baking.

Note: It is sometimes necessary, if time is limited as in school, to reduce the time taken in making bread. In this case time allowed for rising and the second kneading can be reduced or even omitted altogether, provided that the other processes are carried out thoroughly, particularly the kneading before shaping. Bread made in this way will be reasonably satisfactory though not as light and spongy as bread made by the traditional method described below.

1. *Creaming* of the yeast and sugar provides the initial supply of food. Little fermentation occurs at this stage. Fresh yeast should cream easily. Creaming with sugar saves time. The enzyme diastase in flour eventually produces sugar in dough, but in home baking, a little added sugar creamed with the yeast speeds up the fermentation process.

2. *Setting the sponge.* The liquid is added to the yeast and sugar mixture, and rapid fermentation occurs under the right conditions. If this stage were omitted the rate at which fermentation could take place would be reduced. This may be carried out:

a) in a bowl
b) in a well in the flour
c) in a separate ferment

Some authorities think that the home baking method in which the yeast is first creamed with sugar kills some yeast cells and emphasises the 'yeasty' flavour. They advocate the following method:

i) Blend the yeast with the liquid (see also page 157).

ii) Add this to ⅓ of the sieved flour and sugar, beating well to form a batter in which rapid fermentation can take place. Stand in a warm place for 10–15 minutes.

iii) Mix salt with the remaining flour and beat this into the batter to form a soft dough.

3. *Mixing.* During mixing the yeast is distributed thoroughly throughout the dough in order to obtain the maximum amount of food. The protein in the flour absorbs water to form an elastic gluten which is capable of being stretched by the expanding carbon dioxide gas produced by the yeast.

4. *Kneading* or beating will develop the above qualities, i.e. help to spread the yeast throughout the dough.

5. *Rising.* During rising the steady process of fermentation continues. Maltase converts maltose to glucose which is converted by zymase to carbon dioxide and alcohol. The warm conditions during rising are ideal for multiplication of the yeast cells, and enzyme action throughout the flour. The gluten, which has already been developed, stretches more readily, becoming soft and more elastic, resembling a sponge of honeycomb texture, but it will collapse if over-risen.

6. *Re-kneading* breaks down the large bubbles of carbon dioxide into small ones of even size. It also allows the entry of air which rejuvenates the yeast.

7. *Shaping.* The dough is cut and shaped.

8. *Proving.* Fermentation proceeds and more carbon dioxide is evolved. The volume of the dough expands again, but is more uniform in texture. The gluten recovers from the strain of shaping.

9. *Baking.* At first, the dough rises rapidly because the enzymes work more quickly and water vapour is produced to act as a raising agent. Gluten is pressed up by the gases. The starch begins to gelatinise. Then yeast is killed by the heat and no further carbon dioxide is produced. Gluten coagulates around the bubbles formed by the gas – beginning at the outside and continuing until baking is complete. Alcohol vapour and carbon dioxide diffuse out. The baking temperature must be hot at first to destroy the yeast, but must be lowered later to avoid hard bread. The outside crust consists of dextrin with some caramelised sugar.

Basic recipe
500 g plain flour
2 level teaspoons salt
1 level teaspoon sugar
15 g yeast
300 ml warm liquid (milk or water)

Short-time process of bread making

Research in the bread making industry has resulted in the discovery of a number of additives which shorten the process of bread making. This 'Chorleywood Bread Process' eliminates the lengthy bulk fermentation previously necessary to produce the required degree of elasticity in the dough. The main additive or chemical improver is ascorbic acid. The application of the research to domestic bread making involves the addition of ascorbic acid (vitamin C) which can be obtained from chemists in 25, 50 or 100 mg tablets.

Basic recipe

500 g plain flour (strong white, wholemeal or a mixture) ⎫
2 level teaspoons salt   ⎬ Mix together
1 level teaspoon sugar   ⎭

25 g fresh yeast (Dried yeast is not suitable)   ⎫
300 ml warm liquid (water or milk or a mixture)   ⎬ Blend together
25 mg ascorbic acid, crushed   ⎭

15–25 g lard or margarine may be rubbed into the flour before the addition of the liquid.

Method

Keep the ingredients and dough warm at all stages of the process.
Mix the dry ingredients in a warm bowl.
Rub in the fat if required.
Pour the blended yeast into the dry ingredients using a wooden spoon or a palette knife to mix together.
Turn out onto a lightly floured board or table and knead for 10 minutes. Put dough into a greased polythene bag or replace in the mixing bowl and cover, and leave for 5 minutes.
Shape as required into loaves or rolls etc.
Place in lightly greased polythene bag or under greased polythene.
Prove according to size of bread: approximately 40 minutes for a large loaf, 25 minutes for a small loaf, 15 minutes for rolls.

Variations in yeast mixtures

A wide variety of bread and other yeast products may be produced from the traditional or short-time process, e.g. tea cakes, Chelsea buns, rum babas, Danish pastries, pizza, etc.

Important points in bread making
1. Yeast must be fresh and in the correct proportion.
2. Flour must be the strong glutinous variety.
3. Yeast must be worked at an even temperature – blood heat. Draughts should be avoided.
4. Mixing and kneading must be thorough to incorporate the yeast. The second kneading should not be too heavy, or too much gas will be lost.
5. Proving must be done carefully – if proving is too short, bread will not be light; if over-proved, bread will be coarse and sour and might be heavy because of the collapse of the dough. If too hot, the yeast could be destroyed.

REASONS FOR FAULTS IN BREAD MAKING

Heavy 'sad' bread
   a) Stale yeast used.
   b) Yeast destroyed by using too hot a liquid or by too hot conditions during bread making.
   c) Too cool conditions are unfavourable for bread making.
   d) Insufficient liquid was used.
   e) Insufficient time allowed for rising and/or proving.
Note: In the quick method of bread making where some or all of the rising stage may be omitted due to lack of time, this fault may occur.
Uneven texture
   a) Insufficient kneading resulting in uneven distribution of the gases, causing uneven holes.
   b) Over-proving allowing time for the gluten to be overstretched and collapse, resulting in a heavy loaf with a wrinkled outside.
   c) Too cool an oven for the initial cooking period allowing fermentation to proceed for too long.
Note: If bread is proved under too hot conditions, this may result in the yeast being destroyed on the outside. A hard skin will form and cracking will occur.
Sour bread
   a) Use of stale yeast.
   b) Too high a proportion of yeast used. (N.B. Care is needed with dried yeast.)
   c) Over-rising or over-proving of the dough resulting in the development of acids.

19. BATTERS

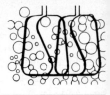

Batters are made with plain flour, milk or water, and usually egg. Occasionally oil or melted fat may also be used.

The mixture is beaten well (batter is derived from the French *battre*, to beat) to make it smooth and to incorporate air. The air expands when heated and acts as a raising agent together with the raising power provided by water vapour produced by the large amount of liquid used.

Proportions

Thin batter – pancakes, toad-in-the-hole, Yorkshire pudding
1 egg
100 g plain flour
¼ teaspoon salt
250 ml milk

Coating batter
1 egg (or 1½ teaspoons baking powder)
100 g plain flour
¼ teaspoon salt
125 ml milk

Fritter batter
1 egg white
50 g plain flour
¼ teaspoon salt
65 ml water
2 teaspoons salad oil

Important points in batter making

1. The flour and salt are sieved into a bowl. A well is made in the centre of the flour.

2. After the egg and a little of the liquid have been poured into the well the flour is incorporated gradually, taking care to avoid lumps.

3. The rest of the liquid is beaten in slowly to ensure a smooth batter. During this process some air is incorporated. There is some controversy as to whether

prolonged beating will incorporate much more air to assist the raising action, but it seems more likely that water vapour provides the main raising power.

4. The theory that batter should stand for a long time is also under dispute. Those in favour claim that the starch grains must be softened by standing, in order to cook more easily, and that coating batters adhere more readily to the foods if they are allowed to stand before cooking. Others claim that batters can be used as soon as they are made. Tests have proved that dishes made by both methods appear to be equally successful.

5. Food to be coated with batter must be dry.

6. When frying batters it is important to ensure that the fat is hot enough or it will penetrate the batter, giving a sad, heavy result, *but* if the fat is too hot the outside will cook too quickly, leaving the centre raw.

20. PRESERVATION

All food is liable in time to deteriorate and decay, but the rate at which this happens depends upon the type of food and the conditions under which it is kept. The aim in preservation is to preserve foodstuffs at their most nutritious stage so that they may be used when fresh food is not available.

CAUSES OF DECAY

Decay is caused by enzyme action. There is a loss of moisture followed by loss of vitamins, growth of mould, yeast and bacteria, and eventual breakdown of the tissues.

Enzymes. Chemical substances present in all living material. They have the effect of speeding up natural processes which would otherwise take place slowly, and their rate of action is increased by warmth. They are destroyed by temperatures over 60°C, e.g. the cut surface of a pear will quickly go brown if exposed to warm air, but browning will be slower if the fruit is put into boiling liquid for one minute because heat destroys enzymes. Their activity is retarded at low temperatures. Enzymes are not harmful in themselves but they will produce over-ripeness leading to decay of fruit and vegetables.

Moulds. Living organisms which in their early stages of growth are difficult to detect. They flourish in warm, moist conditions and will withstand most fruit acids, but not acetic acid. Moulds are present in the atmosphere and will settle and multiply on suitable food, forming a fluffy mass on cheese, fruit, bread or jam, etc. They are not usually harmful, e.g. penicillium is a type of mould from which penicillin has been developed, and moulds are responsible for flavours considered desirable in blue cheeses. The growth of mould can be checked by cold storage in dry conditions. Most moulds are killed at temperatures above 74°C. Acetic acid in sufficient quantity and sulphur dioxide will retard most moulds.

Yeast. Micro-organisms found naturally in the atmosphere and on the skins of fruit (particularly grapes, where they are important in making wine). They will grow readily on any sugary substance in the presence of warmth and moisture, but do not need air. They multiply by budding. Yeasts cause fermentation of jams, fruit juices, syrup, etc. but are destroyed by temperatures over 60°C and will remain dormant below 16°C. Yeast can withstand normal fruit acids, but not acetic acid (vinegar) which is used in making pickles. Growth is stopped by a high sugar concentration, usually above 65% sugar (but yeast can tolerate up to 75% sugar concentration in honey). More than 15% alcohol will also prevent the growth of yeast, e.g. raspberries may be preserved in brandy.

Bacteria. The simplest form of micro-organism. They are minute single cells which reproduce very rapidly by dividing into two when given the right conditions of food, warmth and moisture. Their growth is retarded by freezing, but they can survive very low temperatures. Most bacteria are destroyed by heating to 100°C, but their resistance to heat is increased in the presence of sugar, and a few must be held at a temperature of 116°C for ten minutes or more before they are destroyed. Resistance to heat is reduced in the presence of acids. Some bacteria produce toxins which would be absorbed by the food during storage, rendering the food poisonous. Not all bacterial action is harmful, e.g. lactic acid bacteria play an important part in cheese making.

Aims of preservation

All the organisms causing decay need food, warmth and moisture if they are to multiply. So if they can be deprived of these essentials they will not grow. Heat will destroy them, and coldness will retard their growth. The organisms are always floating in the air, so once they have been removed from the food they must not be allowed to re-enter, e.g. jam jars should be well filled and covered, and bottles of fruit and canned foods sealed.

The aims of preservation are:

a) To destroy the organisms by heat, or to maintain conditions which will render them inactive – cold, dryness or the use of certain chemicals which are unfavourable to the growth of the organisms, e.g. sugar acids. Sometimes several methods are used together.

b) To prevent any fresh organisms reaching the food by sealing it immediately after treatment.

Note: It is useless and may be dangerous to try to preserve food which has already deteriorated.

METHODS OF PRESERVATION

Heat. Will destroy bacteria, yeasts, moulds and enzymes. The temperature must be high enough to kill all organisms and sufficient time must be allowed. Some bacteria are very difficult to destroy. Soil organisms found on vegetables form spores which are resistant to heat.

Dehydration. All micro-organisms need moisture. If water is removed they are unable to grow, and enzyme action is stopped. Dehydrated foods, therefore, will not decay. This is the oldest method of preservation known to man, and was carried out originally by leaving food to dry in the heat of the sun, e.g. dried fruit.

Freezing. The growth of micro-organisms is arrested at temperatures below 4°C. In commercial quick-freezing, temperatures used for freezing are between −30°C and −33°C. Foods are then stored at about −25°C before being distributed to shops. Home frozen foods are frozen at around −25°C and stored at −18°C. During both commercial quick-freezing and home freezing there will be very little enzyme activity or loss of vitamins and no decay due to mould yeast or bacteria.

Chemical preservation

Sugar in large quantities will act as a preservative.

Salt will remove moisture from food by osmosis, thus producing a state in which micro-organisms cannot survive.

Vinegar is acetic acid which prevents the development of micro-organisms.

Sulphur dioxide is a chemical preservative which is poisonous in its natural state, but legal controls permit safe concentrations to be used in foods. Much is driven off by cooking, but some foods containing sulphur dioxide preservative are eaten without cooking, e.g. jams, fruit drinks, pickles.

BOTTLING OR CANNING

These methods make use of heat to kill the organisms, together with sealing to ensure the exclusion of air.

BOTTLING

Most fruits are suitable for bottling. Fruits have yeast cells on the surface and may have mould spores. They also contain enzymes which cause them to ripen and then decay. Bacteria are not often present in fresh fruit because of the acidity of the fruit, but will develop in over-ripe fruit which is sweeter.

Note: Bottling is *not recommended* for preserving vegetables unless a pressure cooker is available, as without one, high enough temperatures to make vegetables safe after storage cannot be attained.

Aim. To sterilise the fruit by killing all the micro-organisms and enzymes and to seal it against the entry of fresh organisms. Sugar may also be used to retard the growth of organisms causing decay and to give flavour.

Fruit. Must be firm, just ripe, an even size, good colour and as perfect as possible.

Preparation

Soft fruit. Pick over and drain..

Hard fruit (apples and pears). Peel, cut in half, core, put in salt water. Rinse before bottling.

Plums. Take off stalks and wipe.

Rhubarb. Peel if necessary or wipe. Cut in even lengths.

Fruit may be bottled in water or syrup. It is ready for use if bottled in syrup and usually has a better flavour, but fruit will rise in the bottle more readily if sugar is used.

Syrup. Use 200 g sugar to 500 ml water. Put half the water in the pan. Add the sugar and boil 1 minute. Check that all the sugar is dissolved and add the rest of the water.

Bottles and jars

Screw band types, e.g. Kilner, have a metal lid with an inner seal ring round the edge. The lid fits over the rim of the jar and is held in place during processing by a metal screw band. Because the latex type sealing substance softens during processing to form a seal a new lid is needed each time the jar is used for bottling.

Closures for jam jars. Porosan caps, perhaps the best known closure for jam jars, consist of a metal cover with an inner ring of latex type material which softens during processing and seals the lid to the jar as it cools. Caps are available for both the 'new' type 63 mm jam jars and for the 'old fashioned' (1 lb) 68 mm jars. The seal should be tested by tapping on the cover which gives a high note if properly sealed. It is not advisable to test by lifting the lid as with other types.

Preparation of jars. Examine for cracks or flaws around the top edge, which would prevent a good seal. Wash thoroughly, rinse in clear water. If the jar is left slightly wet inside, fruit will slip into place more easily.

Packing fruit. Pack closely. Fill right to the top of the jar. Use the handle of a wooden spoon to pack tall bottles. Try to make the bottle look neat and attractive.

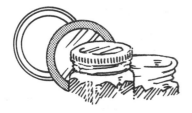 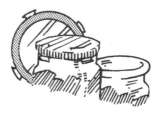

Kilner jars and Porosan caps

Methods of sterilisation

Sterilisation of the bottles or jars and contents may be carried out in several ways, but in no case must the bottles stand within 51 mm of each other.

Oven sterilisation

a) Wet pack method in which the fruit is packed into the bottle which is then filled to within 3 cm of the top with boiling syrup. The lid is placed loosely on top and the fruit placed in the oven pre-heated to a temperature of 150°C for 30–100 minutes, depending upon the type of fruit.

b) Dry pack method, in which the fruit is processed dry in the bottles at 120°C and boiling liquid added after 45–100 minutes, depending upon the type of fruit. This method tends to make the fruit shrivel.

In both methods the lid is adjusted immediately after completion of processing, and is then left to cool during which time shrinkage of the sterilised contents causes a vacuum which effectively seals the containers, thus ensuring that the food is protected from micro-organisms which cause decay.

Water sterilisation

In this method the liquid is added before processing and the bottles heated almost immersed in a bath of warm water which is raised to simmering temperature 80°C in 25–30 minutes and held at that temperature for 2–20 minutes. The bottles are then removed, the tops tightened and left to cool.

This method is more suitable for fruits like damsons whose skins tend to break in the oven method.

Use of a pressure cooker

3 cm of water is placed in the pressure pan and heated to 80°C. The fruit is packed in *warm* bottles, boiling syrup added and the bottles stood on a trivet in the pressure cooker. The tops are not fully tightened.

Note: Jam jars are not intended to withstand pressure of this sort and are unsuitable.

Not all pressure cookers have enough depth to give adequate clearance for the tops of the bottles, which will expand on heating. For suitable bottles, pressure and timing see the manufacturer's instructions.

Testing the seal, when the bottles are *quite* cold.

Screw top type – take off screw top and lift jar by lid.

Porosan top – do not lift by lid, but it should give a 'ringing' noise when the lid is tapped.

Labelling. Label with name of fruit, method used and date.

Storage. Store in a cool, dry, dark place, and examine periodically. Metal caps may be smeared with a little Vaseline to prevent rusting.

CANNING

Most foods can be treated – meat, fish, fruit, vegetables, etc. Home or commercial canning may be done but the special machine required for sealing the cans may make this an expensive method of domestic preservation. Food is packed into cans, the liquid added, and the cans sealed and then heated to sterilise, before cooling rapidly.

Commercial canning uses a higher temperature usually achieved by steam heating in a vacuum. This is much more suitable for meat and fish and milk products, in which bacteria will grow rapidly if not correctly treated, and for vegetables which must be treated at high temperatures to kill off the dangerous soil organisms which may be present.

Tins are made of sheet steel, lined with tin to prevent the metal from reacting chemically with the food. For fruit and vegetables the tins are lacquered to avoid this. An acid-resistant lacquer is used for fruit. Sulphur-resistant lacquer is used for vegetables.

Advantages of canning. Food must be of very good quality or it will not can satisfactorily. Canning is under strict legal control, so there is a high standard and little danger of food poisoning. A normal tin is level or slightly concave at the top and bottom. A 'blown' tin or one bulging outwards is a sign of decomposition inside. These are rare. Inspectors at ports check the standard of imported tinned foods.

The food keeps for many years under most conditions (cans of food have been eaten after being left for years at the North Pole), so canning saves wastage of a glut of food and gives variety to the diet. The quick heat treatment saves much vitamin loss.

Disadvantages of canning. The flavour of some foods may be altered by canning and there may be some vitamin loss and colour loss. The vitamins lost are C and some of the B group which are partially destroyed by the heat – modern quick canning at high temperatures affects vitamins much less. Colour and flavour are often added, e.g. to tinned peas.

DEHYDRATION OR DRYING

Removal of moisture. Dehydration or drying. This is a very old method. Meat, fish, fruit, etc. were dried by sun and wind. It is still done naturally in some countries, but is usually carried out by commercial processes nowadays.

Fish. Still dried naturally in some northern countries where it is hung on racks to dry. Kippers are produced partly by drying and partly by the action of smoke and salt, etc.

Meat. Still dried in some remote areas, e.g. pemmican.

Fruit. Currants, raisins, etc. are produced from partially dried grapes, prunes from plums. The concentration of sugar helps to keep organisms inactive.

Pulses are dried peas, beans and lentils, etc.

Dried eggs. Eggs are sprayed onto heated rollers, dried and scraped off. They need liquid added to reconstitute them. After liquid is added they will not keep long. Dried eggs have lost power to hold air and so are of little use as raising agents. Loss of nutritive value negligible.

Milk. Roller or spray dried (See notes on Milk page 70.)

Dried vegetables and soups. Increasingly used. Usually packed in laminated aluminium foil to help keep them dry. They often have flavouring added. (See Convenience Foods page 209.)

Dehydrated meals. Whole courses in one packet.

Cereals are naturally deficient in water.

Dried foods save storage space. They form a part of the convenience foods. They must be kept dry, or moisture will enable organisms to grow, and they will decay.

Home drying. Mushrooms, apple rings, can be dried in a very slow oven for approximately 5–6 hours. They must be soaked in water before use.

Herbs. Wash and spread out in a warm place to dry slowly, crumble and store in a jar. Put parsley in a hot oven for 1 minute before drying to keep the colour.

FREEZING

Storing at low temperatures. Food is stored at a temperature below that at which organisms can flourish. This does not destroy them, but only prevents their growth; therefore care is needed because organisms will grow again after thawing.

The normal household refrigerator chamber is approximately 4°C, which is not low enough to preserve foods for long periods (see Refrigeration notes page 241).

Home freezing (see Chap. 21 page 172). Home frozen foods are frozen at around −25°C. Since these temperatures are not as cold as those used for commercial quick-freezing, there is a tendency for foods with a high water content and delicate cell structure to soften. The cell walls of the food are broken down by slow freezing. This produces some loss in texture, colour and flavour, e.g. soft fruits such as melons and strawberries, and vegetables such as tomatoes, celery or cucumber.

Quick-freezing. In commercial quick-freezing, temperatures used for freezing are between −30°C and −33°C. There is little damage to the cell structure of food at these low temperatures so that texture, flavour and colour remain intact.

Note: Freezer packaging must be airtight and waterproof to retain flavour and to avoid dehydration.

Frozen foods cannot be kept indefinitely after purchase (see page 178 for storage times).

Freeze dried foods (Accelerated freeze drying)

Quick-frozen foods, which have been marketed in great variety for the past few years, must be stored at low temperatures. Refrigeration is necessary during processing, transport and storage before the food reaches the consumer. As these foods contain all the normal water content they are also bulky to store. Dehydrated foods have all or most of the water removed. They do not need special storage, are light and not bulky, but texture, flavour and colour may be changed and soluble vitamins lost.

Freeze drying is a combination of the above methods but the method of processing is new and has many advantages over the old methods. Food is prepared by removing unwanted parts – bone, gristle, fat, skin, etc. – and is immediately quick-frozen. Trays of the frozen food are placed in a chamber from which the air is extracted to form a vacuum. The temperature is reduced to between $-20°C$ and $-30°C$ and then heat is applied. After some hours the water in the food has been reduced to as little as 2%. The moisture in the food cells has been extracted as vapour not as water. Thus the structure of the food cells is not affected. The product is a honeycomb of cells, is very light and brittle and is little changed in shape and size. Food must be packed very carefully so that it will not be crushed and broken, but it does not need any special storage conditions, e.g. chicken curry, dried mixed vegetables. This method is also used in the preparation of instant coffee granules.

Reconstitution. Very simple to prepare, e.g. add boiling water to coffee granules. Place freeze dried foods in a bowl of water (or in cooking liquid) for a short time to regain water lost during processing, then cook as for fresh food.

Advantages of freeze dried products. Natural flavour, texture and colour is kept. Claimed to retain full nutrients. No special storage conditions needed – can be kept in normal dry food store; very light in weight, preparation for cooking very simple.

CHEMICAL PRESERVATIVES

Make use of certain edible chemicals, salt, sugar, acids (e.g. vinegar) which produce an atmosphere unsuitable for the growth of the organisms which would cause decay.

a) *Sugar.* Must be used in a high percentage in jam, at least 60% of the total, or yeasts and moulds may grow. Sugar is used in jams, canning and bottling. In crystallisation, fruit is impregnated by sugar and the moisture removed by drying.

b) *Acid.* Vinegar (acetic acid) is used in preserving vegetables, usually together with spices, herbs and salt, e.g. chutney, pickles, piccalilli. It is good for home use.

c) *Salt.* Used in salted fish, salt meat, especially bacon, sometimes in conjunction with other chemicals. Salt is used at home for salting beans, where it prevents the growth of organisms and draws moisture from the food by osmotic action.

d) *Use of fruit-preserving tablets*. This is a method using chemical preservatives which is now little used, e.g. Campden Tablets, which dissolve in water to produce a solution of sulphur dioxide that prevents the growth of micro-organisms.

1 tablet + 250 ml water to 400 g fruit.

They are most suitable for stone fruits, e.g. plums, damsons. Fill jar with clean fruit, fill with the solution, seal at once. Do not use metal tops as fumes will attack the metal. Use glass tops or corks waxed over, or waxed paper, to make a good seal. The fruit must be boiled 10 minutes before use to drive off the sulphur dioxide fumes which are poisonous.

Gas Storage. This makes use of sulphur dioxide and is used in ships for bananas and other fruits for short-time storage where lack of oxygen prevents growth of organisms.

Sausages and prepared meats frequently contain chemical preservatives, usually sulphur dioxide, to keep them 'fresh' during the time between manufacture and sale. If sausages contain preservatives the shopkeeper must display a notice to this effect.

REMOVAL OF AIR

Removal or exclusion of air is used in the preservation of eggs. They are coated by painting with special varnishes, e.g. Oteg, or by pickling in a solution of water-glass (sodium silicate). Because this method of preservation is little used nowadays it may be difficult to obtain the materials required.

JAMS AND JELLIES

The making of jams and jellies is an important method of preservation when fruit is cheap. Jams vary in quality, but a good jam has a fruity flavour, a bright clear colour, is well set and keeps well. Jams and jellies are made from fruit, sugar and water.

Fruit

Successful jam or jelly making depends mainly on choice of fruit. Use firm, clean, dry fruit which is not diseased or mouldy. It must be ripe or under-ripe, never over-ripe or it will not set.

Note: When there is a glut of fruit, shortage of time or sugar, suitable fruit may be frozen or canned and made into jam, jelly or marmalade when convenient.

Fresh fruit contains fibre, water, sugar, fruit acid and a gum-like substance called pectin. (Some vitamin C is present in all fresh fruit but some is destroyed by boiling.) Fruit acid and pectin together with sugar help to set jam. There must be the right proportion of each to give the ideal set or 'gel'.

Note: Gelatine is the setting agent used in diabetic jams.

Pectin is found in the cell walls of young fruit and vegetables in varying amounts. Usually the firmer, sourer fruits contain most pectin. Over-ripe fruit contains pectic acid (changed pectin) which is no good for setting, so the use of ripe, or just under-ripe fruit, is advisable – never over-ripe fruit.

Acid helps the extraction of pectin and so improves the set. It helps to prevent crystallisation of the sugar, to brighten the colour of the jam and to bring out the flavour. Acid content varies but is usually high when pectin content is high.

Fruit rich in pectin and acid. Cooking apples, citrus fruits, redcurrants and blackcurrants, gooseberries, damsons, plums.

Fruit poor in pectin and acid. Strawberries, pears and blackberries.

Fruits rich in pectin, e.g. redcurrants or lemon juice, may be added to fruits poor in acid and pectin to help the set, or commercially prepared pectin may be used, e.g. Certo. Care is needed or the flavour of the jam may be spoiled, and the jam may be too stiff.

Fruit may be tested to indicate the pectin content. When the fruit has been simmered and softened, put a teaspoonful of juice in a glass. When cool add 3 teaspoonfuls of methylated spirit. Shake gently and leave 1 minute.

Good pectin content – transparent jelly-like lump is formed.

Moderate amount – clot in 2 or 3 pieces.

Poor amount – clot in many pieces.

Sugar. A jam of good flavour and texture must have the right concentration of sugar, approximately 60% of the total weight of the finished jam. Too much sugar causes crystallisation and spoils the flavour. If there is too little the jam may not keep – fermentation may occur. Sugar must never be added until fruit is cooked or it will have a hardening effect. It must be dissolved before the jam boiling is started. Preserving, granulated or lump sugar may be used. Preserving sugar is said to cause less scum because it is purer.

Important rule for jam making. SLOW COOKING BEFORE AND RAPID COOKING AFTER THE ADDITION OF SUGAR.

Jam pans should be strong, wide and shallow, made from aluminium, stainless steel or enamel. Brass or copper pans are suspected of reducing vitamin C content.

1. *Softening the fruit.* Cook the fruit with the water to soften it and extract the pectin.

2. *Addition of sugar.* Add the sugar gradually and stir until dissolved. It may be warmed first. Sugar must be thoroughly dissolved or it may cause crystallisation. The fruit must be well cooked before the addition of sugar. Boil quickly after addition of sugar until setting point is reached. Boiling too long gives a dark colour and too thick a texture.

Tests for setting

1. *Flake test.* Dip a spoon in the jam, turn slowly sideways and allow the jam to drip back off the spoon into the pan. If set it will form flakes which break sharply.

2. *Cold plate test.* Put a little jam on a cold plate and leave to cool. If setting point has been reached the surface will crinkle when pushed with the finger.

3. *Temperature test.* Use of sugar thermometer. When temperature is 104°C jam should be set. Jam must be stirred first to ensure that a representative reading is obtained. The thermometer should be put in hot water before and after testing.

Note: Check the thermometer with boiling water before use, as climatic conditions may affect the reading.

4. *Weight test.* Weigh empty jam pan. If 60% sugar is used, every 2.4 kg of sugar should give 4 kg jam.

$$\text{Final weight:} \quad \frac{\text{quantity of sugar} \times 10}{6} = \text{yield of jam} \\ (+ \text{ weight of pan and spoon})$$

Covering jam jars

The jars may be covered immediately. If not, they should be covered with a cloth to allow evaporation of moisture as the jam cools. It is wiser to cover the jar while either hot or cold, but *not* warm because when the jam is warm conditions are ideal for the growth of organisms causing decay. Transparent covers for jam jars are readily available and easy to use. If mould forms on the jam it can be seen. Avoid greaseproof and paper covers which hide the surface of the jam. If whole fruit jam is made, allow it to cool and stir it before bottling, and fruit will remain suspended; otherwise strawberries, etc. tend to rise in the jar. Label with name of jam and date. Store in a cool, dark place.

Faults and causes of failure

Mould
   a) Storing in a warm, damp place.
   b) Air between waxed disc and jam.
   c) Jar insufficiently filled.
   d) Use of wet or inferior fruit.
   e) Too little sugar.

Fermentation
   a) Too little sugar.
   b) Not enough boiling.

Crystallisation
  a) Too much sugar.
  b) Too little acid.
  c) Cooking too short a time to convert sugar to simple sugar.
  d) Cooking too long, with consequent over-evaporation.

Jam not set
  Too little acid or pectin. Add lemon juice, etc. and reboil.

Fruit too hard
  Not cooked enough before adding sugar.

JELLIES

Jellies should have a bright colour, be clear and well set, but not too stiff, and have a good fruit flavour.
  Suitable fruit. Fresh, but not over-ripe. Crab-apples, currants, blackberries, gooseberries. Cooking apples are good but insipid and may be mixed with other fruit or have flavouring added, e.g. apple and mint, blackberry and apple.
  Preparation of fruit. Wash and cut up if large. Remove damaged fruit. Use cores, skins, pips, etc.
  Cooking. Cook gently with water until a pulp is formed.
  Straining. Strain through a jelly bag scalded before use. Drain without pressure until dripping stops. If the bag is squeezed, jelly will be cloudy.
  Measure the juice and allow 400 g sugar to 500 ml juice. Then proceed as for jam, but do not use large jars for jelly as it will not set and will tend to 'weep' when the jar is opened.
  Note: If the jelly is allowed to strain overnight the quality of the pectin tends to deteriorate sufficiently to reduce its setting power. The small amount of extra juice obtained does not compensate for this disadvantage.
  If fruit is rich in pectin a second boiling of the pulp with more water may be possible but jelly will be of poorer quality.

21. HOME FREEZING

Home freezers are increasingly being regarded as invaluable extra pieces of large kitchen equipment. They enable the cook to store basic perishable food, e.g. bread and dairy produce, and to prepare food in advance for family meals, parties and emergencies. Commercially frozen food can be stored at home and advantage can be taken of price savings offered in bulk purchases of meat, fruit and vegetables.

TYPES OF APPLIANCES

A freezer can store ready-frozen food and also freeze fresh food. It will be marked with this symbol

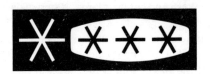

and preferably bear the B.E.A.B. Kitemark. (See page 257.)

The air temperature for normal freezer storage is −18°C, but this can be reduced for freezing fresh food by pressing the fast-freeze switch. (See page 173.)

There are three main types of freezer on the market:

1. *Chest freezers*
   a) Take up more floor space than an upright freezer.
   b) Small people may have difficulty reaching the bottom.
   c) Need defrosting less frequently than an upright freezer (about once a year).
   d) Difficult to see contents at a glance.
   e) Removable baskets available to help with unloading.
   f) Easier to store joints of meat and vegetables in bulk as there are no shelves to break up storage space.

2. *Upright freezers*
   a) A fully loaded freezer is exceptionally heavy on a small floor area.
   b) Need defrosting at least twice a year.

   c) Fixed shelves make storage of large joints of meat and poultry difficult.

   d) Take up little floor space.

   e) Contents easily visible.

   f) Contents easily accessible.

3. *Refrigerator/freezers*

   a) Particularly economical.

   b) Other advantages as for upright freezers.

Fast-freeze switch

The manufacturer's instruction book will recommend the weight of fresh food which can be frozen daily. These instructions should be followed carefully to avoid the frozen food already being stored rising in temperature.

Most freezers have a fast-freeze switch for use when freezing fresh food. Some also have a numbered dial for air temperature adjustment during normal running. The fast-freeze switch should be pressed about 2 hours before the fresh food is put into the freezer and left on for not less than 24 hours after.

Make sure that fresh food does not touch already frozen food as this will slightly thaw the frozen food. There are usually particular shelves on which to pack fresh food in an upright freezer or a separate compartment in a chest freezer. Never exceed the recommended weight of fresh food which can be put into the freezer at one time.

Freezer storage capacity

The storage capacity of a freezer is measured in cubic feet or litres. (1 cubic foot = 28.3 l.) Each cubic foot (28.3 l) of space will hold up to 9.1 kg of food, depending on the type of food and shape of the packages, e.g. square containers take up less space than irregularly shaped cuts of meat or poultry.

A single person or married couple will need a 4–6 cu ft freezer (113.1–169.8 l) but a family with children would need a bigger one. A very large size will be needed for storing meat in bulk or home-grown vegetables.

Running costs

Electricity prices vary in different parts of the country. Each cubic foot (28.3 l) of freezer space will use about 3–5 units of electricity a week.

Power consumption depends on:

   1. How much 'fresh' food is put in.

   2. How often the door or lid is opened.

   3. Where the freezer is kept – more power is used in a warm place.

   4. The time of year – more electricity in warm weather.

Defrosting (See page 245.)

Where to keep a freezer

1. A freezer should be installed in a cool, dry, well ventilated place.

2. Continuous damp may rust a freezer, as well as the mechanical and electrical components.

3. Installing a freezer in a cool place reduces running costs.

4. Leave at least 25 mm of clear space all round the freezer to allow air to circulate.

Suggested sites: kitchen
spare bedroom
laundry or utility room
hall
conservatory or lobby – if dry
garage – if dry
under the stairs – if the door is well ventilated

Power cuts

Frozen food in a tightly packed freezer will be in good condition for up to 8 hours with the power switched off. It is unlikely that a power cut will last long enough for food in a freezer to thaw completely, but it is wise to have an emergency plan – perhaps neighbours with a freezer will help, or share food with friends so it is not wasted. This also applies in a case of freezer breakdown.

1. Keep the door or lid tightly closed.

2. Resist the temptation to peep inside.

3. After a power cut, leave the freezer unopened for at least 2 hours to allow the air to return to the normal storage temperature.

Freezer breakdown

1. Check the plug and fuses.

2. Telephone the manufacturer's local agent for service (see instruction leaflet, guarantee card, telephone directory or 'Yellow Pages'), or the local Electricity Board.

3. Leave the food in the freezer and do not open the freezer door or lid.

4. Food that has only softened on the outside can be refrozen, but may deteriorate in colour, texture, flavour and food value. Food hygiene must be practised. If the freezer has been out of action for some time it is not wise to refreeze food that has thawed and been kept at room temperature for more than a few hours.

Insurance

Most reputable insurance companies will insure against the loss of food in freezers which break down. It is not possible to insure against power cuts. The annual premium will be based on the value of the food likely to be stored in the freezer. Some insurance companies insist on annual servicing and maintenance contract with an approved refrigeration service agent.

Moving house

The contents of a tightly packed freezer will remain in good condition for up to 8 hours. If the journey is completed in this time the freezer can be moved fully loaded. For longer journeys, run down the stock and empty the freezer. Secure the door or lid and make sure it is last on and first off the van. Some removal vans have a socket to plug in a freezer. Make sure there will be somewhere to plug it in on arrival.

PACKAGING MATERIALS

Packaging for freezing must be airtight and waterproof. Most stationers, hardware stores, freezer food centres and larger supermarkets stock a wide range of packaging materials.

Some containers in which food is purchased can be re-used for freezer storage. Foil basins, plates and divided containers and plastic containers for margarine, yogurt, cream, glacé cherries and peel are all useful. If there is no lid, use aluminium foil.

Glass

Glass is not suitable for freezing as it tends to shatter when exposed to extremes of temperature.

Aluminium foil

Foil is useful to wrap unevenly shaped foods such as meat, fish or poultry, but it is not suitable for acid fruit, unless protected by pastry. Foil can be used also for lining earthenware or oven-proof dishes before food is put in for freezing. Once frozen hard, the foil parcel can then be removed and the casserole or the dish re-used. (See page 250.)

Foil dishes

Any foil dish, basin or tray can be used for food freezing but the contents must be covered with foil or with a foil-lined cardboard lid. Acid fruits and tomatoes may react with the foil, if placed in direct contact.

Rigid polythene containers

These can be used indefinitely for freezing, thus justifying the initial cost. They have tightly fitting lids and are available in many shapes and sizes. Square shapes take up least freezer space.

Polythene bags

Extra thick (120–150 gauge) bags with gussets should be used for long-term storage. Perforated rolls of thinner polythene bags are only suitable for short-term storage. Coloured bags are useful for colour coding foods stored in a freezer. Freezer cling film is useful for individual wrapping or interleaving foods to be stored in polythene bags.

Wire ties and labels

Wire ties, either paper or plastic coated, are useful for sealing the twisted top of polythene bags. Plastic and card labels with incorporated wire ties are useful for packs with uneven surfaces on which it is difficult to write or stick an adhesive label.

Freezer tape

Special freezer tape or masking tape should be used, as the ordinary variety will crack and peel off in the freezer. It can be used to seal containers which are not airtight, and polythene bags.

Labelling

An unlabelled, frosted parcel loses its identity in a surprisingly short time. All food frozen at home should be labelled with the contents of the package, the weight and the date of freezing. Coloured or white self-adhesive labels can be bought in sheets.
Marking pencil
Biro, ink, pencil and felt-tip pen become indecipherable during long-term freezer storage. Use a freezer pencil but label rigid containers before chilling as this type of pencil will only write on a warm surface.

Record book

Keep a record of the date of freezing, storage life, number of portions, portion sizes and cooking or serving reminders. Instead of writing details on each package, an alternative is to keep detailed notes in a record book, code the notes and each package with a corresponding number.

HOW TO PACK FOOD FOR THE FREEZER

1. Pack in family or portion sizes.
2. Joint meat into pieces suitable for different occasions.
3. Interleave chops, sausages and layers of cake with polythene, freezer cling film or foil, for easy separation.
4. Pad sharp projections with foil or polythene, e.g. bones, which might puncture the outer wrapping.
5. Exclude all air from packages before sealing to prevent food from drying or becoming tough through long exposure to very cold air.

OPEN FREEZING

Commercially frozen fruit and vegetables are 'flow' frozen in a blast of very low temperature air which keeps them separate. This makes it possible to use any quantity required and store the rest. At home, fruit and vegetables can be frozen uncovered, spread out on a wire rack or baking sheet, for 1–2 hours until hard. They are then quickly packed before the surfaces have time to thaw and stick together.

Foods suitable for open freezing:

vegetables	piped cream rosettes
soft fruit	piped mashed potato
lemon slices	

Freezer burn

Badly wrapped food which is stored for a long time will dehydrate and, although safe to eat, will change in colour, texture and flavour and become unpalatable. Greyish-white marks appear on the surface of poultry, meat or fish and this is known as freezer burn.

Headspace

Liquid or semi-liquid food, such as sauces, soups, etc., expands when frozen. Allow 13 mm headspace in shallow containers and 25 mm in tall, narrow containers.

Making square shapes

Because square shapes take up less freezer space, liquid or semi-liquid food can be moulded in rectangular containers. Line an appropriate sized container with a polythene bag, pour the liquid in, leaving headspace, and seal with a wire tie. Freeze until solid and then remove the rectangular shape from the container for storage.

Lining a casserole

To keep a casserole or serving dish in circulation, it can be used as a mould and then the food can be removed. Line the dish with foil, leaving a generous 'frill', fill with the food to be frozen, leaving headspace and cover, either with the frill or foil or the casserole lid. Freeze until the food is solid, remove from the dish and pack in a polythene bag.

   If the foil is perforated during freezing, a little liquid from the casserole may freeze into the dish. To release the food, hold the dish under hot running water until it loosens.

   When required, thaw the foil package in the dish and remove the foil during or after cooking.

USES FOR A HOME FREEZER

1. Store a wide selection of bought frozen food.
2. Store your own home cookery.
3. Store components of made up meals.
4. Store meat bought in bulk or home produced meat and poultry.
5. Store home-grown produce.
6. Keep 'left-overs'.
7. Prepare for parties in advance.
8. Store Christmas cooking.
9. Prepare packed lunches in advance.
10. Store cooked meals for a household while the cook is away.
11. Reduce waste for small families or single people, e.g. bread.
12. Single people can add variety to their diets by cooking in bulk and storing in single portions.
13. Store meals for the elderly or infirm.
14. Store home-made baby foods prepared in advance.
15. Cater for unexpected guests or emergencies.
16. Prepare food for school holidays so that the family can spend more time together.
17. Keep fish caught by the family.
18. Store dog food bought in bulk, clearly labelled, in a separate section of the freezer.

STORAGE TIMES (see also chart on page 187)

There are widely differing opinions about storage times. This is because people's ability to detect flavour and texture changes varies considerably.

Storage times are determined by the length of time foods can be stored without changes in colour, flavour and nutritive value. The colder the storage temperature, the slower these changes take place. Storage times are considerably affected by the fat content of the food, since fat will eventually turn rancid, even in low temperature storage. Salt increases the rate at which fat will turn rancid. Bacon, butter, fat meat or oily fish and dishes containing these foods will have a shorter storage life than other foods.

Bought frozen foods
Bought frozen foods can be stored for up to 3 months in a home freezer operating at −18°C. This allows for the fact that the food has already been in frozen storage during distribution.

THAWING AND REFREEZING

If food were to be repeatedly thawed and refrozen the cell structure would be damaged and there would be a loss of colour, texture and nutritional value. This is why it is often recommended not to refreeze thawed food. Food treated in this way is not necessarily less hygienic, because food poisoning bacteria will not multiply in a freezer, but it is important to appreciate that bacteria which are present are not destroyed by the freezing process and will be reactivated by thawing.

Taking bought frozen food home
It takes up to 5 hours for a small packet of fish fingers to thaw completely at room temperature. A sensible shopper will buy frozen food last and pack it in the centre of the shopping basket, where it will be insulated by other purchases and hardly thaw at all. Even if the frozen food has started to soften on the outer surface, it can be put back into a freezer or frozen food storage compartment as there will be little loss of quality. An insulated bag or box may be used to transport frozen food.

Retail display cabinets

Retail display cabinets do not operate at low enough temperatures to quick-freeze food, but only to display and store already frozen foods. Food should not be sold if it has thawed and been refrozen as it would not be of the quality required by the customer.

To keep frozen food in perfect condition, it should be stored *below* the load limit line indicated on the cabinet.

How to treat thawed food
If frozen food has thawed completely, it should be treated in the same way as any other fresh food. It is perfectly safe to thaw frozen food, cook it and refreeze it, provided that food hygiene is practised. Food must be cooled rapidly after cooking and kept refrigerated before freezing, e.g. bought frozen pastry can be safely thawed, made into an apple pie and refrozen because it will eventually be cooked before being eaten. The texture and flavour could be affected.

HOW TO COOK FROZEN FOODS

Just as quick-freezing is less damaging than slow freezing to the quality of food, so too is quick thawing. The quickest way to thaw home frozen food is to cook it from frozen. The exceptions are pastry, which must be thawed for rolling out, poultry, and some large cuts of meat.

Poultry

All poultry, whether fresh or frozen must be thoroughly cooked. If frozen poultry is not thawed first, heat may not penetrate sufficiently to the bone to ensure thorough cooking.

If poultry is stuffed before it has thawed, the rate of thawing will be slowed down.

After thawing keep in a refrigerator and cook as soon as possible.

Meat

It is safer and easier to thaw large cuts of meat before cooking as they take a long time to cook from frozen and it may be difficult to achieve a good result. It is necessary to use a meat thermometer to ensure cooking right through to the centre.

Chops, steaks, liver, kidneys and cubed meat can all be cooked from frozen but the cooking should be started at a lower temperature than usual and it will take almost twice as long.

Rolled joints, whether stuffed or not, must be thawed before cooking. Because both surfaces of the meat have been handled and rolled up, thorough cooking is important.

FREEZING AND FLAVOUR

Seasoning

Some flavours decline and others intensify during freezing. Sage and thyme change signifiantly.

It is best not to over-season foods for freezing and to adjust seasoning during reheating. Additional flavouring can usually be added during the final cooking.

Alcohol

This sometimes loses flavour during freezing. To obtain the full flavour, it is wiser to add it during reheating.

FREEZING AND NUTRITIVE VALUES

The freezing process itself does not affect any nutrient. There will be some loss of water-soluble vitamins C and B_1 during the blanching of vegetables. As blanching partially cooks vegetables, less final cooking will be needed so there will be less vitamin loss at that stage.

FOODS WHICH DO NOT FREEZE WELL

Foods which contain a large proportion of water and have a delicate cell structure do not usually freeze well.

Baked Egg Custard – separates.

Bananas – turn black.

Cream (single) – separates. Double or whipping cream will freeze if whipped.

Eggs (hard-boiled) – become tough and watery; the white turns grey.
Jelly – collapses.
Mayonnaise or Salad Cream – separates.
Melon (whole) – collapses; is fairly satisfactory scooped into balls and frozen in syrup.
Milk – separates; homogenised milk stores quite well.
Salad Vegetables – become limp.
Tomatoes – collapse: best frozen as purée.
Yogurt (plain) – separates: the sweetened fruit variety freezes quite well.

FREEZING FISH

Because fish deteriorates rapidly after leaving the water, unless it is refrigerated, it is only truly 'fresh' for a few hours. As only really fresh fish should be frozen at home, it is often necessary to rely on bought frozen fish.

Freshly caught fish should be gutted, trimmed, washed and dried carefully. Interleave cutlets, fillets or small whole fish with foil or polythene and wrap in polythene.

Fish can be cooked from frozen, allowing extra cooking time or it can be made into recipes and frozen uncooked or cooked.

FREEZING MEAT

Meat for the freezer can be bought in bulk from the butcher, freezer food centre or larger supermarkets.
Points to consider when buying meat for the freezer:

1. The butcher may prepare cuts to individual requirements, pack and freeze them.

2. Freezer food centres usually sell individual cuts frozen or bulk packs of smaller cuts such as chops or steaks. As these may not be from the same animal, the quality sometimes varies.

3. Supermarkets frequently stock items a butcher may not offer because of insufficient demand.

4. The cost of a quarter side of beef, half a pig or a whole carcase of lamb is considerable. Make sure it is from a reliable source, as tough meat is not an economy.

5. Unjointed frozen carcases can be a real problem at home.

6. Unfrozen meat bought in bulk can take several days to freeze in a small freezer, as the weight of it will be greater than the freezer's daily freezing capacity.

7. When whole or half carcases are purchased, both cheap and expensive cuts will be included in the overall price.

How to freeze fresh meat

1. Freeze the offal first, then the small cuts and finally larger cuts.
2. Meat waiting to be frozen should be stored in the refrigerator.
3. Do not freeze at one time more than the quantity recommended in the freezer manufacturer's instruction booklet.
4. Small pieces of meat should be packed individually, either in small polythene bags or interleaved with polythene sheeting or freezer cling film.
5. Projecting bones should be padded with foil or kitchen paper to prevent them from perforating the wrapping material.
6. Meat packed in a string mesh sleeve or on a polystyrene tray need only be overwrapped with polythene. Overwrap several flat packs together.
7. Boned, rolled joints take up less room in the freezer.
8. The lean parts of tough or unfamiliar cuts can be minced and used for dishes such as rissoles, shepherd's pie, lasagne or spaghetti Bolognese.

Cooking frozen meat

1. Meat to be roasted can be cooked from frozen but it is usually essential to use a meat thermometer and wrap the meat in foil or a roasting bag. Temperatures and times for cooking can be found in most text books.
2. Rolled joints must be thawed because both surfaces have been handled before being rolled up and thorough cooking is essential.
3. Chops, steaks, offal and kebabs can be cooked from frozen. Cooking should be started at a lower temperature and increased half way through cooking. It will take almost twice as long.
4. *All* frozen poultry must be thawed before cooking to ensure that sufficient heat penetrates the flesh to cook it thoroughly.
5. Poultry should be stuffed after it has completely thawed.

FREEZING VEGETABLES

1. Most vegetables, except salad vegetables which become limp, freeze well and can be kept for up to a year.
2. It is important to blanch vegetables before freezing to halt enzyme activity which causes changes in colour, flavour, texture and nutritional value.
3. All vegetables can be cooked direct from the frozen state, but reduce the total cooking time by the original blanching time.
4. Vegetables should be packed in polythene bags in the most frequently used quantities, as they tend to stick together. If separated vegetables are required, open freeze them on a wire rack or baking sheet. (See page 177.)

FREEZING FRUIT

1. Only freeze fruit in peak condition. It should be dry and firm.
2. Unripe, over-ripe or blemished fruit gives poor results and inferior colour and flavour.
3. Fruit should be frozen on the day it is picked or bought.
4. The way it will be ultimately used will influence preparation and packing, e.g. fruit for sauces and fools should be puréed and for pies left whole.

Methods of preparing fruit

1. *Dry (with or without sugar)*
Suitable for: most soft fruit (not those with stones) e.g. raspberries, strawberries, gooseberries.
Uses: soufflés, sorbets, ice-creams, pies, flans, gâteaux, garnishes, fruit salads.
2. *Sugar syrup*
Suitable for: fruits which discolour when cut, e.g. apples, pears, peaches, apricots.
Uses: pies, flans, fruit salads.
3. *Purée*
Suitable for: liquidised or sieved fruit, sweetened or unsweetened.
Uses: pies, fools, soufflés, sorbets, sauces.
Sugar syrup is made by boiling sugar in water for 1 minute. It should be used cold. The proportions of sugar and water depend on personal preference and the natural sweetness of the fruit.

Light syrup	200 g sugar	⎫
Medium syrup	325 g sugar	⎬ to 500 ml water
Heavy syrup	500 g sugar	⎭

Packing fruit for freezing

1. Pack in polythene bags or rigid containers.
2. Leave headspace when freezing purées. (See page 177.)
3. Crumpled polythene will help to keep fruit submerged in syrup and prevent discolouration during storage.
4. Keep containers upright until the fruit and syrup are solid.
5. Freeze purée in polythene bags moulded by a rigid container. (See page 175.)

Thawing fruit

To be eaten raw: thaw unopened at room temperature for 3–4 hours.
For cooking: heat slowly from frozen.

FREEZING DAIRY PRODUCE
Bacon
1. The salt content of bacon hastens the development of rancidity during prolonged freezer storage. The fat develops off-flavours and sometimes becomes pink.
2. Vacuum packing doubles the freezer life of bacon.
3. Interleave rashers and pack in polythene. Several vacuum packs can be stored in one polythene bag.

Cheese
1. Cheese tends to dry out and become crumbly after freezing.
2. Grated cheese freezes well.
3. Pack in polythene. Store several vacuum packs in one polythene bag.

Cream
Whipped cream freezes well. Single cream, which will not whip, is not successful. Double, clotted and whipping cream all keep fairly well.
1. Freeze in rigid polythene containers, leaving 13 mm headspace.
2. Piped cream decoration can be frozen on cakes or desserts. They should be open frozen (see page 177) and then overwrapped. A cardboard collar can be used for protection, before overwrapping.
3. Cream rosettes can be piped onto a buttered baking tray, open frozen until hard and then transferred to a flat, rigid container. Layers should be interleaved with greaseproof paper. Thaw on the food they decorate.

Eggs
1. Eggs can be frozen, either beaten or separated. Pack in rigid polythene containers or freeze in ice-cube trays and then pack loose in polythene bags.
2. Hard-boiled eggs do not freeze well. They become tough and watery and the white turns grey.

Fats
1. Overwrap greaseproof covered blocks with polythene.
2. Fats in bought rigid containers can be frozen unwrapped.
3. Butter pats or curls should be open frozen and packed in rigid containerrs. Interleave layers with polythene or greaseproof paper.

Milk
1. Homogenised milk freezes well. Other types separate.
2. Store in a sealed waxed carton or polythene container, allowing headspaces.
3. Never freeze milk in a glass bottle.

Yogurt

1. Plain yogurt separates but can sometimes be recombined by whisking.
2. The sweetened fruit variety freezes quite well.

FREEZING BREAD

All bread, bought or home baked, freezes well if it is fresh when frozen.

Part-baked dough

1. Frozen raw dough does not produce well-risen results when cooked.
2. Part-baked loaves and rolls can be kept successfully in a home freezer as long as they are frozen as soon as purchased.
3. Part-baked soft rolls should be open frozen before packing, to prevent them being squashed out of shape.
4. Store part-baked loaves and crusty rolls in the polythene bags in which they are sold, overwrapping them if the bags are perforated.
5. Frozen part-baked dough can be cooked from frozen. Bake at G.M. 7; 220°C. Allow 15 minutes for rolls and 40 minutes for loaves.

Loaves

1. Cut loaves in half if bread consumption is limited.
2. Sliced bread can be toasted from frozen or allowed to thaw for half an hour.
3. Leave loaves in waxed paper and overwrap in aluminium foil or a heavy duty polythene bag.
4. Thaw wrapped loaves at room temperature for 3–6 hours, according to size, and rolls for 1½ hours.

Breadcrumbs

Spread out on a tray to freeze and then pack in heavy duty polythene bags.

Sandwiches

1. Fillings made from cheese, meat, fish and preserves freeze well.
2. Unsuitable fillings are hard-boiled egg, salad vegetables, salad cream, banana and tomato.
3. Season sparingly.
4. Pack individually or in stacks of the same filling.
5. Interleave with foil or polythene and overwrap in heavy duty foil or polythene bags.
6. Label with type of filling, quantity and date.
7. Thaw in wrapping, either overnight in the refrigerator or at room temperature. Individual sandwiches take about 2 hours and stacks of sandwiches take 6–7 hours in a refrigerator.

FREEZING CAKES

Victoria sandwich and whisked sponge mixtures can be made in bulk. Use for basic cake shapes, sponge flan cases or steamed puddings, cooked and frozen in foil basins.

Decorated cakes

Open freeze (see page 177) gâteaux and butter iced cakes until the surface is hard enough to resist finger impressions. Protect the decorated surface with a cardboard collar and pack in heavy duty polythene.

Undecorated cakes

1. Cook in round, oblong or patty tin shapes.
2. Pack, interleaved with greaseproof paper, in plastic containers or heavy duty polythene.
3. Decorations and fillings can be frozen separately so that gâteaux or small iced cakes can be made up as required. Flavour and colours can then be selected at the time of use.

Thawing

1. Thaw all cakes unwrapped.
2. An undecorated cake will take 1½–2 hours at room temperature and a decorated cake from 2–4 hours.

FREEZING PASTRY

Pastry can be frozen before or after baking.

Unbaked pastry

1. Freeze in blocks, rolled into shapes, or made into completed dishes in foil containers.
2. Interleave small items.
3. Freeze uncovered and when hard, wrap in heavy duty polythene.
4. Thaw unwrapped and bake as usual, allowing extra time for thawing.

Baked pastry

1. Bake made-up recipes in the usual way, in foil containers.
2. Cool quickly, wrap in foil or heavy duty polythene and freeze.
3. Thaw 2–4 hours depending on size. Re-heat if required hot.

Choux pastry

1 Open freeze after baking, filling and decorating. Pack in polythene bags or rigid containers.
2. Thaw unwrapped for 2 hours.

APPROXIMATE STORAGE TIMES FOR HOME FROZEN FOOD

Fish

Oily fish	3 months
Shell-fish	3 months
White fish	5 months
Stock	3 months

Meat (uncooked)

Bacon (smoked and unsmoked) –	
joints	3 months
vacuum packed joints	4 months
rashers/chops/gammon	
steaks	1 month
vacuum packed rashers, etc	3 months
Beef	1 year
Chicken	1 year
Duck	6 months
Game	6 months
Giblets	3 months
Lamb	9 months
Mince	3 months
Offal	3 months
Pork	6 months
Rabbit	8 months
Sausages	3 months
Turkey	1 year
Veal	9 months

Meat (cooked)

Casseroles –	
with bacon	3 months
without bacon	6 months
Curry	4 months
Ham	2 months
Meat pies	3 months
Pâté	1 month
Sliced meat –	
with gravy	3 months
without gravy	2 months
Shepherd's pie	3 months
Soup	3 months
Stock	6 months

Vegetables

Most vegetables	1 year
Herbs	1 year
Artichokes	7 months
Mushrooms –	
unblanched	1 month
blanched	4 months
Onions –	
unblanched	3 months
blanched	6 months
Soup	6 months
Tomato purée	1 year

Fruit

Fruit – stoned	1 year
unstoned	6 months
Fruit pies	6 months
Ice-cream	1 month
Mousse	3 months
Sorbets	1 month
Soufflés	3 months

Dairy produce

Butter – salted	3 months
unsalted	6 months
Cheese – hard	8 months
soft	4 months
processed	6 months
grated	3 months
Cooking fat	6 months
Cream – clotted, double	
(whipped) and	
whipping	3 months
Eggs – beaten whole	10 months
separated	10 months
Lard	6 months
Milk – homogenised	1 month
Margarine – salted	3 months
unsalted	6 months
Yogurt – fruit	3 months

Bread, cakes and pastry

Breadcrumbs	3 months
Part-baked dough	4 months
Plain white or	
brown	1 month
Soft rolls	6 weeks
Crusty bread i.e.	
Vienna, French	1 week
Enriched bread i.e.	
milk, fruit, malt	2 months
Sandwiches	2 months
Scones, teabreads	2 months
Cakes – decorated	3 months
undecorated	6 months
Pastry – unbaked	3 months
baked	6 months
Yeast	1 year

Basic meal components

Batter – raw	3 months
cooked pancakes	2 months
Sauces – meat	3 months
vegetable	6 months
white	4 months
Soup – meat	3 months
vegetable	6 months
Stock – fish	3 months
meat	6 months
vegetable	6 months

22. CONTAMINATION OF FOOD

Food may be contaminated by grime or bacteria, or both. Grime on the outside of a loaf may be relatively harmless, although unpleasant, but usually is visible to the naked eye. Bacteria in food may be invisible and so undetectable to the eye. They thrive under warm conditions and are capable of causing illness and death. Both types of contamination can be reduced by food hygiene.

Foods easily infected by food-poisoning bacteria

1. Meat and meat products, especially cooked meats, pies, brawn, tongue, pressed meat, sausages, etc.
2. Made-up fish dishes and shell-fish.
3. Milk foods, synthetic creams, custards, trifles, ice-cream which has been melted and re-frozen.
4. Gravies, soups, stews, etc.
5. Eggs, especially duck eggs and reconstituted eggs.

Susceptible foods are those which are rich in nutritive value and are moist. These foods, especially when they are warm, provide ideal conditions for the growth of bacteria. (See Preservation notes.) In a short time bacteria multiply rapidly under these conditions. In 24 hours a few bacteria can become several million.

CAUSES OF FOOD CONTAMINATION

1. *Bacteria may be present in the food.* Salmonella bacteria can be present in the meat of all animals, in milk, in duck eggs, or in milk powders. Salmonella bacteria may develop in meat or poultry which was insufficiently thawed before cooking, because the cooking time is not sufficient to allow the heat to penetrate and destroy the bacteria.

Note: Diseases such as tuberculosis, typhoid, cholera and dysentery, etc. may be carried and transmitted by food.

2. *Bacteria may be carried by vermin.* Rodents can carry salmonella bacteria in their bodies and transmit this to food in the excreta. Flies can carry and deposit on food salmonella bacteria from decaying matter, e.g. dustbins. (Vermin carry other diseases too.)

3. *Bacteria may be transmitted by man.* Staphylococci bacteria are present in the nose and throat of most people, often on the skin and always in boils, abscesses and sometimes in cuts. Bacterial organisms may be deposited in the food or on food containers by hands which have been in contact with infection, and as they grow there toxins are produced. Staphylococci bacteria may be present in the bowels of a person suffering from an acute case of food poisoning, who may infect food because of failure to wash the hands after visiting the lavatory. Even more danger lies in the fact that the person passing on a disease in this way may be a carrier who has never exhibited any symptoms.

Reasons for increases in food contamination

1. Increase in communal feeding – more people are eating outside the home.
2. More shop-prepared food is eaten – pies, pastries, etc.
3. Careless handling of réchauffé dishes or frozen food.
4. Insufficient thawing of frozen meat and poultry.
5. Employment of untrained food handlers.
6. Lack of attention to personal hygiene.
7. Wider recognition of food poisoning symptoms has led to an apparent increase in the number of cases.

WAYS TO PREVENT FOOD POISONING

1. *Precautions in food handling.* It is likely that staphylococci bacteria will be present in the nose and throat, so care should be taken when handling food. Hands should be washed thoroughly. Avoid putting spoons back in food after tasting it.

Avoid chipped utensils.

Do not use the same cutting board for both cooked and uncooked meat.

Do not store uncooked meat or fish in proximity to cooked foods which are susceptible to contamination, e.g. meat or fish which is allowed to drip on to cooked meat or cream desserts, etc.

Susceptible food must be thoroughly cooked to destroy bacteria and their toxins. If it is to be stored it must be cooled quickly and kept under hygienic conditions.

Do not keep susceptible food for any length of time.

Care is essential when washing up. Use hot water, detergents, and dry by draining rather than using dirty tea towels.

Hygiene must be practised by members of the household – washing hands thoroughly after using the lavatory.

Avoid soiled hand towels and communal roller towels.

Special hygienic practices are needed in the case of infectious diseases – keep food utensils, towels, etc. apart from those of the household. The importance of hygiene at all stages when handling food cannot be too greatly stressed.

2. *Preventing the spread of infection by animals*

Do not use untreated milk.

Thaw frozen meat and poultry thoroughly.

Thoroughly cook all meat and poultry.

Thoroughly cook duck eggs (make sure that they come from a clean source).

Keep domestic animals away from food and food containers. Keep special dishes for their food and wash the dishes separately.

No animals should be allowed into food shops.

3. *Prevention of infection by pests*

Keep the house free of all vermin – flies, cockroaches, mice, etc. The Rodent Officer from the local Council will remove an infestation.

Left-over food should be covered or burnt if not required.

Dustbins should be properly constructed and sensibly used.

Avoid narrow cracks between pieces of kitchen equipment, which harbour dirt and crumbs to attract vermin.

Keep everything, especially sinks and drains, clean and disinfected.

Keep cooked food and laid tables covered.

DOMESTIC HYGIENE RULES

1. Shop where there is a good standard of cleanliness. Draw attention to unhygienic practices, e.g. licking fingers, blowing in bags, not using food tongs.

2. Never take pets into food shops.

3. Keep shopping baskets clean for food carrying. Demand clean wrapping paper for susceptible foods – meat, fish, etc.

4. Keep larders and food stores cool, well ventilated and free from vermin. Keep all kitchen equipment clean and free from flies and vermin, and all kitchen surfaces clean.

5. Wash the hands before handling food. Keep finger-nails short and clean. Cover sores and cuts with clean waterproof dressing. Never handle food if suffering from an infectious disease. Keep an invalid's food separate, if the illness is infectious.

6. Do not smoke when preparing and handling food.

7. Have a good supply of hot water and soap.

8. Always use clean crockery, cutlery, and utensils which are free from chips and cracks. Wash up with detergent and hot water. There is a danger in dirty tea towels; it is better to rinse pots in very hot water and leave to drip-dry.

9. Wash milk bottles before returning and never use for any other purpose.

10. When handling food remember that time, temperature and moisture are vital factors in food poisoning.

11. Avoid accumulations of partially used food. Use food in rotation so that the older food is used up first.

12. Keep premises free from vermin and flies.

13. Use the dustbin properly. Burn as much refuse as possible. Keep the contents dry. Use disinfectant after emptying, especially in hot weather. The bin should stand a reasonable distance from the kitchen window or door. It should be raised, e.g. on bricks, to allow circulation of air.

14. Keep yards and passages, etc. free from accumulations of rubbish and clean to avoid harbouring rodents and insects.

15. Keep drains clean and disinfected. The Environmental Health Inspector will advise if necessary.

16. Keep food *clean* and *cool* and *covered*.

23. STOCKS AND SOUPS

Stock is a liquid containing some of the flavouring constituents (and very little of the nutritive value) of the food used to make the stock, which are extracted by simmering gently for a long time. Stock forms the foundation of soups, sauces and gravies.

PRINCIPLES IN STOCK MAKING

1. The solvent action of the water.
2. The prolonged application of moist heat.

Both these processes are essential in order to extract the maximum flavour.

Aim

1. The extraction of as much as possible of the soluble matter of meat, or fish, or vegetables, in order to obtain a strong, well-flavoured stock.
2. The colour must be good for the purpose required, e.g. brown stock for gravy or white stock for white sauce or fricassée.
3. Freedom from grease is essential to avoid a greasy soup or sauce.

Essential points for good stock

1. Cleanliness and freshness of all the ingredients.
2. Small division of meat and removal of fat.
3. A balanced proportion of ingredients. No one vegetable flavour should predominate. Strong-flavoured vegetables, such as turnip, etc. should not be used.
4. Carefully added seasoning. No one herb or spice should dominate the flavour.
5. Cook meat for a longer period than the vegetables.
6. Remove white scum and fat from the surface.
7. A strong pan with a well-fitting lid should be used.
8. Never leave stock in a warm place. Use as soon as possible or refrigerate when cool.

Suitable foods

1. Meat and bones. Scraps and gristle. Bacon rinds (use with discretion). Giblets of fowl and game. Bones, scraps, etc. of non-oily fish.
2. Liquid in which meat or fowl has been cooked (not salted meat).
3. Vegetables and vegetable liquid (not liquid from green vegetables).

Unsuitable foods

1. Starchy foods – potato, bread, barley, thickened gravy. Would make the stock sour.

2. Green vegetables and liquid in which they were cooked. This will have a bitter flavour.

3. Salty liquor from bacon, etc.

NUTRITIVE VALUE OF STOCK

Very little. A little protein. No carbohydrate or fat. Trace of mineral elements. No vitamins. The value of stock is from the extractives which stimulate the digestive juices.

Types of stock

Best stock. Made from fresh meat, bones, fish, vegetables.
Household stock. Cheaper ingredients are used, liquids from meat cooking, scraps of vegetables.
White stock. Veal bones and chicken bones are used.
Fish stock. Made from fish trimmings, which go sour if cooked longer than 30 minutes.

Nowadays it is considered inadvisable to keep stock longer than twenty-four hours, but if a stock pot is kept it must be boiled up daily and kept scrupulously clean as it is such a fertile breeding ground for food-poisoning bacteria.

Stock freezes well but tends to be bulky to store in the freezer if not reduced in volume. Commercially prepared stock cubes, powders and flavouring liquids may be used in place of home-made stock.

SOUPS

Soup has little nutritive value unless it is thickened, but it is important in the diet because:

1. It stimulates the digestive juices with its flavour.

2. It is a hot start to a meal in cold weather.

3. It is used in invalid cookery to stimulate the appetite. The nutritive value of soup depends on the ingredients used.

4. Unthickened soups can help in dieting by 'blunting' the appetite.

Classification

Thin
consommés (clarified)
broths and
bouillons (unclarified)

Thick

Purées
  a) proper
  b) bound (small amount of liaison)
Thickened
  a) brown
  b) white
  c) bisques (fish soups)

Thin soups

1. *Clear soups*. These are made from meat stock with a little vegetable for flavour. They are of little nutritive value, but are served as a stimulant and an aid to digestion.

2. *Broths*. These are made from vegetables and/or meat with the addition of a cereal such as barley, rice, etc. They have a higher nutritive value because of the presence of the vegetables and cereal, which provide starch and some vegetable protein.

Thick soups

1. *Purées*. These are made from vegetables which may include pulse vegetables. The cooked vegetables are liquidised or sieved which helps to thicken the soup. A liaison or thickening of flour, cornflour, sago, etc. may be used to give a smooth texture and bind the ingredients together. Other types of liaison are a roux of butter and flour or yolks of eggs or cream. Nutritive value depends on the ingredients used.

Essentials of good soup

1. Rich flavour depending on the ingredients used.

Recommended proportion of ingredients to 500 ml liquid
  200 g meat, *or*
  400 g vegetables, *or*
  100 ml soaked pulse.

2. Sufficient seasoning to bring out the flavour.

3. Freedom from grease – resulting from the use of good stock, careful sauté'ing, skimming.

4. A good colour. White soups – vegetables sauté'd not browned.
                    Brown soups – brown stock and roux used.

5. Correct proportion of ingredients. A good consistency of thickened soups – not too thick or too thin, or lumpy. Add liaison carefully. Sieve carefully.

Serving of soup

Consider

1. Quantity. 150 ml of finished soup per person + a little extra for ease of serving.

2. Variety. Do not repeat the flavour of the soup later in the meal.

3. The season of the year. Serve thick soups in winter; cold soups in summer, e.g consommé, cucumber.

4. Colour scheme of meal.

5. The correct accompaniments, e.g. croutons with purées, grated parmesan with some consommés, plain boiled rice with mulligatawny soup, or chopped parsley and a variety of small pasta may be used.

Storage of soups

When cool store in a covered container in a refrigerator for up to two days. (Refer to page 188.)

Freezing of soups
Chapter 21. Pages 177, 187.

24. SAUCES

A sauce is usually a well-flavoured liquid containing a thickening agent. It may be simple or elaborate. The success of many dishes depends upon the quality of their sauces.

This is a very important and often neglected branch of the culinary art. More attention is given to the making of sauces in Continental cookery, but they are being used increasingly in this country.

Sauces serve many purposes

a) Give flavour to dull insipid dishes or impart new flavours to a dish, e.g. parsley sauce with boiled cod.

b) Add to the nutritive value of the dish, e.g. eggs, milk, etc.

c) Counteract the richness of certain foods, e.g. apple sauce with pork.

d) Improve the texture or appearance of certain foods, e.g. minced meat or pieces of meat covered or served in a sauce.

e) Bind food together, e.g. croquettes.

f) Add colour to a dish or meal that might otherwise look dull, e.g. macaroni cheese.

General aims in sauce making

a) Careful blending of ingredients.

b) Judicious seasoning.

c) Suitability of sauce to the dish for which it is made.

d) Preservation of distinctive flavour.

CLASSIFICATION OF SAUCES

1. *Those made with a roux*

a) Household sauces – white and brown.

b) More elaborate types – Béchamel, velouté (white), Espagnole (brown).

2. *Cooked egg sauces*

a) Custard type, e.g. custard sauce.

b) Other types, e.g. Hollandaise, German egg sauce (whipped).

3. *Cold sauces*

a) Mayonnaise type.

b) Chaudfroid.
c) Unclassified, e.g. simple salad dressings, mint sauce, horseradish sauce.
4. *Unclassified sauces*
a) Simple blended – thickened with cornflour, custard powder, etc.
b) Purée type, e.g. apple, bread.
c) Jam, syrup, or fruit sauces.

ROUX SAUCES

Sauces thickened with a roux are particularly important. From the foundation brown and white sauces, more elaborate sauces are built up which give distinction to various dishes. The finished dish is often named according to the sauce that is served with it, e.g. Soles Mornay (fillets of sole with Mornay sauce), Côtelettes de Veau à l'Italienne (veal cutlets with Italian sauce).

It is essential to have complete mastery of the art of making foundation white and brown sauces – the success of a dish may depend on this.

Plain white roux sauce
The roux consists of fat (butter, margarine, etc.) and flour or cornflour in equal quantities. The proportion of these to liquids depends on the consistency of the sauce required.
It may be used for:
a) pouring or serving separately.
b) coating.
c) a panada or binding medium.
The liquid used may be varied according to the type of sauce required. Flavour is very important.
E.g. mixture of stock and milk for savoury sauce;
milk or water for sweet sauces.

Proportions for white sauce
a) *Pouring or flowing sauce*
15–20 g fat
15–20 g flour } to 250 ml liquid
b) *Coating sauce*
25 g fat
25 g flour } to 250 ml liquid
c) *Panada*
50 g fat
50 g flour } to 250 ml liquid

Method of preparation
1. Melt fat in the saucepan. Do not overheat.
2. Add flour, stir in smoothly and stir over gentle heat for about 3 mins. to make a smooth paste. Do not allow to brown. At this stage the starch will begin to cook.
3. Remove pan from heat and add liquid very gradually, especially at first. The mixture must be smoothly blended or lumps will result.

Quick method. For the two thinner sauces, all the liquid can be added at once and a whisk used to whisk the mixture while cooking.

4. Return to the heat, bring to the boil and cook thoroughly for about 3–5 mins., stirring continuously. Boiling is needed to complete the cooking of the starch in the flour, to avoid a raw flavour, to ensure glossiness and to give the correct consistency. Vegetables, herbs, spices, etc. may be added before or after boiling, depending on the type of sauce. Some sauces may need straining.
5. Taste, season, taste, reheat and serve.

Essential qualities of a white sauce
a) Absolute smoothness.
b) Glossiness.
c) Good colour.
d) Correct consistency.

Alteration of consistency
a) If the sauce is too thick, dilute with a little liquid and bring to the boil again, stirring vigorously.
b) If the sauce is too thin, reduce by rapid boiling. Stir all the time, as great care must be taken at this stage to avoid burning.

Proportions for brown sauce
20 g flour
20 g dripping } to 250 ml liquid
carrot, onion, turnip, thinly sliced.
Seasoning.

Method
The same as for white sauce except that roux is cooked until a good brown colour.
1. Heat fat and fry vegetables until brown. (Onion last as it burns quickly.)
2. Stir in flour. Make roux and cook until the roux is an even brown colour, stirring continuously.
3. Remove from heat, add liquid a little at a time, mixing in smoothly.
4. Bring to the boil, stirring all the time, and skim.
5. Simmer for about 30 mins., stirring and skimming occasionally.
6. Skim, season to taste, strain and re-heat.

Essentials for successful sauce
   a) Thorough even browning of vegetables and roux.
   b) Thorough cooking to extract as much flavour as possible and to cook the flour.
   c) No greasiness.

COOKED EGG SAUCES
   a) Custard type.
   b) German egg sauce.
   c) Hollandaise sauce.

Important points
   Underlying principle. To heat the egg albumen to the point of thickening (coagulation of protein) without curdling.
   Curdling. When this occurs, the albumen hardens and shrinks. It then separates from the liquid, resembling curds and whey.
   Consistency. These sauces thicken upon cooling, so should be heated only until the mixture will coat the back of a spoon thinly. Over-heating will result in curdling. Insufficient heating will result in the egg separating from the liquid on standing as it will not have thickened sufficiently.
   Whisked egg sauces. Are whisked until frothy – the whisking entangles air with the egg albumen as it coagulates giving a frothy appearance.

COLD SAUCES
Mayonnaise
Ingredients used are egg yolks, salad oil, malt or wine vinegar or lemon juice, mustard, salt, pepper, sugar, and perhaps cream.
Method
   1. In a large basin mix egg yolk and all seasoning (not vinegar).
   2. Add oil drop by drop, stirring thoroughly with a wooden spoon. At the end add a little more quickly. Add sufficient oil to thicken.
   3. Stir in vinegar carefully.
   4. Taste and add more seasoning if needed.
   5. One or two tablespoonfuls of cream may be added if desired.

Underlying principles in making mayonnaise
   During the thorough mixing of oil with the egg yolk, the oil is broken up into minute particles or globules, and these should become evenly and thoroughly incorporated with the yolk. If added too rapidly, they will not blend properly and the oil will separate out ('curdling'). To avoid curdling keep everything cool. Beat the mixture thoroughly. If it shows signs of curdling add a few drops of cold water and beat again. If the mixture curdles, add it drop by drop to a fresh egg yolk

beating well until smooth. A well-made mayonnaise is smooth and glossy in appearance and is the consistency of thick cream. Will keep 1–2 weeks. If it is to be kept longer, heat the basin over boiling water for 5 minutes while whisking well, and store in a bottle.

Chaudfroid sauce

Used for coating fish, meat, poultry, game, etc. for entrées. A mixture of foundation sauce – Béchamel or velouté (white) or Espagnole (brown), plus aspic jelly and a small mixture of gelatine. Should set firmly with a high gloss and a smooth texture.

Unclassified cold sauces

Simple salad dressings, mint sauces, horseradish sauce.

UNCLASSIFIED SAUCES

a) *Simple blended type (pouring consistency)* e.g. commercial custards, white sauce.

Proportions

15 g cornflour or custard powder ⎫
15 g sugar   ⎬ to 250 ml milk

A savoury white sauce may be made by this method, omitting the sugar and adding seasoning and flavouring, e.g. chopped parsley.

b) *Purée type*, e.g. bread, apple.

The ingredients are cooked to reduce to a thick consistency and sieved.

c) *Jam, syrup or fruit sauces*

These may be cooked to reduce the water content or may be thickened with cornflour or arrowroot.

FAULTS IN SAUCE MAKING

Lumpy: Roux-type sauce. Fat too hot when flour added. Roux not cooked sufficiently. Liquid added too quickly without sufficient stirring. Insufficient stirring during cooking.

Blended type. Insufficient blending of cornflour and cold liquid.

Raw flavour. Insufficient cooking of the roux. Sauce not cooked long enough.

Lacking gloss. Insufficient cooking.

Thin sauce. Wrong proportion of ingredients. Over-cooking causing breakdown of starch to dextrin which is soluble. Under-cooking.

Thick sauce. Wrong proportions used.

Greasy sauce. Too much fat. Over-cooking the roux, causing separation of the fat.

Poor colour. Over-heating a white sauce at any stage results in poor colour.

In brown sauce, uneven cooking of the roux will cause brown specks.

Salads are important as they add colour to meals, making them attractive as well as providing food nutrients necessary for health. Salads add colour to a meal, some bite, and varied flavours.

The nutritive value depends on the ingredients used, and whether these are fresh, raw or cooked. Fresh green salads contain all those vitamins and mineral elements which are extracted or destroyed by heat when cooking, and so are easily lost, e.g. vitamins C and A (carotene), iron, some potassium and some calcium. Salads add fibre to the diet in the form of cellulose. Root vegetables and pulse vegetables add carbohydrate and a supply of vegetable protein. Animal protein may be provided by the addition of eggs, meat, fish or cheese. The water content is important for maintenance of the body fluids – for coolness and refreshment.

CLASSIFICATION AND PLACE IN THE MENU

1. As an hors d'oeuvre (see later notes).
2. As an accompaniment to hot roast meat, poultry or fish. Green salad plants are served with French dressing. Crispness of salad is refreshing.
3. As an accompaniment to cold meat. Green salad, coleslaw, cooked vegetables or fruits served with French dressing, mayonnaise or salad cream.
4. As a lunch, high tea or supper dish in which a green salad and cooked vegetables or fruit are served with a protein food, e.g. fish, cheese, meat, or, for vegetarians – nuts. It is accompanied by bread and butter. Fruit with a sharp acidic taste gives a more piquant flavour.
5. As a filling for rolls and sandwiches.

SALAD INGREDIENTS

Raw green vegetables
Lettuce, cress, cabbage sprouts, chicory, endive, spinach, dandelion leaves, Chinese leaves.

1. Use as soon as possible after picking.
2. Handle as little as possible. Bruising spoils the appearance and reduces vitamin C content.
3. Wash with running water. Drain on a cloth.

4. Discard bruised leaves.

5. Use whole leaves, or break or shred finely using a sharp knife to reduce loss of vitamin C.

6. They should be clean, crisp and dry. They may be revived by putting them in the hydrator tray of a refrigerator.

7. Store dry, wrapped, in a cold place or a refrigerator, or in a pan with the lid on. If left wet they will go slimy.

Raw root vegetables

Carrots, swedes, radishes, onions, celery.

1. Wash well, scrape or peel.

2. Grate carrots and swedes finely, beetroot coarsely.

3. Prepare other vegetables as desired. Onions sliced or diced. Radish cut into 'rose' shape.

Cooked vegetables

Potatoes, peas, cauliflower, etc.

Drain thoroughly, slice or dice. Serve plain or with dressing.

Fruit, fresh or dried, tomatoes

Wash and peel if desired, cut up.

Protein food

Eggs, meat, fish, poultry, cheese, nuts.

Eggs – hard-boiled or scrambled.

Cheese – grated or sliced. May be mixed with herbs or sauces.

Meat and poultry – slice, chop or mince.

Fish – flake or serve in portions with or without dressing.

Nuts – chopped.

Flavouring. Should be used sparingly – pepper, salt, flavoured vinegars, onions – fresh or pickled – garlic, herbs, chopped pickles, capers, nasturtium leaves, dandelion leaves.

Garnishes. Egg white and yolk or whole egg, pimento, olives, red or green peppers, parsley, chives, anchovy or herring fillets, radish roses, curled celery, gherkin tassels, dice or balls of cooked vegetables. Pickled cabbage, onion rings, capers, chopped pickles, chopped aspic jelly.

Winter salads

Great variety is now possible because of the use of foreign imports, hot-house produce and frozen vegetables. Endive, chicory, lettuce, cabbage, cauliflower, celery, beans, potatoes, carrots, etc. are all available during the winter.

Coleslaw is a useful winter salad though it can be made all year round. The basis is finely shredded, raw, white cabbage to which chopped or grated carrots, apples, celery and raw onion are added. Other ingredients may include nuts, sultanas, raisins, pineapple, mandarin oranges and herbs. The mixture is tossed in vinaigrette dressing or mayonnaise or a mixture of both dressings.

Salad gives variety and flavour to winter diet and provides supplies of vitamins C and A.

Assembling salads

A large dish or small individual dishes may be used. A flat dish or tray is easier to arrange and to serve from. Serve salads as soon as possible after assembly. They should appear attractive, unhandled, and should never overhang the edge of the dish.

Salad dressings. The choice should be suitable for the type of salad. The amount should be sufficient to moisten and be palatable, but not over-abundant or it will spoil the flavour of the salad plants. The salad dressing may be served separately, or the salad plants may be tossed in it immediately before serving. Do not soak salad in the dressing, or the oil and vinegar would soften the cellulose and vinegar may stain them.

French dressing.　　⅔ oil　　⎱　+ seasoning – salt, pepper, mustard,
　　　　　　　　　⅓ vinegar　⎰　　sugar.

Lemon juice may replace all or part of vinegar.

Vinaigrette dressing. Add chopped gherkins, parsley and shallots to the above.

Salad creams and mayonnaise. See Sauces.

26. HORS D'OEUVRES AND SAVOURIES

HORS D'OEUVRES

Hors d'oeuvres are served as an appetising preliminary to a meal, often in place of soup. They are intended to stimulate the flow of gastric juices and thus help to digest the foods which are to follow. Hors d'oeuvres consist of a variety of highly flavoured, well seasoned, colourful foods served in very small portions insufficient to satisfy the appetite, though in rare, informal cases they may be modified to form a complete main course. They are usually served cold, and unlike most other foods, hors d'oeuvres may be put on the table before the guests arrive.

Plain hors d'oeuvres. (Hors d'oeuvres variés.) Usually consist of a selection of six varieties of salad foods which may be served on small individual plates, in an hors d'oeuvres dish divided into six compartments, or may be arranged attractively on a flat oval dish. It is usual to include a dressed vegetable, green vegetable and a protein food.

Dressed hors d'oeuvres. Are more elaborate in preparation and garnish and are frequently served alone, e.g. asparagus tips rolled in ham or a crab meat canapé may constitute a dressed hors d'oeuvres. They may be served in a patty case or on a canapé which is a platform of fried bread, on thinly buttered toast, brown bread and butter with the cut edges rolled in chopped parsley, fancy shapes of cheese pastry or small commercial biscuits. Canapés are now frequently served as a part of buffet refreshments and are often more closely associated with this than with hors d'oeuvres.

SAVOURIES

There are two main types of savouries:

1. The titbits eaten with fingers at a cocktail party, which are intended to stimulate the appetite and promote thirst. They also slightly reduce the rate at which alcohol enters the bloodstream – all food eaten with alcohol will have this effect, especially food containing fat. Cocktail savouries are small and piquant and should be easy to eat without risk of smearing the fingers with grease or crumbs.

2. After-dinner savouries are served after the sweet and before the dessert at a formal dinner. They may be hot or cold but must be small, well flavoured and

carefully garnished. After-dinner savouries should clear the palate and help to round off a meal. Cheese is frequently served, e.g. cheese straws, cheese aigrettes. Care must be taken not to repeat a flavour which has already appeared in the meal.

The two types of savouries are interchangeable, and are often similar to dressed hors d'oeuvres.

Foods suitable for hors d'oeuvres and savouries

Vegetables. Lettuce hearts or shredded leaves, sliced chicory, radishes, beetroot, tomatoes, cucumber, celery, peas, asparagus tips, peppers, sweet corn, mushrooms, potato salad or macedoine of vegetables. Olives, green and black, pickles, chutneys, herbs, e.g. chives.

Fish. Oysters, shell-fish, caviare, fish fillets, e.g. anchovy, smoked salmon, roll mop herrings, sardines, smoked eel.

Meats. Smoked meat and sausages, liver, ham, bacon, tongue, scraps of cold chicken, game, etc.

Eggs. Hard-boiled, sliced or chopped and mixed with mayonnaise, etc.

Pulses and Cereals. Haricot beans, rice, shaped pasta.

DANISH OPEN SANDWICHES

These have become increasingly popular in this country. They consist of a slice of bread (rye bread is used in Scandinavia) well buttered with a topping of meat, sausage, fish, including shell-fish, cheese, eggs, etc. garnished with vegetables. They are colourful, attractive and sufficiently filling to be served as the main course at an informal lunch.

27. CONVENIENCE FOODS

In this country many people are out at work all day and require foods which can be prepared and served in the minimum of time. The higher standard of living, increase in foreign travel and willingness to experiment with new foods, together with lack of time, have further increased this demand. Shopping in supermarkets has contributed to the phenomenal increase in the use of convenience foods because they are so well displayed. Modern advertising has also aided their popularity. The use of convenience foods has increased rapidly since the day in 1837 when Alfred Bird, a chemist, first marketed the eggless custard powder he had made for his sick wife.

DEFINITION

What does the word convenience actually mean when applied to food? To people centuries back, flour was a convenience food, and even fifty years ago self-raising flour was thought of as such. Today we think of things such as frozen cakes, pastries and vegetables as convenience foods and we tend to forget that foods we now take for granted such as custard powder and canned meat were convenience foods to our parents and grandparents.

The degree of convenience demanded from foods has risen because people have less time for food preparation but are still looking for more variety and greater economy in the diet. This is a result of the changing pattern of family life and shopping, since many people combine running homes with full time jobs, and they are prepared to pay the higher cost of convenience foods for the sake of the savings in time and labour achieved by their use.

The term 'convenience' may also be applied to the form in which the food may be obtained or stored, e.g. the packet of soup mix or can of peas which are more easily carried home and more convenient to store than the ingredients for soup or the fresh vegetables. The packet itself may act as a protection for the food, e.g. laminated foil envelopes for soup and instant coffee which resist moisture, vapour and heat. Most convenience foods are prepared and packed under hygienic conditions and so the food is protected until the package is opened by the consumer. Recent developments in quick freezing and in canning techniques have made it possible to enjoy out-of-season food throughout the year, e.g. peas prepared when cheap and plentiful and of good quality are available all the year at standard prices. This source is particularly valuable when fresh vegetables are scarce.

NUTRITIVE VALUE

The nutritive value of convenience foods is often equal to that of fresh food, e.g. frozen fruit and vegetables are said to contain as high a vitamin and mineral element content as the fresh food. The apparent extra cost is in many cases offset by the reduction in preparation time and the fact that there is no wastage. This applies especially to frozen fish and vegetables.

DEVELOPMENT OF CONVENIENCE FOODS

This table shows how convenience foods of one age can be superseded in the next:

Wheat	→Flour	S.R. Flour	Cake mixes
Maize	→Cornflour	Custards	Instant desserts
Gelatine	→Gelatine leaves/powder	Jellies	Ready-made desserts
Fish	→Salt/smoked fish	Canned/frozen fish	Prepared fish in batter and sauces
Fruit	→Dried fruit	Canned/frozen fruit	Fruit desserts
Meat	→Salt/smoked meat	Canned/frozen meat	Meat dishes in sauces

Although convenience foods are being continually developed, the developments do not suit all tastes. For example, some people prefer to use plain or self-raising flour in making cakes, rather than use cake mixes, because they prefer the flavour and texture despite the convenience that the packet cake mixes offer.

CHANGING ROLE OF CONVENIENCE FOODS

A convenience food and the part it plays in general eating habits, is always evolving. An example is margarine. Margarine began as a cheap substitute for butter, often used in cooking, then it became an alternative to butter in general use and is used now for its convenience in spreading. Modern margarines are marketed with emphasis on the vegetable oil content, and their low cholesterol content (considered preferable to animal fats since too much cholesterol may contribute to heart disease). Another example is canned fruit. When this was first introduced it was mainly a method of preserving fruit from abroad and fifty years ago it was considered a luxury by many people. Now, as import costs rise canned fruit may revert to a luxury food in the future.

This table shows how the use of some foods has changed.

Food	Stage 1	Stage 2	Current Stage
Tomato Purée	Way of preserving tomatoes.	Seasoning in its own right.	Thickener and seasoning in a variety of dishes e.g. curries; sauces.
Soups Canned/packet	Soup cubes replaced stock pot.	Canned and packet soups used as sauces.	Soups as a complete snack or light meal
Canned Fruit	Way of preserving foreign fruit.	Luxury food.	Basic food – but costs are rising so may revert to luxury food.
Yogurts	Way of preserving milk.	Natural/health food.	Variety of flavoured desserts.

TYPES OF CONVENIENCE FOODS

There are three main types of food made with convenience in mind:

1. *Convenience foods designed to save work*, i.e. labour saving foods, e.g. custard powder, cake mixes, canned and dried soups, canned and bottled sauces, baby foods, stock cubes, canned pie fillings, frozen vegetables, frozen poultry and pies, instant coffee.

2. Foods packed with *storage* as the main consideration for both the consumer and the manufacturer, e.g. processed cheese, fish pastes, canned fruit and vegetables, dried fruit juices, dried milk, 'Long Life' milk, fruit squashes.

3. *Alternative, or non-traditional foods* – some of these may be designed for ecological reasons, some are cheaper than any food they attempt to imitate, and some are new foods in their own right that are impossible to compare with any known food, e.g. TVP, margarine, cream toppings, instant desserts, low fat spreads, coffee creamers.

Labour saving foods

Convenience foods have been developed by the manufacturer to save work for the consumer. This is done at considerable expense to the consumer. Labour saving foods vary from well established convenience foods, such as cake mixes, frozen poultry and frozen vegetables, to their more recent counterparts; frozen gâteaux and dehydrated meals. The more recent convenience foods are preserved for storage but *the prime consideration* is that of saving labour. It is convenient to buy prepared food so cutting out several stages of preparation for which a person may not have time. A flan for a weekday evening meal may be assembled from a ready-made flan case and a can of fruit filling. So a person who goes out to work can still present a meal of interest and variety with the help of labour saving foods and equipment.

Foods preserved for storage

Food may be preserved in a variety of ways: by dehydrating, freezing or canning. Preserved food is convenient to use and easy to store at home. Preservation may change the flavour and consistency of food but this may prove acceptable. Some people prefer the preserved variety to the original, choosing canned pineapples in preference to fresh pineapple, using canned tomatoes instead of fresh tomatoes or processed cheese instead of fresh cheese. Ease of storage makes a wide variety of foods accessible to a person returning home after the shops are closed.

Alternative foods

As world resources diminish scientists are attempting to replace natural foods with alternative foods. Some of these foods may be seen as an improvement on previous foods, and new generations of people unfamiliar with previous versions of a particular food, may enjoy the alternative food in its own right. Some of the foods, e.g. fruit yogurts, originated from traditional foods and yet are no longer compared with the original. Fruit yogurts are so flavoured that their association with natural yogurts is remote. Another example is coffee creamers which are used to replace milk or cream in coffee. Coffee creamers are not a milk product but when the granules are stirred into a cup of coffee the effect is the same as adding milk or cream. (See page 72.)

The alternative food of the greatest significance, however, may well prove to be *Textured Vegetable Protein (TVP)*.

TEXTURED VEGETABLE PROTEIN

People in the western world are used to eating to a high standard and their diet includes a high proportion of animal protein. Animals are an extremely inefficient way of producing protein: a cow needs 12 kg of feed protein to produce 1 kg of meat protein. There is now insufficient meat protein for world requirements and so the expansion of protein foods produced directly from grain is predicted. Vegetable protein is not generally considered as palatable as meat protein and therefore it has been processed to give it the texture and flavour of meat.

TVP was developed about fifty-five years ago although people are only just beginning to appreciate its presence and potential. Since the 1930s soya bean oil and soya bean have been used in the USA in foods such as flour, bread and cooking oil. TVP is extracted from vegetable sources such as soya bean and wheat. In making TVP, particular care has been taken to reproduce the protein, vitamin and mineral content of meat and poultry. Once extracted, the vegetable protein is mixed to a paste with water. Colour, vitamins and minerals are added. It is then partly cooked, extruded, cut into pieces of the required size and either dried or frozen. TVP may be spun in a similar way to textiles to give it the fibrous texture of meat before being partly cooked and cut.

There are two main types of TVP.

1. Meat extenders

These are generally dried in chunks or as mince. Once rehydrated in stock they are added to fresh meat and poultry to make it go further. Generally, they take their flavour from the food to which they are added, so they could supply additional protein to dishes such as stews. Some people consider that meat extenders improve the texture of some convenience foods such as beefburgers and shepherd's pies.

2. Meat substitutes

These are frozen or dried and are intended to replace the total meat portion in any meal. They are available in chunks, pieces, and as mince. Some need to be thawed before use, some are cooked directly from their frozen or dried state. Meat substitutes are particularly suited to dishes with a strong flavour, such as curries or risottos.

TVP is light in weight and presents few storage problems. There is no wastage of fat and gristle as on fresh meat, so a smaller amount per person per meal is required. TVP is quick to prepare and comparatively cheap to buy. To make a complete meat substitute is technically very exacting and, like margarine, TVP may take years of improvement before it is generally accepted.

THE USES OF CONVENIENCE FOODS

In addition to people with full time jobs there are others who can benefit greatly from the existence of convenience foods:

1. Handicapped people can be more self-sufficient and continue their interest in cooking.

2. The elderly, particularly those living alone, may benefit from the single portions of foods available in convenience packs, as may young people living away from home, perhaps in a bedsitter with only limited cooking facilities.

3. People living in caravans where cooking facilities are limited or on 'self catering' holidays will find convenience foods useful.

4. Convenience foods can be held as emergency supplies in the case of illness, bad weather or unexpected visitors.

5. Take-away foods, e.g. fish and chips or Chinese meals are convenient, hot meals.

It is the *way* in which convenience foods are used that determines their success. Someone who plans a meal to be cooked in an automatic oven while at work, and includes in that meal the sensible and imaginative use of convenience foods is using their equipment, food stores and cooking skills wisely. The discerning choice of pre-packed convenience foods for the store cupboard or home freezer helps to provide a variety of meals for the family. Many people prepare their own convenience foods by freezing main dishes, desserts and cakes, fruit and vegetables and by making jams and pickles so that these are readily available.

Convenience foods are often so cleverly packed and advertised that they have instant appeal and the household budget may suffer. However, it is the wide variety and availability of foods, both home produced and foreign, together with the labour they save, and possibly the economy they offer, that is the strength of convenience foods on the market at the present time.

28. PRESENTATION OF FOOD

Food should be served on a dish which is large enough to allow the food to be fully appreciated. There should be room for a sauce if desired and for the appropriate garnish to be seen to best advantage. The food should not overhang the edge of the dish; this is particularly important in the case of salads. Hot foods should be served on hot plates. A casserole, au gratin or entrée dish may be used in some cases in preference to a flat oval dish as it will help to keep the food moist and make sauces easier to serve. The consistency of foods is important. Care is needed when making sauces, particularly coating sauces which will set unevenly if the consistency is wrong. It is important that food looks appetising but there should be as little handling as possible during the presentation stage particularly in the case of foods which are susceptible to contamination.

TABLE LAYING

Modern table settings are usually fairly simple, but care is needed to ensure that cutlery, dishes, etc. are ready to hand, that the food is easily served and looks attractive and appetising. Much time and labour can be saved if table laying is planned. Linen, china and cutlery should be stored so that they are easily available. Everything used should be clean; the colour scheme of cloth, dishes, food, flowers, etc. should balance if possible.

1. Count the number of people to be served.
2. Consider the food to be served, number of courses, style of serving, etc.
3. Table mats should be placed for hot plates or dishes.
4. A table-cloth or mats may be used for lunch or dinner. An attractive cloth is used if the table is laid for afternoon tea, or tea may be served on a trolley. A seersucker or checked cloth may be used for breakfast, an informal supper, or children's meals.
5. Place cutlery in order of courses, i.e. cutlery for the last course nearest to the plate. Always set for a right-handed person. Knives should have the cutting edge turned inwards.
6. Tumblers or wine glasses should be placed on the right hand side above the knives.

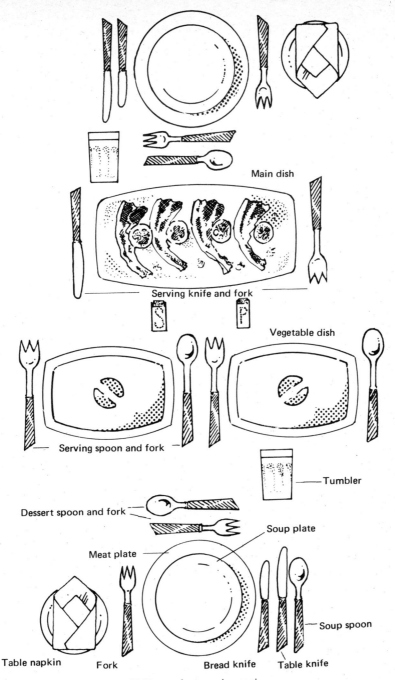

Main dish

Serving knife and fork

Vegetable dish

Serving spoon and fork

Tumbler

Dessert spoon and fork

Soup plate

Meat plate

Soup spoon

Table napkin   Fork   Bread knife   Table knife

Table set for a main meal

7. Table napkins made of cloth or paper may be placed on the side plate or in the centre of the setting. They are usually folded simply.

8. Flower or fruit decoration should be kept low to avoid obscuring people's view of each other.

9. Water should be served ice-cold.

10. Salt and pepper containers should be filled and fresh mustard made.

11. Serving cutlery should be conveniently placed.

The host or hostess carves or serves the main dish. Guests usually help themselves to vegetables. Dishes may be served from a side table or sideboard.

12. Tea or coffee cups and saucers should be placed near to the person who will pour.

13. Serve hot food hot and cold food as cold as possible. Plates should be hot or cold as required.

Meal-times should be enjoyable occasions for the hosts as well as the guests. This is only possible with careful planning and attention to detail.

GARNISHING AND DECORATION

Garnishing and serving are important; a dish may consist of much valuable food, but if it does not look attractive and appetising it will not appeal to the eye and palate, and enjoyment will be impaired. It is particularly important to make food attractive for invalids and young children, but all food is enjoyed more if it is 'mouth-watering' in appearance.

The term garnishing is used for savoury dishes; sweet dishes are decorated.

Aim. To make the dish look as interesting, attractive and colourful as possible, to add to flavour, and to be appropriate for the dish. Colour and design should harmonise. Garnish should be cooked if necessary. Avoid over-garnishing.

Raw garnish. Gives fresh colour and flavour. Easy to apply. It can supply vitamin C.

Cooked garnish. Should be simple, quick and easy to apply to avoid cooling the dish. For hot dishes the garnish must be hot.

Use of garnish. A bold enough design to be readily visible should be used. Garnished food should look fresh and unhandled. Try to decide beforehand what the finished pattern is to be, to avoid moving the garnish and spoiling the surface of the dish. As it is so difficult to find the centre accurately, it is advisable to avoid designs based on the middle.

Suitable garnishes

Parsley – fresh chopped or in sprigs, or fried. Watercress. Cress. Lettuce. Chives. Vegetables cut into shapes, e.g. dice, strips, balls, etc. Cucumber, mushroom, tomatoes, beetroot. Red or green peppers. Lemon slices, wedges or butterflies.

Gherkins. Capers. Olives – green and black. Onion rings. Cocktail onions – red, green and white. Radish roses. Curled celery. Paprika pepper. Egg – sliced or quartered. Sieved yolk of egg. Chopped white of egg. Chopped aspic jelly. Croutons of fried bread.

Decorations

Glacé cherries – red and green. Angelica. Nuts, chopped or whole, fresh or roasted. Sweets, e.g. crystallised fruits, chocolate drops. Grated chocolate. Chopped jelly. Jelly glaze. Coloured sugar. Meringue. Whipped cream. Piped fresh cream or butter cream. Icings.

FLAVOURING

Training and knowledge are necessary if one is to cultivate a discriminating palate and the ability to identify, for example, some of the individual flavours in the blend of a curry. Time must sometimes be allowed for the mellowing of flavours, e.g. Christmas cake, chutney, cheese and wine, all of which are the better for being kept. Home-killed meat is usually well flavoured but the flavour of inferior meat may be improved by the use of herbs and spices. The development of storing meat by chilling and refrigeration and the increased sales of meat may mean that meat is not hung long enough for lactic acid to develop flavour and tenderness. This must be overcome during cooking. Food can be treated by marinading, e.g. herrings which are steeped in an acid liquid – vinegar, wine or cider – which will develop the flavour and partially pre-digest the food.

The correct preparation of food will influence flavour and colour. For quick cooking, vegetables, e.g. onions, are chopped finely so that they will disintegrate quickly, but in stews which are cooked slowly for a long period the vegetables are left in large pieces which will give flavour but will still be recognisable in the finished dish. Sauté or fry to seal in the natural juices and flavour of meat and develop flavour in vegetables. Pressure cooking does not allow time for much development of flavour. It is important that seasoning should be sprinkled on to the prepared, washed and drained vegetables, etc. before they are placed in the cooker. As with other methods of cooking, it is advisable to make full use of the cooking liquid in which some flavour will be dissolved. Some flavours are easily volatilised during cooking and for this reason may be added towards the end of the cooking process, e.g. vanilla and almond essences.

To remove strong flavours
1. Salt or pickled meat or fish may be soaked in water and the liquor discarded.
2. Meat, e.g. rabbit, may be blanched both to whiten it and to remove strong flavours.
3. If food is too salty a little sugar will sometimes counteract this.

USE OF CULINARY HERBS AND SPICES

The use of herbs and spices dates back to biblical times – when they were very important as a source of wealth. Parts of tithes were paid for in herbs and spices.
  Herbs are usually the leafy part of plants.
  Spice is obtained from the root, stem, flower or seed of plants.
  Herbs and spices have no specific nutritive value, i.e. supply no appreciable quantity of protein, kilocalories or vitamins, etc. Their function in cooking is to excite the appetite by heightening flavours and so stimulate the gastric juices which will assist in digestion and assimilation of food. Their flavours are very strong, and they are therefore used only in very small quantities. The flavour is due to some essential oil or fixed oil or blend of both. The quality of flavours varies with the variety, maturity of the plant, climate, storage and method of preparation. The flavour deteriorates with storage, and freshly ground spices are always superior. They should be bought in small quantities. In the old days every large house had a herb garden and home-grown herbs were dried and stored. The use of herbs was a culinary art; old recipes reveal many ways of using them. Herbs and spices are also used for medicinal purposes, as antiseptics and germicides in soaps and dentifrices, and are often the basis of perfumes and liqueurs. Many herbs, e.g. parsley, mint, chives, thyme, dill, borage, rosemary, can be grown easily in this country and are both useful and ornamental. Use approximately half the quantity to dried herbs.

HERBS

  Angelica. Has been native to Britain since the sixteenth century. It is a member of the umbelliferae family. The thick hollow stems are crystallised and used in cake decorations, added to rhubarb jam and to liqueurs – green chartreuse.
  Balm. An old-fashioned herb with a hairy leaf. It has a pleasant lemon/mint flavour and is used in salads, iced drinks and cider, in perfumes and pot pourri.
  Basil and *sweet basil*. Have a sweet-scented, pungent, clove-like flavour. They should be used fresh very sparingly in salads, soups and sauces.

Bay leaf. Comes from a tree of the laurel family. The leaf is dark green and shiny. It is dried quickly to preserve the flavour. Bay leaf is used in soups, stews and custards. It is a component of bouquet garni.

Borage. Has characteristic greyish green leaves and stems covered with fine white prickly hairs. The flavour is similar to cucumber. It is used in iced drinks, claret and cider cups, pickles, salads and sauces.

Chervil. Another member of the umbelliferae family which has a large white flower similar to parsley, but is sweeter and more aromatic. The small green leaves are used in French cookery with fish, sauces, salads and soups.

Chives. A hardy perennial easily grown. They have a mild onion flavour but are more easily digested. They are chopped and added to salads or mixed with cheese in sandwiches, omelettes and scrambled egg.

Dill. Finely chopped dill leaves are used sparingly with fish and in salads, soups and stews. It has a bitter flavour similar to caraway. In America dill is used to give spiciness to cucumber. Dill water is used for digestive troubles.

Fennel. May be used to counteract the oiliness of rich fish, e.g. mackerel or salmon; it is sprinkled on to the fish or made into a sauce. Fennel was a popular Roman vegetable and is a constituent of gripe water.

Garlic. This is a plant of the onion family. Each bulb consists of several smaller bulbs called 'cloves'. The powerful acrid taste of garlic comes from the oil it contains. It should be used sparingly to flavour savoury dishes and salads. Quarter or half a clove is usually sufficient to flavour a soup or stew for four people. Often it is sufficient just to wipe round a salad bowl with a cut clove.

Marjoram. Has a pleasantly aromatic flavour. It may be added to 'mixed herbs'. It is used to flavour savoury dishes and the leaves are used in salads.

Mint. Probably introduced to this country by the Romans. It is made into mint sauce, mint jelly, etc. served with lamb. A sprig of mint is added during cooking to new potatoes and green peas. Freshly chopped mint adds flavour when sprinkled on green salads, potato salads, or used in the stuffing for lamb. It can be made into mint tea. In the north of England mint is sometimes used to flavour fruit pasties. There are many varieties of mint – apple mint, peppermint, eau de Cologne mint, etc.

Parsley. It is used in salads, soups, sauces and sandwiches and as a colourful garnish.

Rosemary. Introduced to this country by the Crusaders returning from the Holy Land. It is used in stuffings and in savoury dishes. The young leaves can be sprinkled over meat before roasting. It should be used sparingly as it has a strong flavour.

Sage. Has a strong flavour and is used sparingly in stuffing, especially for pork, duck or goose.

Tarragon. Grown for oil of tarragon used to flavour tarragon vinegar, which is made by steeping the fresh leaves in white wine vinegar. Tarragon vinegar is one of the components of French or Continental mustard, and is also a flavouring for tartare sauce.

Thyme. Easily dried and stored. It is used for stuffings. Lemon thyme is particularly valuable for stuffings and sauces to be eaten with veal, fish and chicken as it has better flavour and larger leaves.

Bouquet garni. A bunch of herbs used to give a savoury flavour to foods cooked in stock or water, e.g. stews. Bouquet garni consists of an assortment of herbs and spices – parsley, a sprig of thyme, half a bay leaf, a blade of mace, peppercorns and a clove. They are usually wrapped in muslin. They should be removed before the dish is served.

Fines herbes. Equal quantities of chopped fresh parsley, chervil, chives and tarragon, which may be sprinkled on salads, haricot beans or butter beans, or may be used in omelettes and scrambled eggs.

Mixed herbs. This is a prepared mixture of dried sage, parsley, thyme and marjoram, but other herbs may be included. They are used for savoury dishes, dumplings and stews.

Herbs used in salads. Basil, borage, chervil, chives, dill, fennel, garlic, marjoram, mint, parsley, sage, tarragon and thyme.

Herbs used with meat. Basil, bay leaf, chives, garlic, marjoram, mint, oregano, parsley, rosemary, sage, thyme.

Herbs used with fish. Bay leaf, chervil, dill, fennel, marjoram, parsley, thyme.

SPICES

This is a general term covering a wide variety of aromatic seasonings, used to flavour savoury and sweet dishes. Spices are sold both individually or in combination. They are always associated with the East, and are used to a greater extent in hot countries.

Allspice. This is also known as the pimento or Jamaican pepper. It is the berry of a small tree of the myrtle family, which grows in South America and the West Indies. The flavour is reminiscent of several spices, particularly cinnamon, cloves and nutmeg, hence its name. It is sold whole or ground. It can be used in stews, gravies, savoury dishes, puddings and preserves.

Caraway. These are the small, hard, black seeds of a small plant similar to parsley. They may be used whole or crushed, and are nowadays obtained chiefly from Holland. The seeds are used in confectionery, in bread, rolls and cakes, also combined with sugar to make sweets. In Austria they are used in salads, for sprinkling over potatoes and in stews. Caraway is an ingredient of Kümmel liqueur.

Celery seeds. These are used to flavour dishes when fresh celery is out of season. They are used in soups, stews, sauces and gravies. Celery vinegar is used for salad dressings.

Cinnamon. This is the dried inner bark of a small laurel-like tree growing in Sri Lanka. It is sold in scrolls, quills, or powdered. It is pleasantly aromatic and is used to flavour sweet dishes, cakes, biscuits, puddings, stews, sauces, chutneys, etc.

Cloves. These are the dried unopened flower buds of an evergreen tree which grows in hot, moist climates – Zanzibar, India, Malaya. They are rather like small nail heads in appearance. They contain an oil which has a strong, fragrant odour and a pungent taste. They are used whole for flavouring sweet and savoury dishes, the flavour blending well with apple. They may be ground for use in cakes and biscuits, in bread sauce and with ham.

Coriander. The seeds and leaves are used in curries and pickles, and with fish and meat.

Curry powder. Refer to page 222.

Ginger. This is the underground stem and root of a plant which grows in many tropical countries. Jamaica ginger has greater flavour. African ginger has greater heat and strength. It may be prepared as either black or white root ginger. Black ginger is the unscraped root, white ginger is scraped. The root is dried and crushed to make ground ginger, or boiled and crystallised in syrup. Ground ginger is used in cakes, biscuits, puddings, chutneys and savoury dishes. Root ginger is used in pickling and in some sweet and savoury dishes where it is removed before serving. Crystallised ginger, sliced or chopped, is used in cakes and puddings and fruit salads. Stem ginger is preserved in syrup. Its flavour is far from being so hot and pungent as that of root ginger, and it may be eaten alone as a sweetmeat or used in cakes, etc.

Mustard. This is made from the seeds of a very small plant which is grown on the Continent, but which can also be cultivated in this country. The Dutch variety is best. There are two types – yellow and brown mustard – and the seeds are crushed and mixed together to make table mustard. Mustard is used as a condiment, mixed with various liquids and perhaps other flavours. The seeds are used whole in pickles, chutneys, etc. and as an ingredient of pickling spice. Ground mustard is used in curries and chutney, and may be added to all savoury dishes. It complements the flavour of cheese and counteracts fattiness.

Nutmeg and mace. The nutmeg tree is a tropical evergreen, and the nutmeg used in cooking is the dried kernel of its fruit. The kernel is surrounded by a fibrous husk which is harvested and dried separately and is known as mace. Nutmeg is used in both sweet and savoury dishes, or grated over milk puddings, custards and junkets. Nutmeg is sold whole or ground. Mace is sold in chips or 'blades', or ground, and is used in both sweet and savoury dishes, and in pickles, sauces and fish savouries. Ground mace is a component of mixed spice.

Pepper. Peppercorns are the dried fruit of a vine which grows in the tropics. The fruit grows on spikes rather like blackcurrants. The berries change colour as they ripen from green to red and finally to yellow. The fruit is gathered when turning red and dried in the sun or by a fire until black, to make black pepper. To make white pepper the fruit is allowed to ripen until yellow, and after drying it is soaked and the skin removed. Another method is to soak the black peppers in a solution of hydrochloric acid and lime to bleach them. Pepper has the rare ability to complement the flavour of almost any food. It is widely used as a seasoning in all savoury dishes. Freshly ground pepper has a better flavour. Peppercorns are an ingredient in pickling spice. At one time pepper was the most valued commodity in the spice trade between the East and Europe.

Paprika. This is the dried fruit of a type of capsicum, or Hungarian red pepper. It is used to add colour, as a garnish in savoury dishes, in making goulash and other savoury stews and soups.

Chillies and cayenne. Chillies are the dried red pods of a type of capsicum grown in the tropics. Cayenne pepper is a bright red pepper which is ground from the chillies. Chillies and cayenne pepper are exceedingly hot and should be used very sparingly. Chillies are used in pickles and sauces. They are a constituent of pickling spice. Cayenne pepper is used in savoury dishes.

Pickling spice is a mixture of the following: whole spice, mace, cassia (cinnamon family), allspice, coriander, mustard, cloves, ginger, black pepper, chillies and cardamom seed.

Saffron. Obtained from the stigma of a type of crocus. It is expensive and is used in small quantities to flavour Cornish saffron cake. It imparts a rich golden colour to rice, served with chicken, fish or stew.

Turmeric. This is a yellow powder ground from the tubers of an East Indian plant. It is used to colour custard powders, curry and piccalilli.

Spices used in sweet dishes. Allspice, caraway, cinnamon, cloves, coriander, ginger, nutmeg, turmeric.

Spices used in savoury dishes. Allspice, celery seeds, cloves, coriander, cumin, mustard, mace, peppercorns, paprika, cayenne and turmeric.

FLAVOURING ESSENCES

Essences were originally solutions of essential oils or other flavouring ingredients in alcohol, but nowadays are often synthetic substances produced much more cheaply, and while they resemble the natural flavouring fairly closely, they lack the true flavour of the natural food. Essences, whether natural or synthetic, will enhance the flavour of foods to which they are added and will help to give variety in the diet. Essences should be used sparingly and because they volatilise easily should be added towards the end of the main cooking.

Almond essence is obtained from almond oil by distillation and used to flavour biscuits, cakes, puddings and sweets. Synthetic almond essence is made from benzaldehyde.

Fruit essences are usually synthetic as it is difficult to prepare them from the pulp and rind of fresh fruit. The most common are lemon, orange, pineapple and raspberry.

Vanilla is a climbing plant of the orchid family grown in tropical countries. The flavour is obtained from the fermented seed pods which turn brown and become covered with crystals of vanillin. Vanilla pods may be used whole, e.g. a vanilla pod may be kept in the sugar jar and will flavour the sugar, or a pod may be infused in the milk for milk puddings and removed when the desired flavour is achieved. Vanilla essence is more commonly used. It is made by soaking the pods in alcohol or spirit of wine to extract the flavour and colour the resulting liquid brown. Synthetic vanilla essence is made from oil of cloves and has a much inferior flavour. Good-quality vanilla essence is convenient to use in cakes, puddings and icings often in conjunction with almond essence.

Other essences – peppermint, rum, anchovy.

Meat extract, e.g. Bovril.

Vegetable extract, e.g. Marmite.

Colourings are frequently added to foods to improve their appearance, e.g. turmeric is added to custard powder to imitate the colour of egg, to make it resemble an egg custard. Colourings are added to icings and sweets. A wide range of colours is available in liquid or powder form. The early red colours were from cochineal, the crushed bodies of insects. Nowadays most colours are synthetic.

Monosodium glutamate

Monosodium glutamate is a natural product derived from the glutamic acid of vegetable proteins. Although not in itself a seasoning, because it adds no flavour, it helps to bring out the flavour of the food to which it is added. Savoury foods, meat, fish and vegetables, contain small amounts of glutamic acid which help to enhance their flavour. Glutamic acid is a non-essential amino-acid. Monosodium glutamate is a natural sodium salt of the acid in the form of white crystals.

Uses of monosodium glutamate

1. Convenience foods, e.g. packet soups, frozen foods, where it is useful as it is not affected by high or low processing temperatures.

2. In canned vegetables it helps to retain the original 'fresh flavour' which may be lost as the glutamic acid content decreases after picking.

3. It is useful in a low-salt diet where foods might otherwise be insipid.

4. It can be added to re-heated dishes, rubbed in to the cheaper cuts of meat before cooking, used in some soups, gravies, cheese and salads.

Addition of monosodium glutamate

It is advisable to follow the manufacturer's instructions with regard to the amount and method of incorporating monosodium glutamate, but it can be added during the preparing, cooking, or before serving the food – according to taste.

Note: Monosodium glutamate does not enhance the flavour of all foods, particularly those foods which are rich in acids, e.g. pickles, fruit and sweet or fatty foods. Foods which contain a good supply of natural salts, e.g. milk, are not usually improved in flavour by the addition of monosodium glutamate.

CURRY

The word curry is derived from a Tamal word, *kari*, meaning sauce. Although curry is mainly associated with India, it is eaten in many areas of the East as traditional food, and is popular all over the world. Curry powder consists of a number of blended spices which vary according to taste in particular regions. Traditionally the chosen spices are ground together just before the dish is cooked. Prepared curry powder or paste can be obtained in various mixes and strengths.

Meat, fish, shell-fish, eggs and vegetables are used to make various types of curry.

Accompaniments

Rice, shredded coconut, chutneys, cucumber, tomatoes, sliced banana, poppadums, chappatti.

To boil rice for curry. (Refer to page 98.)

Gelatine was originally used in savoury dishes only. It is found naturally in foodstuffs used in savoury dishes. The collagen of meat yields gelatine on cooking with moisture. Most collagen is found where there is most muscular tissue: head, feet, legs and tail – calves' feet, pigs' feet, ox tail, veal, shin beef.

Commercial gelatine. This is obtained from the tendons and connective tissue – bones, horns, hooves, etc. The resulting gelatine is purified, the moisture is evaporated. It is powdered and then granulated and sometimes sheet or leaf gelatine is produced. Size is an early stage in gelatine production. Acid is used in purifying gelatine.

TYPES OF GELATINE

Powdered or granulated. Dissolves very quickly. The final result is improved if allowed to soak in water for a few minutes.

Sheet or leaf gelatine. Is more difficult to measure accurately. It has to soak longer.

Isinglass. Prepared from the swimming bladder of the sturgeon. It is the purest form of gelatine, but is expensive.

Note: *Agar Agar* is a setting agent obtained from seaweed. It is suitable for use in vegetarian cookery because it is not obtained from gelatine or other animal products but can be used to achieve similar results. (See page 37.)

NUTRITIVE VALUE OF GELATINE

Gelatine is of low biological value, even though it is an animal protein, but it can act as a supplement to other proteins. Although the nutritive value of gelatine itself is low, it helps to make appetising dishes of nourishing foods – milk, eggs, fruit juices, meat, etc.

Savoury. Moulds of meat or fish, e.g. brawn, jellied stocks for pies. Glazes. Aspic jellies.

Sweet. Diabetic jams. Stiffening agent for jellies and creams, soufflés. Glaze for flans. Sweets, e.g. Turkish delight.

IMPORTANT POINTS IN THE USE OF GELATINE

1. Use a good quality. To use cheap gelatine is false economy – this will result in a poor set and a poor flavour.

2. Measure the quantity accurately – excess gives a poor flavour – 10 g to 500 ml for most recipes.

3. Dissolve separately from the rest of the ingredients in a little water over hot water. The acid used in purification may curdle milk or cream. A jelly or cream, etc. will set more quickly if most of the liquid used is cold.

4. Allow to soak in a warm place before use – this will ensure that the gelatine is dissolved and reduce the time of setting.

5. Do not prolong heating the gelatine – the water will evaporate and the gelatine become thick and will not mix easily with the other ingredients.

6. If gelatine is added quickly to a cold mixture it will set in globules and give a ropy result. It is best to pour the gelatine from a height in a thin stream and stir in well. In cold weather it may be advisable to warm the mixture slightly before adding the gelatine.

7. Allow sufficient time for the mixture to set. Avoid leaving the dishes made with gelatine in the refrigerator or freezer for long periods or the gelatine may go hard and tough.

8. If a jelly contains any ingredient likely to settle out, e.g. milk jelly or fruit in jelly, it should be moulded when on the point of setting.

GELATINE DISHES

Uncleared jellies. Made with milk, eggs, fruit purée or flavoured water. Use 10–12 g gelatine to 500 ml milk according to the thickness of the foundation liquid.

Cleared jellies. Savoury or sweet; made by heating gently and whisking the liquid, flavouring and gelatine (10 g to 500 ml) with egg-shells and whites usually in the proportion of 2 crushed shells and whites to 750 ml liquid. The egg-shell filters the jelly and the egg white collects the impurities as it rises to the surface in a froth after whisking. The jelly is heated to almost boiling point, allowed to stand 5 minutes and then strained. The impurities are removed and the resultant liquid is clear.

Aspic jelly. A transparent, savoury, cleared jelly made from well-flavoured meat or chicken and vegetable stock stiffened with gelatine and cleared by egg shells and whites as above. It is used to make moulds of meat, fish, eggs and vegetables. Commercial preparations of aspic jelly may be obtained.

Sweet cleared jellies. Fruit juices or wines may be used to flavour a sweet jelly which may be served alone or with fruit set in it.

Creams. Sweets stiffened with gelatine and served in individual dishes or moulds. The richness of the dish depends on the ingredients used, e.g. cream, evaporated milk (boiled in the can for 20 minutes and chilled overnight), custard, fruit purées, egg whites, flavouring and gelatine, 10–12 g to 500 ml, depending on the thickness of the liquid used. There is a wide variety of creams ranging from the simple fruit cream to the elaborate cream, e.g. Charlotte Russe.

Frozen dishes. The use of gelatine when making ice-cream will help to prevent coarse crystals forming and will help to stabilise the mixture.

30. KITCHEN PLANNING

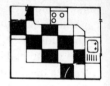

HISTORY

Throughout the centuries the kitchen has been the heart and soul of the household and a centre of social life. In the first primitive homes, one room with a central hearth served the whole family for every purpose. In castles and manor houses the kitchen was the meeting place for all household servants. In rural areas the kitchen has always stood first in size and importance. In many cottages it covered practically the whole of the ground floor and in farmhouses the large kitchen was the hub of numerous activities of employers and servants. These kitchens were usually dominated by a fireplace which had cooking and heating utensils ranged round it. This fireplace was often very large and made in the shape of an inglenook in which several people could sit in warmth and comfort and shelter from the cold and dampness.

During the eighteenth and nineteenth centuries, the kitchen became degraded and was situated in any dark corner of the house, as employers usually took little interest in domestic life and servants were cheap and plentiful. This influence had an effect on the type of smaller house built in the late nineteenth century and early twentieth. Kitchens were so small that it was often impossible to fit in some of the essential furniture.

Architects are now paying more attention to the position, size and decoration of kitchens. Equipment has been developed to save labour and time. Many people have full-time jobs and need facilities which will enable them to produce meals for members of a household and for guests as efficiently as possible in surroundings which are pleasant to work in. The dining area may be part of the kitchen or an extension to the kitchen. We appear to be returning to the concept of a kitchen as the centre of household activities.

KITCHEN PLANNING

When a house is built, the position of the kitchen should be planned in relation to the rest of the house to save time and unnecessary work. A kitchen should be sunny or it would be cheerless to work in, but if it faces directly south it might be too hot to work in comfortably. It should be near to a dining-room, with a through hatch if possible.

A kitchen is usually closed off from the rest of the house to avoid cooking odours but extractor fans are available which should remove smells and steam. With developments in kitchen planning, fitments and decoration, a kitchen can be most attractive and one of the 'show places' of a house. The size and type of kitchen depends upon the circumstances of the household. In too small a kitchen it is difficult to fit in all the necessary equipment, but too large a kitchen may be inefficient, waste time and be tiring to work in. A kitchen need not be situated at the back of the house. It may be positioned at the front so that the person working can see what is happening outside and the view over a back garden is seen from a living room.

There are various types of kitchen, e.g. a) a working kitchen, b) a working kitchen with room for dining, c) a kitchen-living room, etc.

Ventilation

It is important that ventilation is adequate because of cooking odours, steam and heat. Cross-ventilation is desirable. Windows must be large enough, but may need venetian blinds for sunny days. An extractor fan will help to remove cooking smells, and may be fitted to a window or an outside wall. A canopy or cooker hood may be fixed over the cooker which will lead odours and steam outside or will absorb them in charcoal.

Lighting and electric points

It is most important to plan lighting and power points to try to ensure safe, efficient and comfortable working in a kitchen. There should be the best possible natural and artificial light which will not cast a shadow on working surfaces and which will provide light for the selection of stores and equipment from cupboards. Fluorescent lighting has advantages in that it does not cast shadows as readily as tungsten lighting because of the length of the tube. (It is necessary to have the tube parallel to the main working surface.) This type of lighting is economical in running cost and in the life of the tube. However, some people consider that the light given is cold and unflattering and that the designs of the fitments are unattractive. They prefer to use tungsten lighting positioned at the various working areas of the kitchen. Whatever lighting system is adopted, it must be considered carefully. It should be noted that the choice of decoration affects the light in any room. Light coloured, glossy surfaces will reflect light while dark matt surfaces will absorb light. Sufficient power points at a convenient height must be provided according to the amount of electrical equipment used. Changing over plugs is inconvenient and could be dangerous. Trailing flexes are *most* dangerous.

Heating

A certain amount of heat will come from a cooker, depending on its use and degree of insulation, but a kitchen can be cold in winter, especially in the morning. Heating may be part of the central heating system which will be timed to supply heat at times most convenient for the household. If individual heating is used in the various rooms of a house, a heater which will supply heat immediately may be the most satisfactory arrangement for the kitchen but preferably it should be fitted to a wall or ceiling for safety.

Decoration

Obviously this will depend on individual taste. In the past, colour schemes for kitchens tended to be in cool, light colours which were considered to be restful to work in and which would show up any dirt. Blue is thought to be a good colour for kitchens because it is supposed to repel flies. Now there is such a variety of colours and patterns in kitchen fitments, large and small equipment, wall coverings and floor coverings, that choice may be difficult. There are a number of books and brochures available. It is advisable to have basic colours in fitments and large equipment and to ring the changes in wallpaper, paint and small equipment.

Surfaces

Walls should withstand moisture, condensation and grease, and should be easy to clean. Tiling satisfies all these conditions but is expensive and the choice of colour and pattern needs careful consideration. Many types of paints are available but a matt finish is preferable to a gloss finish to reduce condensation. Vinyl coated wallpapers are attractive and easily washed.

Floor. The surface finish may depend upon the sub-floor, if this is of wood or concrete. Clay tiles are hard wearing but may be cold and tiring to work on. Rubber is not recommended for kitchen floors as it might be damaged by spillages and could be slippery. There is a wide variety of plastic floor coverings in an assortment of colours and patterns. Some types have a layer of plastic foam sandwiched between a top layer of vinyl and a backing material to make them comfortable and warm. There may be a layer of clear vinyl on top of the pattern to protect it and remove the need for polishing. Care is needed to avoid damage to vinyl flooring by the movement of heavy equipment. Clay tiles could be laid under fitments and heavy equipment and a more resilient vinyl flooring provided for the traffic areas.

Working surfaces

The surface should be impervious to grease and to acids and alkalis found in food and household materials. However, plastic will scratch, cut or chip and one should never chop or cut on a plastic surface but use a wooden chopping board. If wood is used for working surfaces, it is necessary to use a hard wood such as teak which will not soften when wet. Most surfaces are damaged by heat from pans taken directly off a cooker hob or by dishes taken from an oven. It is necessary to provide an area of material such as stainless steel which is resistant to intense heat or to use a pan stand. A working surface should be continuous, if possible, so that there are no cracks to hold dirt. The average height of a working surface is about 800–900 mm but this depends upon personal choice and the work being done. The correct height is one which is comfortable for the task being carried out.

The placing of equipment

If planning a kitchen in a new house, or replanning a kitchen, consider the placing of fitments and equipment to make the most efficient working arrangement. Try to place a preparation surface between the cooker and the sink. Storage for food and equipment should be at the most convenient place for use. Store cleaning materials and equipment separately from food. Use high and low storage areas for equipment and materials which are used infrequently. It may be necessary to place some large pieces of equipment outside the kitchen. Freezers may be placed in a garage, outhouse or utility room. Laundry equipment may be positioned in a utility room. Some authorities recommend that the laundering of clothes should never take place in a kitchen because of the danger of bacteria from soiled clothing being transmitted to food or crockery.

Common faults in kitchens

Too small a kitchen for the size of the household.
   Badly sited in relation to the other rooms, especially the dining-room.
   Sinks and other equipment in a bad light. General lighting bad.
   Insufficient working surfaces or surfaces at the wrong height.
   Poor ventilation, resulting in a stuffy atmosphere.
   Poor storage facilities. Shelves too high and too deep, wasting space and time.
   Little or no storage for perishable foods.
   Slippery floors which could cause serious accidents.
   Condensation on walls.
   Equipment wrongly placed for efficient working.
   Narrow cracks between equipment which harbour crumbs and dirt and cannot be cleaned easily.
   Steps up or down to the hall or dining-room so that wheeling trolleys or carrying trays is difficult.

CHOICE OF LARGE EQUIPMENT
Cupboards

The cupboard space needed depends upon the size of the household and the amount of materials and equipment to be stored. The placing and size of cupboards depends upon the dimensions of the kitchen. Different sized shelves and drawers are needed for the storage of various materials and equipment. Try to store as much as possible under cover to avoid grease, etc. Plan to avoid wasted space. Storage is needed for dry and perishable goods, cooking utensils, crockery, laundry equipment and cleaning equipment. Cleaning equipment must be stored separately from food and cooking utensils.

Sinks

Sinks may be made from fireclay, stainless steel, fibreglass, nylon and stoved enamel. If possible provide two sinks which will prove useful in the preparation of meals and in clearing up. Sinks and draining boards which are made in one piece do not have crevices which could harbour dirt and moisture. Waste disposal facilities should be provided. These may range from a fitted waste disposal unit to a container for waste matter. As for all working surfaces in a kitchen, the height of a sink must be related to the person using it and there should be good natural and artificial light.

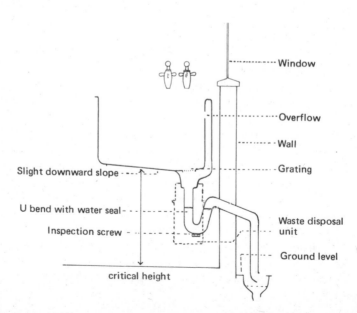

Care of the sink
1. Do not allow bits of food, tea leaves, etc. to go down the drain.
2. Always flush the sink after use with hot and then cold water.
3. To dissolve grease use synthetic detergents or soda crystals and boiling water. Clean with a solution of detergent. If necessary use a paste or liquid abrasive. (Care is needed to avoid scratching stainless steel.)

Clearing a blocked sink
1. Pour boiling water down.
2. Poke with soft wire.
3. Suction – using dishcloth or forcing cup.
4. Place a bucket under the inspection screw and undo and examine.
5. Send for plumber.
Try the above remedies in that order. The blockage may be caused by tea leaves or bit of food, shreds of dishcloths, etc. and/or grease. Always try to avoid these. Always give a final rinse of cold water to make sure the seal is full of fresh water.

Waste disposal units are a hygienic and effective way of disposing of kitchen waste. The unit can be fitted under a sink, connected to the sink outlet and the waste pipe, and it works by grinding up waste into small particles which are washed away down the drain. These units are particularly useful in high rise flats, etc.

COOKERS

It is usually a personal decision as to which type of fuel is used for cooking and which model of cooker is chosen but the decision may depend upon the fuel available in the area. There is a wide variety of cookers available and each model offers certain advantages. Split level cookers are becoming increasingly popular. The hob and the oven can be built into kitchen units at convenient working positions and it is possible to use a combination of fuels, e.g. gas-fired hot plate and electric oven. New designs and new materials developed for cookers assist efficiency in use and cleaning. The local Electricity or Gas Showrooms will offer advice on the choice, use and maintenance of a cooker. Other organisations will assist in the case of solid fuel appliances. The use of electronics is resulting in further developments, e.g. a 'listening/talking' cooker.

Points to consider when choosing a cooker
  Number of people to be catered for.
  Quantity and type of cooking to be done.
  Space available.
  Price that can be afforded.

Is the cooker:

      easy to control and regulate?

      quick to heat and efficient to use?

      easy to clean?

      a convenient height for the user?

  Does the cooker have any particular features which are required, such as large hob, high level grill, double oven, spit-roaster or automatic controls?

Oven temperatures

The table shows the gas marks, electric oven temperatures and equivalent Celsius temperatures. It can be seen that the Celsius cooking temperatures are roughly one half of the Fahrenheit.

Gas Mark	Electrical Scale	Celsius Scale	Heat of Oven
Below thermostat setting	200°F	100°C	Very cool
¼	225°F	110°C	Very cool
½	250°F	120°C	Very cool
1	275°F	140°C	Cool
2	300°F	150°C	Cool
3	325°F	160°C	Warm
4	350°F	180°C	Moderate
5	375°F	190°C	Fairly hot
6	400°F	200°C	Fairly hot
7	425°F	220°C	Hot
8	450°F	230°C	Very hot
9	475°F	240°C	Very hot

Solid fuel cookers

Solid fuel can provide a cheap form of heat for cooking and water heating. Solid fuel cookers are less easy to regulate and slower to respond to regulation than gas or electricity, but with experience they are very satisfactory in use. The oven is usually placed on one side of the firebox, and may be heated by hot gases from the fire which circulate through cavities or flues round the oven. The rate at which the gases flow is controlled by dampers. Heat storage cookers store heat in metal around the fire unit, and this is transferred to hot plates as these are used and to ovens by the operation of thermostats. Hot plates are capable of storing a considerable amount of heat. Like the oven, these are well insulated and are covered when not in use. There are usually two plates, one hot and one for simmering. There is a roasting or baking oven and a slow cooking oven which are easily controlled. Solid fuel cookers are easy to clean. Some may also heat water and could provide some central heating. They are always ready for use if stoked correctly. But some types are difficult to regulate, need regular stoking with the fuel recommended for the particular stove, and the soot deposited in the flues must be removed weekly as it is a bad conductor of heat. Economical, efficient working of solid fuel cookers depends on the type of stove and on the degree of insulation. Fuel consumption will depend on the amount of use the cooker has and how efficiently it is operated. Pans used should have flat, smooth, thick bases which will come in contact with the solid plate and utilise conducted heat.

Electric cookers

Electricity enables heat to be produced without combustion. It is therefore a clean fuel producing no fumes or soot. The heat is easily controlled and in most cookers an automatic timing device can turn the oven on at a pre-set temperature at any pre-selected time during the day, and turn the current off at a pre-set time when the food will be cooked. This is particularly valuable for people who are out at work during the day. They can prepare a meal, leave it in the pre-set oven and return to find a cooked meal ready for them. If they return later than expected the food should not be spoiled, as the heat will have been turned off. Electric oven temperatures are controlled thermostatically.

Ovens may have fan circulation which provides even heat for even cooking throughout the oven. Dishes can be positioned anywhere in the oven. It is possible to use four loaded shelves at the same time, so giving economy in use. It is claimed that meat shrinkage is reduced. Because the sides of the oven do not get so hot, there is less risk of burning and so cleaning is easier.

Cooker hobs
Radiant rings. The heating element comprises a flat grid or tubular sheathed elements. Heat is transferred by radiation and conduction and the ring is quick to heat up. There may be dual control to enable the whole or the centre of the ring to be used. The hob cover usually hinges up for cleaning and there is a spillage tray.
Solid hot plates. Heat by conduction, and care is needed in the choice of pans (see page 247). The hot plates do not lose heat quickly and this residual heat should be used in cooking. Care is needed when cleaning. There is usually a dimple in the centre to prevent distortion.
Ceramic hob. Consists of a smooth ceramic cooking surface which transfers heat from elements situated underneath. Each 'ring', which may provide large or small heating areas, is controlled separately. Ceramic hobs are tough and non-porous. Cleaning is not difficult provided that instructions are followed. Choice of pans is as for solid hot plates.

Hobs may incorporate simmer controls or sensing devices to maintain a given temperature.

Grills
Position varies according to cooker design. May be a separate unit, or may be positioned in a small oven or the main oven. This could cause problems if the grill is needed when the oven is in use. Some grills have controls to enable the whole or part of the grill to be used.

Safety
Most electric cooker control knobs are placed out of reach of small children. Always turn off the main cooker control switch before cleaning.

Ovens may have stay-clean linings. Self-cleaning ovens are available which heat to 480°C, reducing dirt and grease to smoke which is passed through an eliminator. Only a small amount of ash remains.

It is important to use the correct type of pans on' electric plates for the most efficient working. Pans should have flat, smooth bases which will make contact with the plates, heat up quickly and not waste heat.

Microwave cookers
Microwave cookers cook food by electronic energy. An electronic device called a magnetron generates microwaves which are invisible short electro-magnetic waves. The waves form an energy pattern by bouncing off the metal lining of the microwave oven. In the roof there may be a paddle or stirrer to help distribute the microwaves so that they enter the food evenly from all angles. Some cookers have a turntable to achieve this action.

Microwaves are attracted to moisture in food. As the microwaves are absorbed, they cause the molecules to vibrate so generating heat to cook the food. Microwaves penetrate the food to a depth of 4–5 cms and heat is then passed on by conduction. Foods with a high moisture content or a porous texture will cook through more quickly. In bulky food such as joints of meat or whole fowl, the heat generated in the outer layers is passed to the centre more slowly. When the outside is cooked the food is taken from the oven and given 'standing time' according to the type of food to allow the heat to penetrate and cook the centre.

Containers must allow microwaves to pass through to the food. China, plastic, paper and glass – heat resistant or ceramic – are all suitable. Metal, including aluminium foil, is not suitable as it reflects the microwaves. Frying cannot be carried out in a microwave oven because of the danger of overheating the fat. Food may be cooked straight from the freezer. Basic cookers have an 'on/off' switch, a 'cook' or 'start' control and a timer. Browning steak, sausages, etc. is not possible in a basic oven. A browning skillet is available which is pre-heated to attract microwaves to a specially prepared base. When food is placed on the hot base it will sear and brown. More elaborate models have defrost controls or variable power controls, automatic programmes, temperature probes, and built-in browners or grills which will brown foods before or after cooking.

Cleaning. The oven cavity, door and seals should be cleaned according to the instructions provided.

Safety. The cooker cannot operate with the doors open. There are stringent tests for leakage and microwaves. The cooker will remain cool inside and out during cooking, and the containers only heat where the food is in contact with them. Cookers should be serviced at regular intervals according to manufacturer's instructions.

Gas cookers

Cooking by gas is quick and efficient. The size of the flame can be quickly and easily regulated. Ovens are automatically controlled by means of a thermostat which regulates the flow of gas and maintains the required temperature.

In most gas ovens there are three zones of heat. The thermostat setting refers to the middle of the oven – it is warmer above and cooler below. Thus dishes requiring different thermostatic settings can be cooked together in the oven at the same time. Some new ovens have more efficient heat circulation which gives even heat throughout the oven. Gas ovens heat up very quickly and so it may not be necessary to pre-heat the oven before cooking. All modern gas cookers have automatic, or semi-automatic, ignition for all burners. Automatic ignition means that the gas will light as soon as the tap is turned on. With semi-automatic ignition the burner lights up if a push-button is pressed at the same time as the control tap is turned.

Grills can be at waist height or high level, or can be obtained as separate units and mounted at any height. As no bending is required, high level grills can be easier to use and clean but care should be taken when lifting a loaded grill pan and inspecting contents cooking at 'eye level'. Gas cookers are available with automatic cooking controls. The controls incorporate a clock and a minute timer and can be pre-set to turn the oven burners on and off automatically to maintain the required temperature. Adjustments can be made at any time and it is possible both to finish off cooking a dish manually, although it has been started automatically, or to start the cooking manually and set the oven to turn off automatically.

Pan supports, whether individual or paired, are light and easily removed for cleaning. Some new gas cookers are fitted with special oven linings that help to clean themselves. Fat splashes on the lining are spread over the special porous matt finish of the oven. The fat is absorbed into the surface and slowly oxidised by the air, helped by the heat during cooking. Abrasive scourers and chemical cleaners must not be used on special oven linings.

Safety

Care should be taken that gas cookers are not placed too near a window if possible as burners on a low setting could blow out if there is a draught or breeze from an open window, though this is not common. A recent safety development is the incorporation of a re-ignition device in some cooker ignition systems. If the burner flame accidentally goes out the spark ignition will automatically come into operation and re-ignite the burner.

Flame failure devices are also fitted to gas ovens to prevent gas escaping if the main flame goes out. If the pilot light goes out the main supply of gas to the burner is cut off. Only when the pilot has been re-lit can gas flow through to the main burner again.

Many gas cooker taps must be pressed in before they can be turned on so that it is almost impossible to knock them on accidentally.

Natural gas is non-poisonous. It is given the characteristic smell of manufactured gas so that leaks can be detected.

A gas thermostat

The thermostat is a simple device for controlling the temperature in refrigerators and some water heaters as well as cooker ovens. There are two types of thermostat, the *rod* thermostat and the *liquid* thermostat.

Rod thermostats are used in water heaters and some cooker ovens. The action of the rod thermostat depends on the fact that some metals expand more than others when heated. In the diagram the brass tube B encloses rod A made of special steel, which is attached to valve C. The valve regulates the flow of gas to the burner. Rod thermostats in cookers are used in conjunction with a numbered thermostat dial which regulates the amount that valve C can close, so that sufficient gas is allowed through to maintain the oven at the desired temperature.

When the gas is burning the brass tube becomes heated and expands, carrying with it the inner steel rod A, which expands very little. This brings the valve head C closer to its seating, thus reducing the flow of gas to the burner. If the air in the oven cools down, the brass tube also cools, contracts a little and moves the valve C

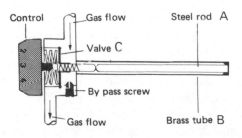

A rod thermostat

slightly away from its seating, so allowing more gas to pass to the burner until the set temperature is reached again. The by-pass allows sufficient gas through at all times to keep the burner alight. In cookers rod thermostats are always placed with the head immediately above the oven door and the rod lying directly under the oven roof.

METERS

The number of units of electricity consumed and the volume of gas used are both registered by meters which give readings on which the suppliers' bills are based.

To read a gas meter

There are two types of gas meter – the dial type and the more recent cyclometer or direct reading index type. Both types measure gas in cubic feet.

Dial type. Only read the lower four dials numbered 1–4 (the top two dials are for test purposes). Write down the readings in the order they appear. Where the hand stands between two figure, write down the lower one. However, if the hand stands between 0 and 9, write down 9.

Cyclometer type. The actual figures are all in a line. Read only the first four figures.

To calculate the amount of gas used in hundreds of cubic feet since the last reading deduct the figures for the previous reading, which are shown on the gas bill, from the new reading. E.g. the dials on the meter show *3,072*. If the previous reading had been *3,044* the difference would be *28* hundred cubic feet.

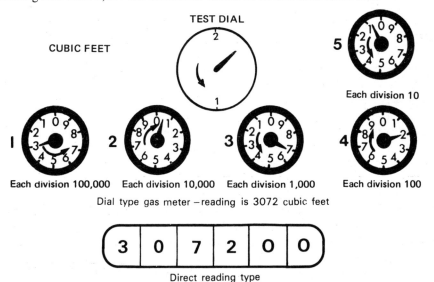

Dial type gas meter – reading is 3072 cubic feet

Direct reading type

Gas bills

Gas is always measured in cubic feet, but charged for in therms as the bill is calculated on the amount of heat which that gas supplies. A therm is 100,000 British Thermal Units (B.T.U.). To change cubic feet into therms it is necessary to know the calorific value, or heating power of the gas. This is shown on the gas bill, but is usually between 1,000 and 1,035 British thermal units per cubic foot of natural gas.

On the bill the gas supplied is shown in hundreds of cubic feet, each supplying 1,000 B.T.U.

$$\frac{Calorific\ value \times hundreds\ of\ cubic\ feet}{1,000} = therms$$

Therefore, if the meter reading shows that 28 hundred cubic feet of gas has been consumed, with a calorific value of 1,000, the number of therms consumed is:

$$\frac{1,000 \times 28}{1,000} = 28\ therms$$

To find the total cost of the gas, multiply the number of therms used by the charge per therm. In addition, a quarterly standing charge is usually payable. This, like the charge per therm depends upon the local tariff and upon the amount of gas used. Details are available at local Gas Showrooms.

To read an electric meter

There are two types of meter – the dial type and the more recent cyclometer type. Both types register ten thousands, thousands, hundreds, tens and single units. A unit or kilowatt hour is 1,000 watts. Any appliance, e.g. an electric fire, rated at 1,000 watts can be used continuously for 1 hour for 1 unit. A lamp marked 100 watts will burn for 10 hours for 1 unit.

Dial type. Read the dials from left to right. If the pointer is between two figures, write down the lower figure, except when the pointer is between 0 and 9 – in that case, write down 9. If the pointer is directly on a figure, e.g. 7, write down the next lower figure, i.e. 6, unless the pointer on the next dial has just passed 0 – in that case put down the figure that the pointer is actually on. The meter shown here reads *14,960* kilowatt hours or units. If when it is next read it shows *14,975* it means that *15* units have been used between two readings.

Cyclometer type. This type is read straight along.

When calculating approximate running costs consideration should be given to appliances that are thermostatically controlled since they will not be using electricity continuously. For example, an iron which is rated at 1,000 watts and has a thermostat can in fact be used for about 2 hours for 1 unit of electricity.

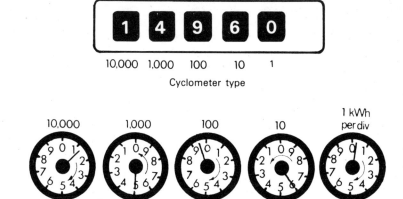

Cyclometer type

Dial type electricity meter — reading is 14960 units

Tariffs

Tariffs vary from one local Electricity Board to another so must be checked according to the area. There are various tariffs available, such as 'Off-Peak' tariff for storage space heating and water heating during night hours, or 'Day/Night' tariff which means all electricity can be paid for at two rates; day, and a much cheaper night rate. Local Electricity Boards will supply details of all tariffs.

DISHWASHERS

A dishwasher now forms part of the basic large equipment in a number of kitchens especially in large households. Apart from the obvious advantage of freeing a person from the time-consuming task of washing up dishes, cutlery, glasses and saucepans, the dishwasher is a hygienic method of washing up as the water is heated to 65°C which is much hotter than hands can bear. The crockery and cutlery, etc. are stacked in the machine according to the directions. When the door is closed and the machine is switched on, hot water and detergent are sprayed on to the contents. There are usually at least two rinses in clear water before the contents are dried by hot air. It is important to follow the instructions for use carefully and to use the detergent recommended by the manufacturer. Machines are loaded either from the front or from the top and can usually be left to complete the programme of washing, rinsing and drying once they have been turned on. The capacity is generally measured by the number of place settings the machine will take at one time and can vary from 4 to 12 place settings.

As with a washing machine a choice of washing programmes is usually available, e.g. a gentle programme is recommended for glasses if washed alone.

REFRIGERATION

Refrigeration is a form of preservation: keeping food at a temperature at which food bacteria cannot multiply easily – approximately 4°C.

Frozen food storage compartments

In 1964 a British standard for frozen food storage compartments in new refrigerators was introduced. Until that time most refrigerators had an ice-making compartment, which was only cold enough to make ice cubes and store frozen food for up to one day. The new standard took the form of 'star marking'. The number of stars marked on the frozen food storage compartment indicates the storage temperature in the frozen food compartment and consequently the storage time of frozen food in the compartment.

✳	−6°C	up to 1 week
✳ ✳	−12°C	up to 1 month
✳ ✳ ✳	−18°C	up to 3 months

This star marking is also shown on bought frozen food packaging, with an indication of appropriate storage times.

Home freezers – see chapter 21.

Advantages of refrigeration

Safe storage for food whatever the weather. Less risk of food poisoning in susceptible foods – milk, meat, fish, etc.

Easier shopping, can buy in bulk. Can buy at mid-week when foods are cheaper.

Less waste of food – left-overs can be stored safely.

Can be used as a cold cooker for cold sweets, etc.

Choice. Governed by various factors.

Size of family – approximately at least 1 cubic foot (28.3 litres) for each member of the household should be allowed.

If shops are near and time available for shopping.

Amount of entertaining done.

Space available for fitting the refrigerator, need for table top?

Money available.

Supply of fuel available – electricity, gas or oil.

Look for

Good finish to interior and exterior.

Easy-to-clean finish.

Well-fitting shelves.

Automatic defrosting.

Well-fitting, easily opened doors.

Size of freezing compartment and its star rating.

Easily adjustable thermostatic control.

Good use of storage space, back of door storage, etc.

Principles of use

Refrigeration is based on the principle that when a liquid evaporates it takes heat from its surroundings. So a liquid is made to evaporate near the refrigerator storage chamber and take heat from it, thus cooling it.

Note: It is essential to have a refrigerator well insulated and to keep the door closed as much as possible to prevent warm air from the kitchen entering.

Absorption type (See diagram)

Absorption units generally use a mixture of ammonia and water as the refrigerant. The liquid ammonia evaporates in a series of tubes set in sheet metal which form the frozen food storage compartment. The heat needed for this change of state comes from food placed inside the refrigerator and from the air inside the refrigerator chamber.

Boiler B containing ammonia solution is heated by a small gas flame (or electricity or oil). Hot ammonia gas is given off which passes upwards to condenser C. Here cooling takes place and heat is lost to the outside air. Because of the pressure inside the system and the drop in temperature, ammonia gas condenses into a liquid. Liquid trickles to the frozen food storage compartment F inside the refrigerator, where it evaporates forming ammonia gas and taking heat from the refrigerator interior. This process is assisted by the presence of hydrogen gas which ensures that the total pressure is the same throughout the system. Thus the pressure of ammonia gas in F is kept low. Because of this, liquid continues to evaporate. The gases pass immediately into the absorption chamber – absorber A – where the ammonia gas readily dissolves in the dilute solution which has been driven over from the boiler. A concentrated ammonia solution is less dense than a dilute one, so after absorption of the gas the concentrated solution passes back to the top of the boiler for re-heating. Hydrogen gas being insoluble in water returns to the evaporator.

This type is completely silent. No moving parts, so less wear and no interference to television, etc. Thermostatic control, but the range of temperatures is less than in the compression type. Running cost is slightly higher than compression type.

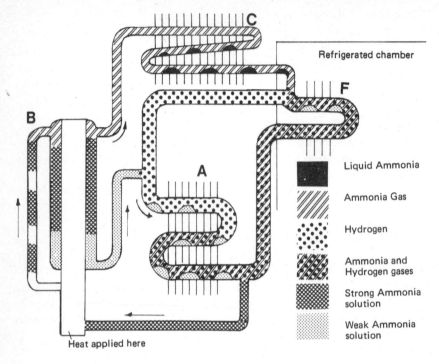

Absorption type refrigerator

Compression type (See diagram)

(Majority of refrigerators.)

The refrigerant is usually dichloro-difluoromethane or one of the Freon compounds, e.g. Freon 12 or R12. The compressor, which is driven by a small, sealed electric motor, exerts pressure on the heat laden, gaseous refrigerant forcing it into the condenser where the combined effects of pressure and heat lost into the room by convection cause the refrigerant to revert to liquid form. The liquid then passes via a capilliary tube to the frozen food storage compartment where it expands and evaporates taking heat from inside the refrigerator cabinet. A drop in pressure causes the gaseous refrigerant to be drawn back to the compressor to be liquefied again as the cycle is repeated. The controlling thermostat is in the form of a gas operated bellows which disconnects the electricity supply to the motor as the temperature falls. The temperature within the refrigerator is usually maintained between 3.8°C and 8°C.

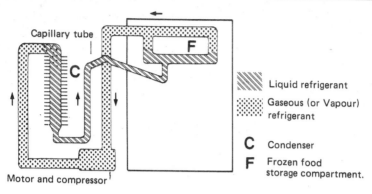

Compression type refrigerator

Use of refrigerator

If possible a refrigerator should occupy a cool position away from a stove or radiator. A well-constructed refrigerator is well insulated to prevent heat getting in, but experiments have proved that there is a rise of 2°C inside for every 6°C rise outside, so room temperature does affect a refrigerator. Warmer air will enter every time the door is opened and so avoid this as far as possible. Place in a light position so that the contents can be readily seen, and the door closed quickly (may have interior light).

Avoid putting in hot food as this raises the temperature, fills the inside with steam which condenses on the shelves and lining, and causes a rapid build up of frost on the frozen food storage compartment. Keep down condensation by covering foods and wiping the inside if condensation is apparent.

Storage of food

Do not crowd foods together and prevent circulation of air. The placing of food depends on the position of the frozen food storage compartment.

Never put tainted food in a refrigerator. Cover all strong-smelling foods, e.g. cheese. Cover foods to prevent evaporation.

Milk. Store in a bottle on the top shelf or in the door.

Uncooked meat, bacon or poultry. Wrap in paper or plastic. Keep on the middle shelf.

Butter, fats or cheese. Keep in wrapping paper, wrap cheese in plastic or foil, store in the door or away from the frozen food storage compartment.

Uncooked fish. Do not keep more than one day. Wrap loosely in paper or foil and store in the drip tray.

Eggs. Store unwrapped in the rack, pointed-side down.

Cooked food. Cover, cool, and store on middle shelf.

Vegetables and fruit. Wash or wipe dry. Put in container with lid or put on low shelf wrapped in foil or plastic.

Frozen foods. The length of the storage period depends on the nature of the frozen food and the temperature in the frozen food storage compartment. This is indicated by the star marking in the refrigerator (see page 240). Obey manufacturer's instructions.

Cleaning refrigerator

It needs to be defrosted when the frost on the frozen food storage compartment is about 5 mm thick, or at least once a fortnight. If allowed to become too thick frost will act as an insulator and increase the running costs, and also tend to hold food odours.

Quick method of defrosting. Turn control to 'off' and empty refrigerator. Replace the drip tray. Empty the ice tray and fill with hot water, and close the door. The heat will melt the ice. Wipe cabinet dry. Re-fill ice tray with fresh cold water, turn on the control and replace food.

Normal method of defrosting. Turn the control to defrost. Remove all frozen food. Leave until the frost has melted. Empty drip tray, put fresh water in ice box, turn back the control, replace any frozen food. If needed wash interior after defrosting.

Washing. Wash the interior with a solution of bicarbonate of soda, 1 teaspoonful to 1 litre of warm water – *never* use soap, washing up liquid or detergent – and dry thoroughly.

Note: Never try to hasten the defrosting process by chipping at the ice. This could damage the refrigerator.

Automatic defrosting mechanisms

Push button defrosting. When the defrost button is pressed it operates a delay mechanism incorporated in the thermostat. This ensures that the temperature in the frozen food storage compartment must rise high enough to melt the ice coating before the thermostat can return to its normal cycle. It is advisable to remove frozen food from the refrigerator in the normal way before defrosting.

Accelerated defrosting. Here the defrost button operates a valve in the compressor system which causes hot refrigerant to be passed directly to the frozen food storage compartment where the temperature is rapidly raised high enough to melt the ice coating. When the ice has all melted the refrigeration cycle is automatically restarted.

Fully automatic defrosting. This system requires no attention. The refrigeration unit cuts out automatically when defrosting becomes necessary and cuts in again when it is completed. Defrosting is so quick that frozen foods and ice cream do not have time to thaw. The cabinet must, however, be cleaned regularly.

HOME FREEZERS

Almost any food can be stored in a home freezer provided it is protected by airtight and moisture-proof wrapping. A freezer usually maintains a temperature of −18°C for normal storage, and, if the fast freeze switch is depressed, can reach a temperature as low as −25°C for the freezing of fresh food. (See Chapter 21.)

Defrosting

Defrosting will depend on:
1. How often fresh food is put in.
2. How frequently the lid or door is opened.
3. The humidity of the air admittèd to the freezer.

Defrosting should be carried out when stocks of frozen food are low. While defrosting, food still being stored in the freezer should be placed in boxes, wrapped in newspaper or stored in a refrigerator.

How to defrost a freezer

Follow the manufacturer's instructions, which will usually cover the following points:
1. Switch off the electric current and pull out the plug.
2. Place plastic bowls or buckets of hot water in the freezer to melt the 'frost'.
3. Place a thick absorbent towel in the bottom of the freezer to collect the water as the ice thaws. Some freezers have a drain plug to let out the water during defrosting.
4. Wipe the inside surfaces, shelves and baskets with warm water and dry.
5. Replace the drain plug, switch on and keep the door or lid closed for up to an hour before reloading.
6. Occasionally, clean the outer surface with a mild detergent and polish with silicone cream.

CHOICE OF SMALL EQUIPMENT

A wide selection of small equipment is available, both in type and variety. It is important to decide what equipment is necessary for efficient working in any particular household. When this has been acquired, less essential items may be purchased. Advice is usually given to buy the best which can be afforded and this is true of much small equipment. Electrical equipment should be of a good quality and have passed a test for safety. (See page 257.) Pans and cutlery usually repay the money which is spent on them. However, glass, pottery and plastic ware which is colourful and attractive in design may be purchased at reasonable prices.

Consider the size and shape of equipment in relation to the storage available. Consider the cleaning of equipment and choose designs without crevices which would make cleaning difficult.

Glass

Examine for rough edges, flaws and bubbles. Tumblers and glasses should be well balanced so that they are not easily knocked over and wide enough to be cleaned easily. Consider the advantage of dishes which will stack for storage. There is some beautiful glass produced which, if it can be afforded, is a delight to use but consideration must be given to the question of breakage. There are some good designs in the cheaper ranges of glass ware.

Heat-resisting glass. Buy a good quality. Choice as above. This toughened glass will stand oven temperatures. Some types crack if put out of the oven on to a cold, wet or metal surface. Dishes are made in attractive shapes and food can be served in the cooking dish. Glass pans are available which will stand direct contact with flame.

Glass in a freezer. (See page 175.)

Glass for a microwave oven. (See page 234.)

Pottery

May be earthenware, stoneware, bone china or porcelain, depending on the clay used, and methods of firing. Decoration varies and may be under-glaze or over-glaze decoration. Under-glaze usually gives longer wear. Choose suitable shapes and sizes, and consider position of handles for good appearance and balance and for easy washing, with no crevices or ridges. Lids should fit properly, and cups sit well on saucers. Buy a standard pattern if possible, so breakages can be replaced.

Plastics

This is a term used to denote substances which can be moulded by heat and pressure – Polythene, Nylon, Melamine, Polypropylene. Plastic is used for a variety of household equipment – bowls, crockery, containers, brushes, sieves, strainers, tools. Plastic can be clear or opaque and is produced in attractive colours.

It is flexible and does not break although the cheaper types will crack and are easily scratched. It is non-porous, thus waterproof, and will not hold flavours which makes it suitable for food storage. Plastic bags and plastic food wraps are used both commercially and in the home for the storage of food and for home freezing. (See page 175.) Some plastics soften with heat and will eventually melt, but Melamine will stand quite high water temperatures and Polypropylene basins may be used for steaming food.

Cutlery

Choose cutlery of a reliable make and it should last for years. Table cutlery may be made of electro-plated nickel silver (E.P.N.S.), stainless steel or silver, with a variety of materials used for the handles, wood, ivory, xylonite (to imitate ivory), nylon, bone and plastic. Stainless steel knives may be made all in one piece for easy cleaning. Cutlery should fit the hand comfortably, balance well, be a good shape and easily cleaned. Kitchen knives are usually made of stainless steel. Some large kitchen knives may not be stainless because of the need for a sharp cutting edge which can be resharpened easily. However, new techniques of producing cutting edges enable stainless steel to be used increasingly.

Pans

A saucepan should be chosen to suit the type of cooker on which it is to be used. Electric cookers and solid fuel cookers need fairly heavy, flat, ground-based pans which will give close contact with the cooking plate. A heavy pan will give much longer wear and is more efficient in use, but it will not heat up so quickly as a thin pan and will be more expensive. The base should be large enough to make full use of the cooking plate. Metals used for pans should not be affected by the food cooked in them. Because metal conducts heat very quickly it is efficient for heating food, but the pan handles and lid handles must be made of a material which does not conduct heat, and so will be cool to touch. Handles should be firmly attached. Lids must fit well to avoid evaporation of the contents of the pan, causing burning. The inside of the pans should be smooth to prevent food sticking and there should be no grooves to hold grease and dirt.

Types of pans

Aluminium. This metal is widely used for pans but its efficiency and wear depends on the quality bought. Heavy quality aluminium with ground bases will give years of good service, but thin aluminium pans will burn easily, will dent and lose shape so that they do not make contact with cooking plates and the lids will not fit closely.

Enamel on metal. Enamel-coated saucepans are of two types. The cheaper type of pan is tin coated with enamel, which chips easily and has restricted use. Heavier pans are made from cast iron coated with enamel. They have good heat retention but are very heavy in use.

Stainless steel. This metal is very hard wearing, looks attractive and is easily cleaned, but it does not always conduct heat evenly. The better type of stainless steel pan has a copper-coated base. These will give many years of wear but are expensive. Some of the newer types of stainless steel pans are said to conduct heat more efficiently.

Copper. This metal is an excellent conductor of heat and looks very attractive. It is often used by professional cooks, but most people dislike the frequent scouring and polishing which is necessary to keep the metal clean and safe to use. Copper pans are thought to reduce the vitamin C content in fruit and vegetables cooked in them. They are tin-lined to prevent contamination of food.

Cooking pans are available in very attractive designs and colours. Whatever type is chosen it must be used sensibly and kept clean to give the most efficient working life.

Non-stick finishes

Non-stick finishes for pans, baking tins etc. are produced by coating the specially prepared pans with polytetrafluoroethylene (PTEFE). PTEFE treated articles are sold under trade names such as Teflon and Fluon. No food should stick to this coating. It should be heat resistant up to 230°C and is resistant to most household chemicals. Recent developments have improved the adhesion of the coating to the pan base and thus the scratch resistance.

Care of non-stick pans

Follow the manufacturer's instructions.

1. Oil lightly before using for the first time.
2. Do not overheat especially before putting food into a pan. Care is needed to avoid overheating frying pans.
3. Wash in hot water and detergent. Use a soft nylon brush if necessary. *Never* use abrasive powders, steel wool, or pan scourers.
4. It is advisable to use wooden or plastic utensils with PTEFE pans even if they are claimed to be scratch resistant.

SMALL ELECTRICAL EQUIPMENT

Food Mixers and Processors. These appliances vary considerably in power and capacity. The simplest are hand-held mixers for cake mixtures and doughs. The most complex have attachments for mixing, blending, sieving, grinding, shredding, slicing, peeling, mincing and juice extracting. Choose according to household requirements.

Portable ovens/grills/rotisserie spits. May be used in addition to, or instead of, a full sized cooker.

Infra-red grills. Cook snacks – eggs, bacon, sausages, sandwiches and steak very quickly by the use of black heat which is reflected through the food.

Toasters. Traditional upright toasters have adjustments for the thickness and type of bread and for toast colour. Open toasters will cook savouries and sandwiches as well as bread. Toaster ovens are available which grill and toast.

Kettles. An electric kettle provides boiling water very quickly and can save electricity. New models have an automatic switch-off device or will switch over to simmering. There should be some form of safety cut-out in case the kettle should be plugged in while empty, or boiled dry.

Electric jugs. Are thermostatically controlled to hold liquids at a required temperature.

Tea Makers. May be primed with materials and pre-set to produce tea at a required time which is indicated by an alarm.

Fry pans. There is automatic control for frying, baking and roasting.

Deep fat fryers. Consist of a pan, lid and frying basket. Thermostatically controlled for safe and efficient deep fat frying.

Casseroles. A heavy pottery casserole set in metal with an electric element in the base. Very economical to run. Will casserole, stew and braise.

Coffee Makers

Percolators have an electric element in the base. They may be made of metal, aluminium or stainless steel, or pottery. The newest types have strength selectors and will keep hot.

Drip filters. Boiling water is directed through a small tube to drip on to finely ground coffee. The coffee liquid is collected in a jug which stands over a heating element.

Cona coffee maker. May have a separate heating element or be used on a cooker hob. Consists of a double glass bowl. Water is placed in the bottom bowl and coffee in the upper bowl. When the water boils it rises through a glass tube over the coffee in the upper bowl. Then the coffee liquid filters back into the bottom bowl which has a lip and may be used to serve the coffee.

KITCHEN PAPERS AND WRAPPINGS

Aluminium foil is pure aluminium rolled to wafer thinness. In this form it is moistureproof, greaseproof, vapourproof, non-inflammable, light but strong, malleable and a good conductor of heat. It is invaluable in the kitchen for cooking, wrapping and storing food and can be used to line cake tins, to form a lid for casseroles, or as a lining for casseroles containing food to be frozen. When the food has been cooked and frozen it can be lifted out in the foil lining, wrapped in more foil for storage in the freezer and the casserole used again. Foil pudding basins, baking dishes, individual pie dishes, plates and patty tins are all available for food freezing. They should be covered with foil or a foil-lined cardboard lid.

Food cooked in foil retains its flavour and nutritive value, tends to shrink less and splashes on the oven lining are prevented. Left-overs may be wrapped in separate parcels of foil and later re-heated in the foil, provided that the usual food-hygiene rules are observed. Foil may sometimes be used to line baking trays and grill pans where spilled foods may tend to burn.

Note: Care must be taken to avoid allowing the foil to come into contact with electric elements as it is a conductor of electricity. Foil is available in two widths to fit wall dispensers. Heavy duty foil is available (but not essential) for use in freezers. It is less liable to puncture than normal duty foil so forms a better seal.

Absorbent kitchen paper roll is double thickness soft paper embossed to increase the surface area thus making it even more absorbent. Paper may be plain, coloured or patterned. It is expensive but invaluable for mopping up spilled liquids, draining fried foods, cleaning greasy or wet surfaces, or as a quick way to 'blot' fruit dry after washing. Can also be used as a soft polishing cloth. It is easily disposable and usually sold in double roll packs of standard width to fit wall dispensers.

Greaseproof paper is grease resistant and used for wrapping small quantities of food, e.g. cut cheese, sandwiches and picnic foods, for lining cake tins and covering steamed puddings during cooking. Can be used for disposable icing bags, but these tend to burst as the paper gets wet, and as a tracing paper for preparing chocolate and sugar cake decorations. Available in sheets or rolls. Greaseproof paper cases are used to shape individual small cakes.

Non-stick baking parchment e.g. Bakewell parchment, is a vegetable parchment similar in appearance to greaseproof paper but is stronger when wet so is very useful for paper icing bags. Its non-stick surface makes it ideal for meringues which peel off the paper easily when cooked. Can be used for interleaving chops and steaks in the freezer. Available in sheets or on roll with special cutting edge.

Waxed paper is waxed on both sides. Discs of waxed paper are used to seal the surface of hot jam before jars are covered. Waxed paper is used as a base on which sugar icing flowers etc. are made because it peels off easily when sugar is dry. Food for the freezer can be interleaved with waxed paper. Waxed paper lining from cereal packets is an economical wrapping which keeps sandwiches moist.

Polythene bags are useful for storing food and have numerous other uses about the house, e.g. lining bins. Heavy duty bags are available for use in the freezer (alternatively two thinner bags can be used double). Sold in boxes of single or assorted sizes, clear or opaque, and in tear-off rolls.

Transparent cling film is a strong, transparent plastic wrapping which will cling to itself and to any other surface, thus forming an airtight seal which retains food flavour and reduces the risk of food absorbing odour from strong-smelling foods stored nearby. It is used for covering prepared food and is particularly useful for sealing cut foods such as lemon or for covering leftovers. It is specially useful in the freezer when an airtight seal prevents 'freezer burn'. It is advisable to use the special thicker film in the freezer (or double thickness of standard film) because thin plastic film is easily punctured.

Clear roasting wrap is made from transparent heat resistant plastic film with foil strips at the edge. It does not cling to food but the foil provides enough support to allow it to be shaped round a joint and then sealed by twisting the foil edges. The wrap prevents fat splashing over the oven during roasting and it allows meat to baste itself and brown while shrinkage and loss of meat juices by evaporation are reduced. It may also reduce cooking times. Sold in rolls with special cutting edge.

Note: The wrap must be pierced with a fork to allow air and steam to escape during cooking. It is *not suitable* for use in oven temperatures above 190°C, G.M.6, or for lining tins or grilling.

Clear roasting bags are made from the same materials as roasting wrap. The food to be cooked is put in the bag, the bag is punctured to allow air and steam to escape, the open end sealed with a wire closure. If desired the tenderness of the meat can be checked during cooking by piercing the bag with a metal fork. When the food is cooked the top of the bag is slit with a knife, the meat removed and the juices can be poured out to make gravy. Bags can also be used for cooking fish, chops, ham and vegetables.

31. SAFETY IN THE HOME

Statistics show that more people are killed and injured by accidents in the home than in any other way. There is danger everywhere in the home if care is not taken, especially for children and old people. The main causes of home accidents are ignorance, carelessness, apathy, faulty equipment and installations. Most accidents could be avoided with reasonable care.

It is important to realise where the dangers may be. Equipment should be examined and kept in good repair and used correctly. The house should be planned carefully, especially the kitchen, to reduce the possibility of accidents.

The most frequent household accidents are burns, scalds, cuts, falls, poisoning and suffocation.

Burns, scalds and cuts

Every year in Britain approximately 700 people die and 50,000 are injured by burns and scalds. Many are under 5 or over 65 years of age. Most accidents are caused by unguarded or inadequately guarded fires. Laws forbid the sale of unguarded fires. under the *Children and Young Persons Act*, if a child of 12 or under is seriously injured or dies from burns resulting from unguarded heating appliances, the person responsible may be fined.

Safety precautions – burns

1. The placing of fires is important – place electric fires out of reach of children (high on the wall). Do not use electrical appliances in bathrooms unless they are fixed to walls or ceiling, and the switch should be outside the room or of the cord type.
2. Do not hang mirrors over a fireplace.
3. Do not use inflammable clothing for children. Use pyjamas rather than nightdresses.
4. Keep matches out of children's reach. Use safety matches.
5. Never use paraffin to start fires.
6. Never leave newspapers to draw up a fire.
7. Do not have curtains hanging near a stove or open flame.
8. Never use cheap electrical fittings or equipment.
9. Do not use tea towels or other thin cloths to lift dishes from the oven.

10. Take care when heating fat, e.g. clarifying.

11. Overhaul electrical equipment at regular intervals. No amateurs should service this equipment.

12. Use safety gas and electric fittings which carry recognised approval marks. (See page 257.)

13. When wiring a plug remember the correct colour coding. Appliances bought after 1st April 1971 must have flex with the international colour coding. Many appliances still in use will have the old colour coding. The new and old colours are as follows:

New Colours		Old Colours
Green/yellow	EARTH	Green
Brown	LIVE	Red
Blue	NEUTRAL	Black

Important

Connect the coloured wires to the appropriate terminals.

Secure the flex with the protective cover inside the flex holder.

Tighten the screws at each terminal so that the wires are held securely.

Use the recommended fuse for the appliance.

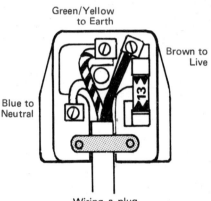

Green/Yellow to Earth

Brown to Live

Blue to Neutral

Wiring a plug

Safety precautions – scalds

1. Keep all hot liquids and all types of kettle out of children's reach.
2. Handles on pans should be turned in – a special guard is available.
3. Avoid trailing table cloths which could be pulled by small children.
4. Use hot water bottle covers for children and old people.
5. Bath water must be carefully tested before use.

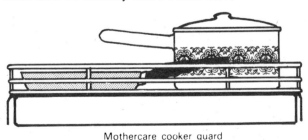

Mothercare cooker guard

Safety precautions – cuts

1. Keep all sharp edged or pointed utensils in a safe place. Pointed knives, etc. should be kept in a sheath or have a cork on the point.

2. Used razor blades should be wrapped and disposed of in the dustbin.

3. The use of a sharp knife or tool is safer, as it is easier to use and less likely to slip.

4. Rusty or dirty utensils may result in infected cuts.

Falls

1. Keep floors in good repair, not slippery, especially under mats. Have no trailing flexes.

2. Have no loose stair carpet or rods. Keep stairs clean and in good repair.

3. Lighting must be good, especially on stairs.

4. Use safety gates where there are young children.

5. If possible avoid odd stairs when planning a home.

6. Toys should not be left lying around.

7. Do not stand on too low a ladder to reach up or over. Ladders must be safe.

8. Do not wear old shoes with loose soles.

9. Do not open a window at the bottom if young children are about. If possible use bars on children's bedroom windows and make it difficult for them to climb up to window sills.

10. Equipment must be sensibly placed to avoid falls.

Poisoning

1. See that all poisons and medicines and chemicals are locked up safely, especially those resembling sweets and lemonade, etc. Many medicines safe for adults are fatal for children.

2. Cleaning materials which are harmful, e.g. bleaches, must be kept out of reach of children.

3. All tins and bottles should be clearly labelled. Keep poisons in distinctive bottles, e.g. never put bleaches in bottles which have contained drinks.

4. Throw away all unused medicines.

Suffocation

If air is prevented from entering the lungs, suffocation or asphyxia will result from lack of oxygen.

May be caused by:

1. Choking.

2. Smothering by:

Solids, e.g. cushions or pillows.

Fluids, as in drowning.

Gases or fumes, e.g. coal gas.

Paralysis of the muscles of breathing, e.g. by an electric shock.

Safety precautions

1. Do not leave small articles, e.g. buttons, within reach of small children.

2. Have safety taps and other devices on all gas and electric appliances, and check the equipment, piping, wiring, etc. regularly.

3. Do not leave gas on low where there is a draught.

4. Do not use soft pillows and mattresses in babies' cots.

5. Keep pets away from young babies, especially when the babies are sleeping.

6. Do not leave a feeding bottle with a baby. Do not use soft, thin plastic bibs which can be drawn in to the face during breathing.

7. Care must be taken with baths of water, pools, etc.

8. Do not allow young children to play with plastic bags.

Keep all equipment in good repair and use it correctly. Remember it is foolish to attempt amateur repairs on dangerous equipment, e.g. cookers, televisions. Try to plan the home with safety precautions in mind. Have a knowledge of simple first aid.

SIMPLE FIRST AID

Keep a readily available first-aid box in the house. It should contain:

Sterile bandages.	Cotton wool.
Burn dressings.	Lint.
Adhesive plaster.	Antiseptic.
Scissors.	

Small cuts. Wash with dilute antiseptic solution and cover with a dry sterile dressing.

Larger cuts. (Bleeding from a vein.) Raise the limb above the level of the head to reduce the rate of bleeding. Apply a clean pad, bandage and send for the doctor. Keep the patient lying down and warm.

Arterial bleeding is most dangerous. The blood will be bright red in colour and coming out in spurts. Apply pressure at both sides of the bleeding point. A tourniquet is not recommended for use on an arm, but in emergencies may be used elsewhere provided that pressure is released after 20 minutes. Bandages used should be saved so that the doctor will be able to estimate the amount of blood lost. While waiting for the doctor treat the patient for shock – keep him warm, lying with his head low, and, if conscious, give him hot, sweet, strong tea as a stimulant.

Nose bleeding. Hold the head forward so that the patient will not swallow the blood. Apply a cold compress to the bridge of the nose and the forehead. In the case of severe bleeding, *do not* plug the cavity, but allow the blood to run freely and send for the doctor if necessary.

Slight burns or scalds. Apply cold water; pat dry and apply a clean, dry dressing.

Extensive burns or scalds. Cover with clean, dry cloths and send for doctor.

Flames. Smother the flames by rolling the patient in a rug, coats, etc. and treat for shock. Send for doctor.

Fainting. Loosen the clothing at the neck, hold the head between the knees and apply a cold compress to the forehead. *Do not* give anything to drink until the patient is conscious.

Breaks or fractures. Do not move the patient or give any treatment apart from supporting the limb. Do not give anything to drink in case it is necessary for the patient to be given an anaesthetic. Keep the patient warm until the doctor arrives.

Food poisoning. Give an emetic – warm water with mustard, or put a finger down the throat. *But* for caustic poisons, strong acids or alkalis give milk or diluted olive oil.

Electric shock. Switch off the current *before* touching the person.

Gas poisoning. Open or smash the windows. Turn off the gas, leave the door open. Send for the doctor and apply artificial respiration if necessary.

APPROVAL AND SAFETY MARKS

When choosing equipment look for the recognised approval symbols which show that the product conforms to the rigorous requirements of the British Standards Institution. The two BSI marks are the Kitemark and the Safety Mark.

The BSI Safety Mark was introduced in 1975. It indicates that a product has been thoroughly tested to a British standard dealing only with safety and conforms to safety standards laid down by the European Economic Community (EEC).

BSI Safety Mark

The Kitemark can also be seen on products and indicates standards of quality, performance and durabilty as well as safety.

BSI Kitemark

The British Electrotechnical Approvals Board (BEAB) carry out tests on all electrical household goods, e.g. cookers, kettles, blankets, refrigerators, etc. The presence of the black and yellow label is a safeguard indicating that the article will work safely and that there are no exposed 'live' parts or other hazards. Local Electricity Showrooms only stock electrical goods which conform to the standard.

BEAB mark

The British Gas Seal of Service is carried by all domestic gas appliances sold by British Gas and its Authorised Dealers. It indicates that the appliance has been tested by British Gas for performance, durability, reliability, etc. The Seal of Service guarantees 'Superflame' appliances for two years and other appliances for one year. During the period of the guarantee, British Gas will repair or replace any faulty part and provide a free breakdown service provided there has been no misuse or damage by the customer. The Seal of Service also guarantees that spare parts will be available throughout the working life of the appliance. The certification of gas appliances for safety is carried out by the BSI Quality Assurance Council. Appliances carry the BSI Safety Mark to show they meet BS 5258, the appropriate British Standard.

British Gas
Seal of Service

INDEX